THE PASSIVE SOLAR HOUSE

THE REAL GOODS INDEPENDENT LIVING BOOKS

Paul Gipe, Wind Power for Home & Business: Renewable Energy for the 1990s and Beyond

Michael Potts, The Independent Home: Living Well with Power from the
Sun, Wind, and Water

Edward Harland, Eco-Renovation: The Ecological Home Improvement Guide

Real Goods Solar Living Sourcebook: The Complete Guide to Renewable Energy
Technologies and Sustainable Living, *Ninth Edition, edited by John Schaeffer*

Athena Swentzell Steen, Bill Steen, and David Bainbridge, with David Eisenberg,
The Straw Bale House

Nancy Cole and P.J. Skerrett, Union of Concerned Scientists,
Renewables are Ready: People Creating Renewable Energy Solutions

David Easton, The Rammed Earth House

Sam Clark, The Real Goods Independent Builder: Designing & Building a
House Your Own Way

James Kachadorian, The Passive Solar House: Using Solar Design to
Heat and Cool Your Home

Real Goods Trading Company in Ukiah, California, was founded in 1978 to make available new tools to help people live self-sufficiently and sustainably. Through seasonal catalogs, a periodical (*The Real Goods News*), a bi-annual *Solar Living Sourcebook*, as well as retail outlets, Real Goods provides a broad range of tools for independent living.

"Knowledge is our most important product" is the Real Goods motto. To further its mission, Real Goods has joined with Chelsea Green Publishing Company to co-create and co-publish the Real Goods Independent Living Book series. The titles in this series are written by pioneering individuals who have firsthand experience in using innovative technology to live lightly on the planet. Chelsea Green books are both practical and inspirational, and they enlarge our view of what is possible as we enter the next millennium.

Ian Baldwin, Jr.
President, Chelsea Green

John Schaeffer
President, Real Goods

THE PASSIVE SOLAR HOUSE

James Kachadorian

CHELSEA GREEN PUBLISHING COMPANY   White River Junction, Vermont

Special thanks to George Philip Kachadorian for his editing help, and to my clients who believed in me and from whom I learned. Also, no business succeeds without devoted people, and much credit for the success of Green Mountain Homes is due to the efforts of Wayne Chalmers, Kendall Spaulding, and Wally Killian, who ran the factory; to Dolores Zick, who ran the office; to Gary Delaney, who helped out with drafting in the early years; and to my wife Lea, who handled our advertising and contributed artwork, and who has never wavered in her support of my activities.

The tables in Appendices 2, 3, and 5 are reprinted with permission from the American Society of Heating, Refrigerating, and Air Conditioning Engineers, Inc. The tables and data are reprinted wholly or in part from the 1981 and 1993 ASHRAE *Handbooks of Fundamentals*. ASHRAE, Inc. retains the exclusive copyrights to this reprinted material.

Cover design by Ann Aspell
Book design by Andrea Gray

Printed in the United States of America

00 99 98 97   1 2 3 4 5

First printing May, 1997

Although great care has been taken to insure the accuracy of the information in this book, the publisher and author accept no liability for printing or typographical errors, nor for personal injury, property damage, or any other loss or damages arising from actions inspired by this book.

Library of Congress Cataloging-in-Publication Data

Kachadorian, James.
     The passive solar home : using solar design to heat and cool your home / James Kachadorian.
         p. cm. -- (The real goods independent living books)
     Includes bibiliographical references and index.
     ISBN 0-930031-97-0
     1. Solar houses. 2. Solar heating--Passive systems. 3. Solar air conditioning--Passive systems. I. Title. II. Series: Real goods independent living book.
     TH7414.K33 1997
     690'.8370472--dc21   97-3264

Chelsea Green Publishing Company
Post Office Box 428
White River Junction, Vermont 05001

This book is dedicated to the memory of
Nathaniel E. Kachadorian
July 6, 1973 – November 21, 1992

Contents

APPENDICES

Preface

All houses are solar. The sun shines on almost every home, many days throughout the year. The question is, to what extent are you utilizing the sunlight? This book has been written to help you to take advantage of this free resource.

The first part of the book will acquaint you with the basic concepts involved in solar design. Notice that we have included ten easy-to-follow "Solar Principles," each one illustrating a key consideration in building solar homes. As you progress through the chapters, the discussion will get more specific and more technical, incorporating many formulas and equations needed to actually factor the solar principles into effective solar home designs. Do not be discouraged if you do not instantly grasp the mathematics. What is important is that you understand the concepts so that, with the help of a professional designer, you will be able to include solar features in the plan for your home.

Great care has been taken to provide accurate and factual information based on over twenty years of solar home-design experience. I wish that I could make competent solar designers and builders out of every reader, yet the disciplines needed to design and construct homes take years of education and apprenticeship to learn. If you do not possess these skills, please consult with or hire professionals. While this book's technical data and equations will be widely applicable for the technically trained, hopefully the book will also spark an enthusiasm among non-technical readers for the limitless potential of solar energy.

Wouldn't it be nice if your house, too, could spend next winter heating itself, naturally, with free heat from the sun?

THE PASSIVE SOLAR HOUSE

1

LET NATURE
HEAT YOUR HOME

During the summer of 1973, the U.S. economy was booming. We were all whizzing down the highway at 70 miles per hour, the legal speed limit. Gasoline was about 39 cents per gallon, and the posted price of Gulf crude oil was $2.59 per barrel. That year, my wife Lea and I had purchased a lovely old Vermont farmhouse, heated by a coal-stoking boiler that had been converted to oil. The base of this monster boiler was about three feet by six feet, and when it fired, it literally shook the house. We tapped our domestic hot water directly off the boiler, so we had to run the unit all four seasons: Every time we needed hot water, the boiler in the basement fired up. We were burning about 2,500 gallons of fuel oil each year, and in the coldest winter months, it was not unusual to get an oil delivery every two weeks.

Since we had no other way to heat our home, we were entirely dependent on the oil-gobbling monster, and on our biweekly oil deliveries to survive the Vermont winter. Our only alternative source of heat was an open fireplace. Though aesthetically pleasing, the fireplace actually took more heat out of the house than it gave off.

At that time, I was the vice president and general manager of a prefabricated post-and-beam home operation. Like others, I shared the industry opinion that the heating contractor's job was to install the heating system that the homeowner wanted. As designers and home producers, we were not responsible for that part of new home construction. Home building plans were typically insensitive to the position of the sun. Our prefabricated home packages were labeled simply "front, back, right side, left side," not "south, east, west, north." We offered little or no advice on siting, except that we needed enough room to get a tractor-trailer to the job site.

To give you an idea how little energy efficiency was considered in house design (an area of home construction that has since received enormous attention), our homes had single glazed windows and patio doors; R-13 wall and R-20 roof insulation were considered more than adequate. ("R" is the thermal resistance of any housing component; a high R-value means a higher insulating value. Today's homes typically have much higher R-values.) Homeowners in the 1970s rarely asked about the R-values of their home components, and our sales discussions were less about energy efficiency than about how the house would look and whether it would have vaulted ceilings.

The point is, we were not yet approaching the task of design and construction in an integrated, comprehensive way. We had not yet recognized that all aspects of a design must be coordinated, and that every member of the design team, including the future resident, needs to be thinking about how the home will be heated from the first moment they step onto the site.

THE OIL CRISIS

In 1973, an international crisis forever changed the way Americans thought about home heating costs. After Israel took Jerusalem in the "Six Day War," Arab oil-producing nations became increasingly frustrated with the United States' policy toward Israel. In the fall of 1973, these oil-producing nations began to utilize oil pricing and production as a means to influence international policy. In October 1973, the Organization of Petroleum Exporting Countries (OPEC) met and unilaterally raised oil prices 70 percent. The impact of this price hike on U.S. homeowners who heated with oil was spectacular. Fuel oil prices soared.

Then the oil embargo hit. In November 1973, all Arab oil-producing states stopped shipping oil to the United States. By December 1973, the official OPEC member-price was $11.65 per barrel—a whopping 450 percent increase from the $2.59-per-barrel price of the previous summer. Iran reported receiving bids as high as $17.00 per barrel, which translated to $27.00 per barrel in New York City.

In addition to giant price increases, oil supplies became uncertain and the United States, which depended on foreign oil for fully half its consumption, was facing the real possibility of fuel rationing for the first time since World War II.

Richard Nixon was president, and his Secretary of State, Henry Kissinger, spent most of that winter in what was termed "shuttle diplomacy," racing from country to country attempting to bring a resolution to the crisis. He didn't succeed until March 18, 1974, when the embargo against the United States was lifted. It had lasted five months.

As the international oil crisis was played out over those five months, every oil delivery to our home was marked by a price increase, invariably without notice. Worse, our supplier could not assure delivery. My wife and I had two small children, an energy dinosaur of a house, and no other way to keep warm but to burn huge amounts of oil. We couldn't even "escape" to a warmer climate, because there were long lines at the gasoline pumps. We had never felt so dependent on others as we did that winter. It was plain scary!

THERE HAD TO BE A
BETTER WAY

I have a background in engineering, and the energy crisis of 1973–1974 provided an incentive for me to investigate solar heating. It was obvious to me that as a country, we had forgotten the basics of good energy management. I just knew that there must be a better way to design and build houses that would capture the sun's heat and work in harmony with nature. I also have a background in business, and I realized that the energy crisis had opened up a market ready for new ideas about how to heat homes. The energy crisis had shaken us all into action.

The years immediately following that energy crisis saw a remarkable emergence of new ideas about solar energy. Solar conferences were held, and the public was treated to frequent articles that described new solar home designs in popular magazines. The results of this collective effort were largely positive. Many new ideas were tested. Some succeeded, and others failed, but building specifications focused on energy efficiency developed during that time have now become standard practice. For example, double-pane high-performance glass is now used almost universally in windows and patio doors. Standard wall insulation is now R-20. That was previously the roof standard; standard roof insulation is now R-32. The science of vapor barriers took huge leaps forward, and highly effective vapor barriers are now standard. Exterior house wraps, such as Typar and Tyvek, are applied on most new construction to tighten up air leaks. Appliances are now more energy efficient. Heating systems have undergone major improvements. These days, it is even common for "smart houses" to monitor lighting and to turn lamps and heating equipment on and off according to need. In sum, we are now building better energy-efficient houses, in large part due to the wake-up call we got in the winter of 1973–1974.

WHY FEAR SOLAR?

Unfortunately, as we near the end of the century, it seems that we might be suffering from collective amnesia. We still import more than half of our oil from foreign sources. State by state, we see the speed limit raised back to 1970s levels; some states have eliminated speed limits entirely. A Vermont utility recently announced a plan to reward consumers who use *more* electrical energy this year than last year. Are we headed toward another energy crisis?

Back in the 1970s, I designed and patented what I saw as a partial solution to the energy crisis—an innovative solar house design. All of our homes, as far south as North Carolina and as far west as Kansas, are still functioning as well today as when they were first built. This design will work for you, today.

And yet from my work building solar homes over the past twenty years, I've found that people resist solar for four main reasons. They are afraid that the house will get too hot. They are afraid that the house

will be too cold. And they are afraid that a solar house has to be ugly and futuristic-looking and will require expensive, fickle gadgetry and materials, with walls of glass, or black-box collectors hanging from every rooftop and wall. None of these fears are well-founded.

The design and building strategies presented in this book are carefully engineered for building solar homes with traditional features, while incurring no added expense in the process. The solar approach is really a rearrangement of materials you would otherwise need to build any home. In fact, the only feature you sacrifice using this design is a basement, but you gain so much in energy savings and by living in a large, cheery, well-lit place, that I think that you'll find this trade-off is more than worthwhile.

Here are a couple of other considerations to keep in mind when reading this book. First, I came to the design and building of solar homes as a businessman and engineer, and this book reflects that approach. I've aimed for a practical, step-by-step, how-to treatment. Every building strategy presented in this book has been proven out in the real world.

Siting a house with sensitivity to the sun's daily and seasonal patterns, and using conventional materials wisely, you can build a traditional-looking solar home that largely heats itself.

Moreover, though I've chosen one type of design to describe in detail, this book also offers a wealth of practical information for designing *any* solar home, whether you use the Green Mountain Homes approach or not. A wealth of engineering data is included in the hopes that this book will become a welcome addition to any complete library of solar design.

GREEN MOUNTAIN HOMES: A SOLAR SUCCESS STORY

The ingredients for my decision to go into the business of designing and manufacturing solar homes were all in place just after the oil crisis hit. My engineering and home manufacturing background offered the stepping-off point. I had been doing research on solar designs throughout 1974, and by mid-1974, the idea of starting a business devoted to producing pre-fabricated solar homes seemed more exciting than ever before. The concepts for the business and formulation of the solar design were finalized by late 1975. Green Mountain Homes was incorporated on January 1, 1976, and was the first United States home manufacturer dedicated solely to designing and manufacturing solar homes in kit form. I purchased twenty acres of commercial property in Royalton, Vermont, and in June 1975, left my job as vice president and general manager of the prefabricated post-and-beam home operation.

In January 1976, I visited Sheldon Dimick, the president of the Randolph National Bank in Randolph, Vermont. In the business proposal, I included plans for a dozen affordable solar homes. My wife Lea, with her Middlebury College art background, had drawn pencil renderings of the homes, which later became the basis for our first brochure. Shel, my banker, was immediately taken by the idea. In just a few weeks, we had put together a financing package with his bank, the Vermont Industrial Development Authority (VIDA), the Small Business Administration, and a personal loan backed by our farmstead, the one with the oil-thirsty boiler in the basement. The irony did not escape me that my energy dinosaur of a house was helping to finance an energy-efficient housing business.

While I was arranging private funding to start Green Mountain Homes, a business that would ultimately design, fabricate, and ship almost three hundred solar homes, the state and federal governments were getting involved in solar, offering tax incentives to encourage use of solar energy. The U.S. government spent on the order of a quarter of a million dollars to install domestic solar hot water collectors over a

The Green Mountain Homes factory practiced the lessons we preached: the building where our houses were fabricated was itself solar-heated, energy-efficient, and largely lit by daylight.

covered parking lot at a nearby resort hotel. To the best of my knowledge, those solar collectors have long since been disconnected because of mechanical problems and leaks. The state of Vermont, with some other states and the federal government, was instituting tax credits for investments in solar technologies. But credits were offered only for add-ons and retrofits of existing homes. These credits were for the "additional equipment needed," in the state's view, to provide solar energy. As a result, passive solar homes like the ones I intended to sell were almost completely left out of the tax-credit programs. Green Mountain Homes' buyers had difficulty obtaining solar credits, since the principle of my design was to utilize and rearrange the materials that you are already committed to purchase for building any style of new home, solar or not. Fortunately for my buyers, nighttime window and patio door insulating devices, extra insulation, and elements of the solar control system were considered add-on features and therefore qualified for solar credits. Yet the credits thereby earned were never significant enough to be the motivation for us or our clients to build solar homes instead of conventional ones. The real incentives were the ease, reliability, and comfort derived from solar heating. Paradoxically, since the solar water-heater collectors at the nearby resort were an add-on feature, the resort probably got more money from the U.S. government through solar credits than all of the Green Mountain Home solar homeowners combined. The federal government's solar subsidy program was completely dismantled during the Reagan years.

OUR MODEL HOME AND SOLAR FACTORY

When I was first working on my solar home design, I participated in a seminar led by Professor A. O. Converse of the Thayer School of Engineering at Dartmouth College. My role in the seminar was to provide the students with practical house construction information. When I explained my plan to build a prototype model solar home, Professor Converse offered to provide independent monitoring, using some of Dartmouth's resources, with funding and equipment supplied by the local power company, Central Vermont Public Service.

Construction of Green Mountain Home's solar-heated factory and the model home, which also served as my office and sales center, began in March 1976. The design was so successful that the energy savings (in both heat and electric lighting costs) paid the real estate taxes on our twenty acres each year.

A Green Mountain Home built in 1984 and located in northeast Pennsylvania.

With our borrowed money, we started an advertising campaign. We also decided to erect a state-approved off-site road sign on one of Vermont's major interstate highways, indicating the location of our business. The Vermont state highway department objected to the placement of the sign, so I asked my wife, Lea, to represent us at a hearing in Montpelier. As Lea was explaining the need for our placement of the sign, she described our new solar home business. A woman who sat on the board was so impressed with the idea that she sent her son to see us. He liked what he saw, and his home was delivered early in the fall of 1976.

Not long after, Lea was working in her mother's grape arbor and noticed a stranger approaching. He had seen an ad for Green Mountain Homes in a magazine, but the return address was to our home, not our factory/model-home complex nearby. The gentleman explained that he had spent most of the day looking for Green Mountain Homes and had finally stopped at the post office for help. Since ours is a small town, the postmaster knew about our new venture and sent the gentleman to my mother-in-law's home. By coincidence, Lea happened to be there. It turned out that the gentleman was a graduate of Worcester Polytechnic Institute, and was most supportive of our new solar home business. His home was delivered late in the fall of 1976; he has always maintained that he was the first buyer, because he ordered his home first.

Green Mountain Homes was launched. The company doubled in size yearly, and we were often hard pressed to keep up with the workload. I can remember many a Christmas when we were late to our own party because we were loading a tractor-trailer with that year's last home.

Potential buyers almost always traveled to Royalton, Vermont, to examine the model solar home, and to attend my Saturday morning solar heating seminars, which were followed by lively question-and-answer sessions. It was fun. Our customers came from all walks of life, and they accepted this new technology with enthusiasm. One man

Solar Principle #1

Orient the house properly with respect to the sun's relationship to the site.

Use a compass to find true south, and then by careful observation site the house so that it can utilize the sun's rays from the east, south, and west during as much of the day and year as possible. In orienting the house, take into account features of the landscape, including trees and natural land forms, which will buffer the house against harsher weather or winds from the north. Deciduous trees on the sunny sides of the site will shade the house from excess heat during the summer months, but will allow the winter sunlight to reach the house and deliver free solar energy.

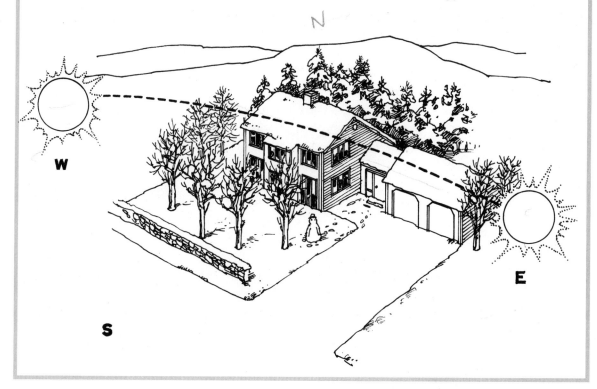

who bought a Green Mountain Home was asked to speak about it to the local Rotary Club. He protested, claiming that he didn't know how his house worked. Since he had a good sense of humor, the Rotarians thought he must be joking, so they asked him to speak anyway. The fact is, he really *didn't* know how his house worked, even though he and his brother had built it from our kit. When the Rotarians asked about the house's operation and about how much work he had to put in to keep it heated, he informed them that the day after it was completed, he had set the thermostat on 68 degrees and hadn't touched it since. This man had called me shortly after moving in to let me know that he and his brother had forgotten to put in the second floor heating ducts. And the house was *still* warm. We learned from our customers as we went along; in this case we found out that we could cut back on ductwork.

NEWS OF OUR SUCCESS SPREADS

Since Green Mountain Homes was a private venture financed through conventional bank loans, we had to succeed on our own merits without public or government funds. And we did succeed, because the design worked so well, both in tests on our prototype and in the comfort it delivered to the people living in actual homes. We also tried to help advance the solar movement by speaking at our own expense at various meetings and conferences. Our success story was featured in dozens of publications, including *Solar Age, Better Homes and Gardens, House and Garden, New Shelter, Farm Equipment News, The Muncie Star* (Indiana), *The Winchester Evening Star* (Virginia), *The Boston Herald, The San Francisco Chronicle, Money Magazine,* and *The Sierra Club Bulletin,* to name just a few. We also received enthusiastic mail from our customers through the years, for instance this from happy solar homeowners in Bethlehem, Connecticut:

> In the winter, we are warm. In the summer, we are cool. There are no unusual contraptions involved to store heat or regulate the temperature. We spent no additional money on "solar features" when we built this home. All materials were available at local lumberyards—nothing exotic. However, it was important to let common sense take precedent. We did, according to our instructions, face the broad, multi-windowed side of our house to the south. (Consequently, we gave up the "parallel to the road.") The north side has few windows, and many closets, and that side is also sheltered by a windblock of pine trees. The "heat-producing" kitchen is also placed on the north side of the house. Our floor is made of tile, which absorbs the heat from the sun, so in

winter the tile is never cold to our feet, as the tiles and Solar Slab underneath store the warmth. (The reverse is true in the summer, when the tile retains the coolness of the night during much of the day.)

And this letter from Susquehanna, Pennsylvania:

One of the greatest satisfactions about our home is that even though we are designed to be solar energy efficient, it placed very little restraints on how we designed the floor plan. Our home has a real feeling of spaciousness because of the view and use of windows. Even during the horrendous winter of '93, we didn't get "cabin fever."

Due to the collapse of the housing industry in 1990, Green Mountain Homes' production facility was closed down. Now semi-retired, I have continued to consult and to design solar homes. The patent for the Green Mountain Homes Solar Slab is now in the public domain, which means that our particular solar design now belongs to "the people of the United States." This book explains how to use the information formerly protected by that patent. Hopefully, it will benefit other solar designers and future home builders.

THE
PASSIVE SOLAR
CONCEPT

2

A French engineer named Felix Trombe is credited with the simple idea of building a solar collector comprised of a south-facing glass wall with an air space between it and a blackened concrete wall (see the illustration on page 16). The sun's energy passes through the glass, and is trapped and absorbed by the blackened wall. As the concrete warms, air rises in the space between the glass and the blackened concrete wall. Rectangular openings at the bottom and top of the Trombe wall allow this warm air to flow to and from the living space. This movement of air is called thermosiphoning. At night the blackened concrete wall will radiate, or release, its heat to the interior.

The process can, unfortunately, reverse at night bringing warm air from the living space over to the cold glass. As this warmer air is cooled by the glass, it drops to the floor which, in turn, pulls more warm air from the living space. In the process, thermosiphoning is reversed. The colder it is outside, the more the Trombe wall will reverse thermosiphon. One way to control this heat loss is mechanically to close the rectangular openings at night and to reopen them when the sun comes out.

The Trombe wall is the "Model A" of passive solar design; that is, it is elegant in its simplicity and dependability, but has been largely supplanted by more modern technology. The Trombe wall example, however, illustrates some important principles. The system requires no moving parts, no switches to turn motors on or off, and no control systems; yet when it is functioning properly, it will collect, store, and then radiate heat back into the living space, even after the sun has gone down.

By contrast, an active solar collector is an ancillary system; instead of incorporating heat collection, storage, and release into the structure

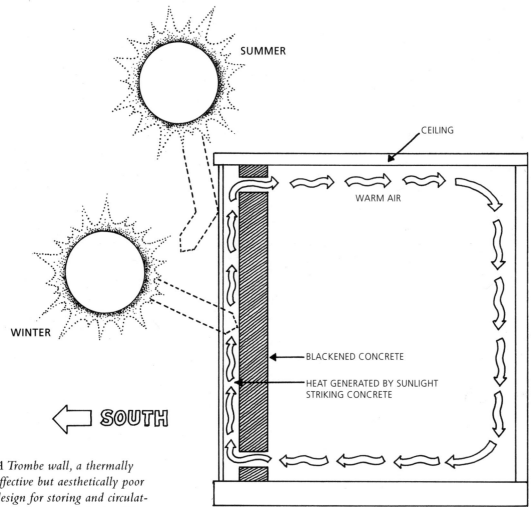

SUMMER

CEILING

WARM AIR

WINTER

SOUTH

BLACKENED CONCRETE

HEAT GENERATED BY SUNLIGHT
STRIKING CONCRETE

*A Trombe wall, a thermally
effective but aesthetically poor
design for storing and circulating sun-warmed air. At night,
the process can reverse, and
warm air may be drawn back
out of the living space to
escape through the cool
glazing.*

of the building, active systems are made up of devices attached to the
structure. (Active systems also represent "add-on" expenses for a home—
"add-ons" are features that are additional to those that you would normally purchase.) Active systems will not work without a pump or blower
operating. Typically, solar collectors are placed on the roof. Water pipes
deliver water heated by the collectors to a storage tank and heated
water is pumped out of the storage tank as needed. These systems will
not work by themselves, as they need to have sensors "tell" switches to
turn on pumps or blowers to mechanically activate the circulation of
water.

The "passive" Trombe wall and the active solar collector system represent the technological range of solar heating systems from most basic to most complicated.

KEEP IT SIMPLE AND
LET NATURE HELP YOU

Given the challenge of designing and building a naturally solar-heated home, the most widely applicable system is simple, passive, and does not add cost to construction of the home. Let's look at the materials which one has already committed to purchasing. Used properly, these materials become the building blocks of the naturally heated home. We need concrete to build the base of the house, and we all like windows and patio doors. Also, let's take a critical look at the building site, because much can be done to make home orientation and vegetation function as heating and cooling assists.

Let's start by finding a south-facing house site. For the sake of discussion, let's locate this house in Hartford, Connecticut, which is at north latitude 41°5', or "41 degrees 5 minutes." If the home faces true south, you will get the maximum solar benefit, but as you rotate your home off true south the solar benefit is reduced. At solar noon in February in Hartford, Connecticut, the cost of being oriented at an angle other than true south is indicated in Table 2–1.

TABLE 2-1	
TRUE SOUTH	100% SOLAR BENEFIT
Rotate 22½ degrees off true south to south-southwest or south-southeast	92% solar benefit
Rotate 45 degrees off true south to southwest or southeast	70% solar benefit
Rotate 67½ degrees off true south to west-southwest or east-southeast	36% solar benefit

As you can see, the reduction in solar benefit increases exponentially as you rotate the home's orientation away from true south. Within 20 degrees or so of true south, the cost of variation in lost solar benefit is minimal, which allows some latitude in placing the house on a site that presents obstacles such as slopes and outcroppings.

Ideally, the north side of the site will provide a windbreak, with evergreen trees and a protective hillside. These natural features will protect the home from the harsher northerly winds and weather. Deciduous trees on the east, south, and west will shade the home in summer, yet drop their leaves in winter, allowing sunlight to reach the home. Note in the drawing on page 11 how the south glass would be shaded in summer, yet the ease with which sunlight will penetrate through the deciduous trees in winter.

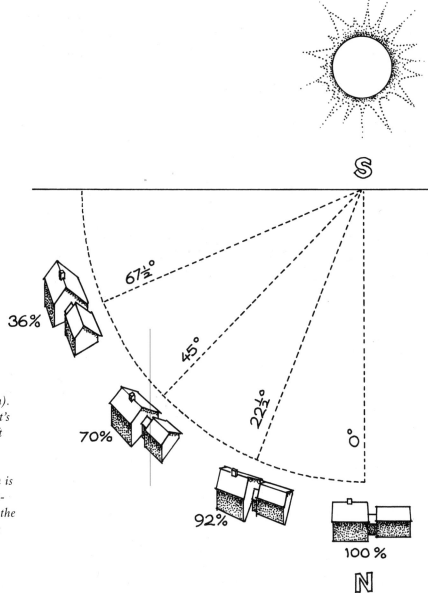

The ideal orientation for a solar house is with its long axis perpendicular to true south (or 0° on the diagram). Because of various factors, it's sometimes necessary to shift the orientation somewhat. Within 20 degrees of true south, the cost in solar gain is minimal, but as the orientation shifts more drastically, the house will significantly lose solar benefits.

KNOW YOUR SITE

Spend some time on your proposed home site. Try camping on the site to learn about its sun conditions in different seasons. Make a point of being on the site at sunrise and sunset at different times of the year. Develop a sense for which direction the prevailing wind comes from. Use your imagination in order to picture the view from each room. Mark the footprint of your new home on the ground, and develop a "feel" for what each room will be like after the home is constructed. In addition to solar orientation, consider access, view, wind direction, snow removal, power, septic, and of course, water. Carefully investigate your water source. If it is to be non-municipal, consider dowsing to find the best location for a well. (The American Society of Dowsers in Danville, Vermont, can refer you to a qualified water dowser in your area.) Sometimes it's advisable to drill the well in advance of building your home just to be sure of the cost, quantity, and quality of your water.

The long axis of a solar home should run east to west, presenting as much surface area to the sun as possible. If your new home measures 24 by 48 feet, maximize the amount of surface that the sun will strike by siting your home with the 48-foot dimension running east-west.

USE WINDOWS AND PATIO DOORS AS SOLAR COLLECTORS

If you locate the majority of the windows and patio doors on the east, south, and west elevations of the home, they can act as solar collectors. One often sees pictures of solar homes with huge expanses of south-facing glass tilted to be perpendicular to the sun rays. Let's remember that you want your home to be comfortable all year-round. Tilted glass, though technically favorable during certain heating months, is

Taking into account the sun's angles at three representative times of year.

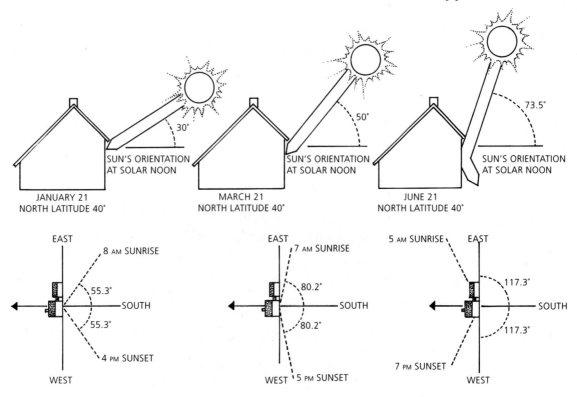

TABLE 2-2	
DATE	BTUS PER SQUARE FOOT
September 21	200
October 21	234
November 21	250
December 21	253
January 21	254
February 21	241
March 21	206
April 21	154
May 21	113
June 21	95

very detrimental in summer. One has to design on a 12-month basis, and understand where the sun is at each time of the year, in order to comprehend how the sun may be most beneficial to your home.

The diagram on page 19 shows the sun's angles at three different times of the year—January 21, March 21, and June 21, at north latitude 40 degrees (see also Appendix 2). We can see in January that the sun's low altitude almost directly strikes the south-facing vertical glass, which demonstrates again the importance of facing a home true south.

The March 21 and June 21 illustrations show that as the days grow longer, the breadth of solar aperture widens, meaning that a home will gain more solar heat and light from its eastern and western windows. Meanwhile, the altitude of solar noon rises to 50.0 degrees on March 21 and 73.5 degrees on June 21.

MAKE USE OF THE LOW SUN ANGLE IN WINTER

In Vermont at the winter solstice (December 21), the sunlight shining through a south-facing patio door will penetrate twenty-two feet into the home. On the summer solstice (June 21), the sun will only enter the building a few inches.

A dentist in New Hampshire placed a small round dental mirror flat on the sill of his south-facing patio door, and each day at noon he made a mark on the ceiling where the reflected sunlight hit. In twelve month's time, can you guess what kind of geometrical pattern was on his ceiling? An elongated figure-8. The mark closest to the south wall was made at the summer solstice, and the mark farthest from the wall was made at the winter solstice.

Let's examine south-facing glass at solar noon. If you plant a deciduous tree on the south side of your home, the sun's rays will shine through the canopy in winter when the leaves are gone. Yet in summer, the tree's canopy will absorb almost all of the sun's heat. Plant deciduous trees at a distance from the home, based on the height to which the tree is expected to grow and the size of the anticipated canopy. If deciduous trees exist on your site, cut down only those that directly obstruct the clearing needed to build the home. Thin adjacent trees' branches after you have gained experience with their shading patterns in both winter and summer.

Because of the high angle of the summer sun, its heat will bounce off vertical south-facing glass, unlike the almost direct horizontal hit your solar collectors will get in winter. This "gadget" called a solar home will "automatically" turn itself on during the coldest months

Solar Principle # 2

Design on a 12-month basis.

A home must be comfortable in summer as well as winter. When designing a solar home, carefully plan to accommodate and benefit from the sun's shifting patterns and other natural, seasonal cycles. Before finalizing a building plan, spend time at the site at different times of day and year, and pay attention to the sun, wind, and weather.

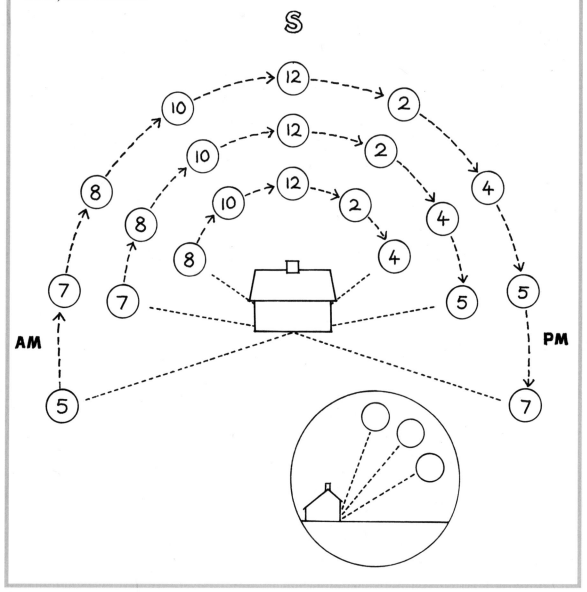

and shut itself off during the summer months, so that solar collection is maximized for heat gain when you need the extra heat, and minimized when heat would be uncomfortable. As you grasp these basic dynamics, you have started to let nature work for you. Table 2–2 shows the amount of energy received by vertical south-facing glass at solar noon at 40 degrees north latitude.

As you can see, the amount of energy received by vertical south-facing glass in December or January is almost triple the amount received in June.

What about east- and west-facing glass? We frequently hear about south-facing glass, but at the beginning and end of the heating season, as you can see from the illustration on page 19, east- and west-facing glass make good solar collectors, as well. In March, sunrise is at 7:00 AM versus 8:00 AM in January and 5:00 AM in June. Due to the angle of the sun being perpendicular to east-facing glass as the sun rises, and perpendicular to west-facing glass as the sun sets, east- and west-facing glass do not "turn off" as solar collectors in summer. We have to be more careful about the amount of east- and west-facing glass we use. We also have to consider location as more of a factor in the distribution of east- and west-facing glass. For example, a solar home located in Pennsylvania, which requires energy for summer cooling, should have less east- and west-facing glass than a home located in northern New England. In chapter 4 we will discuss other techniques to control the gains and losses of windows and patio doors.

Now that you understand how effectively windows and patio doors function as solar collectors, you will see why I continue to emphasize that you should use the windows and patio doors that you are already committed to purchase to not only enhance the livability of a new solar home, but also to serve as an automatic solar collection system.

STORE THE SUN'S FREE HEAT FOR NIGHTTIME USE

The other important material we have already committed to purchase for our new home is concrete and/or concrete building blocks. To store heat we need to have *mass*, or a body of material that can hold heat. Water is the storage medium of choice in active solar systems because it holds 62.4 Btus per cubic foot per degree Fahrenheit, making it an excellent theoretical storage medium. Concrete holds only about 30 Btus per cubic foot per degree Fahrenheit, but has an advantage: when building a new home, we have already committed to buy tons of it. Used properly, concrete becomes another integral component in a household solar heating-and-cooling system.

I have described the way in which the Trombe wall utilizes concrete as part of a solar collection system. In chapter 3 we will look at another way this durable heat-storage material can be used.

A solar house uses trees, hills, and the varying angles from which the sun strikes a home during the year to enhance its ability to collect sunlight and store its heat. I have emphasized the importance of facing a home south, and we've begun to think about rearranging materials that we would have purchased anyway, such as windows and concrete. Ideally, your new solar home will not cost you any extra money.

And there are other, non-monetary characteristics of a well-built solar home, including tightness of construction, absence of air leaks, and judicious venting to supply plenty of fresh air without wasting heat. Layering the walls to prevent heat loss and providing proper venting are crucial to energy-efficiency, and we will discuss these practices in depth in chapter 4.

Let me quote from another letter from an enthusiastic solar homeowner, this one in South Harpswell, Maine:

> We find it takes a special way . . . dealing with life and the environment. . . . We have come to feel great pride in our woodpile. It is not a beautiful piece of garden architecture, but you sure feel secure when you look at it. And the house has to be set exactly right to catch the sun's rays in the colder months, and our southern deciduous trees do not cast shadows to interfere with maximum solar energy. Our daily lives and routines have been altered somewhat—keeping woodboxes filled, stove work done regularly, thermal shutters closed at about 4 PM once winter sets in. You develop a whole philosophy of working with nature and you become committed to a life style in which your house is almost a family member that you care for. There's extra work for sure, but the pleasure you get is worth the extra effort, as we seem to watch the world around us as we never did before. It is important to us now to know when the sun will rise and set—and the direction and velocity of the wind—and the temperature of the air.

THE
SOLAR SLAB
AND BASIC SOLAR
DESIGN

3

Heating-system designers think in terms of heat transfer from warmer to cooler. The typical home furnace warms air to 140 degrees, and the warm air is delivered to the various rooms in the home via ducts. When the thermostat reads 72 degrees or another desired setting, the furnace shuts off. Heat has been transferred from the warmer body (the furnace at 140 degrees) to the cooler body (the house at 72 degrees). The design of a conventional heating system represents a straightforward problem that has a direct solution: determine the heat loss of the building, then size the furnace and ductwork in order to provide a continual or "on-demand" supply of replacement heat.

Active systems are easy to visualize—boilers, ductwork, pipes, and radiators—whereas the elements of a passive heat collection and storage system may be almost "invisible." When faced with the problem of designing a solar home, early solar designers tried to assimilate the elements of an active, furnace-based system. Exterior solar collectors were utilized to build up high temperatures using water or air. This heat was then stored in a high temperature "heat sink" using beds of rocks or tanks of water ("heat sink" is a physics term for a medium that absorbs and stores heat—for example, water, concrete, or masonry, in particular arrays). Ducts or pipes transported the heat back and forth from the sun-exposed exterior collector components to the interior storage components of the system. Such active systems are complicated; they tend to require added-on costs to the home, and are sometimes difficult to justify financially. Further, some of them simply didn't work very well or were plagued with mechanical problems, especially over time, necessitating continuous oversight and maintenance.

IT'S HARD TO GET
A DRINK IN A DRIZZLE

"Solar gain" is the free heat derived from the sun. Sunlight is ubiquitous, but diffuse. Systems that involve rock beds and solar hot-water storage tanks attempt to concentrate a diffuse form of energy. It is both difficult and expensive to concentrate, build, and hold high temperatures in solar heating systems. Solar energy can be compared to a drizzle: there are tons of water in the air but it's very difficult to get a cupful to drink. Almost all attempts to build active solar homes are based on trying to build up heat in some sort of storage reservoir that will have a temperature substantially higher than room temperature.

Since the Trombe wall, for instance, needs to build up a temperature greater than normal room temperature in order to transfer heat to the adjacent living space, the home can become overheated during the day. If, as described in chapter 2, the Trombe wall reverses its air flow at night, the home may be subjected to uncomfortable cold flows of air. If we remember that our naturally heated home needs to stay comfortable all day and all night, twelve months a year, these wide variations in temperature should be avoided.

In this chapter we are going to examine a solar heating system that stores heat in the floor at a temperature no greater than comfortable room temperature, and a system that uses windows and patio doors as solar collectors.

The solar system technique described in this book is a departure from conventional heating design. As mentioned in chapter 1, most heating systems are designed by specialists working independently from those producing the general house design. This practice usually results in a worst-case design, with oversized furnaces and ductwork. Oversized equipment will necessitate higher construction costs and will also cause higher operating costs, as oversized equipment inefficiently cycles on and off.

Passive or natural systems represent transient engineering problems; many elements of the calculations necessary to design these systems occur simultaneously, making the processes they involve difficult to analyze. Most heating designers don't like this kind of "fuzzy" problem, and often they are not given all the site information necessary to design on anything more subtle than a worst-case or generic basis.

It is a straightforward calculation to size a furnace on a worst-case basis and to provide a system of ducts to carry heat from a 140-degree furnace to areas of 72 degrees. However, to calculate exactly what is going on when heat is entering the home from the sun is much more complicated: some heat is being used directly to heat the home; some is being stored; and some is being lost back to the outside. Moreover, each one of these events influences each of the others. From the perspective of the conventional heating and cooling technician, this is a "fuzzy" or transient problem. We will simplify this transient problem by looking at temperature averages for the day, month, and year.

In fairness to the conventional system designer, it's important to acknowledge that their job is to guarantee adequate heat and coolness with a wide margin to cover seasonal variation. Experimentation can sometimes lead to "call backs" or other expensive liabilities if a system doesn't work to the homeowner's satisfaction. A system designed on a worst-case basis may cost more to buy and operate, but it also doesn't represent a potential liability to the designer as it will always be more than capable of doing the job. The same principle is invoked by highway builders who construct a four-lane expressway because once a year, on the Fourth of July, all four lanes will be utilized by the traffic.

ROOM TEMPERATURE STORAGE

Engineers and designers schooled in heating and ventilating have found the idea of creating heat storage at or below room temperature to be strange. Early on in the development of the system described by this book, some of the typical responses were: "Can't be done"; "Remember Newton's Laws of Heat Transfer—heat only goes from hot to cold"; "Low-temperature room storage will take heat from the living space. You'll create the equivalent of an ice cube in the drink." (That is, the drink remains at 32 degrees Fahrenheit until the last ice cube melts; in this case the "drink" is the living space and the "ice cube" is the heat storage in the floor. The skeptics are concerned that the floor won't let the house come up to temperature.) Or, "The heat sink will act detrimentally to the comfort of the living space."

KEEP THE FURNACE OFF

We will use daily averages to help analyze this transient heat problem. Let's start by thinking in terms of how we can keep the furnace off. If the furnace doesn't have to run at all, and instead heat is being supplied naturally and free to the house from the sun, isn't that the name of the game?

The Trombe wall described in chapter 2 is elegant in its simplicity but aesthetically crude. Pictures of a blackened concrete wall along the south side of a home certainly would not survive among glossy photo spreads in *Better Homes and Gardens*. In addition it blocks out a good portion of

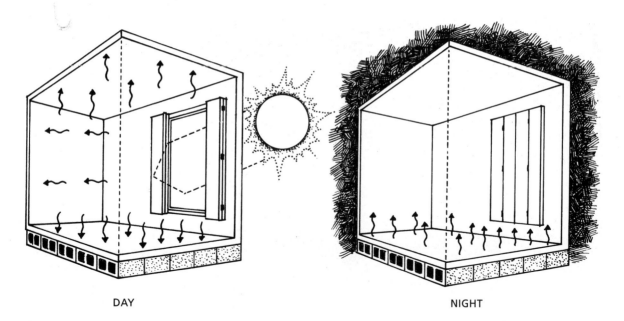

DAY   NIGHT

Thermal mass is comprised of building materials that absorb heat effectively, charging up like a thermal battery and then yielding this heat back into the home's living space through periods of time when the building is not actively gaining heat from the sun or from some other source.

the cheery southerly sun. From a technical standpoint, the movement of warm air over the surface of a smooth vertical wall will cause laminar flow; that is, a thin boundary layer of air will build up and the warm air passing over this boundary layer will not readily give up its heat to the concrete. An airplane wing is an example of a surface that produces laminar flow. There is very little heat being transferred to the wing as it slips smoothly through the air.

On the other hand, a rough surface interrupts the flow of air causing turbulence, which in turn causes greater heat transfer. Picture the fins in a baseboard radiator versus a smooth pipe along the baseboard. The fins provide much more surface area per running foot than smooth pipe would provide. This increase in surface area allows the heated water inside the pipe to give up or transfer its heat to the air. This concept will be crucial when we discuss the construction of the Solar Slab.

Remember the goal described in chapter 2 of utilizing materials you are already committed to purchase for your new home, and rearranging them in a different configuration in order to collect and store heat. Consider what we would need to buy for a full basement. The cellar floor will require a 4-inch concrete slab and we will need a poured or concrete block cellar wall. That gives us tons of material with which to work. Let's see how we can rearrange these materials.

Start by moving the 4-inch concrete slab from the cellar floor to the first floor, eliminating the basement. This is the equivalent of placing the concrete Trombe wall horizontally flat. Next, let's take some of

The Solar Slab utilizes completely conventional materials, including concrete blocks and poured concrete. Construction of this foundation is neither difficult nor costly, yet the result will be a house with exceptionally effective thermal mass as its base.

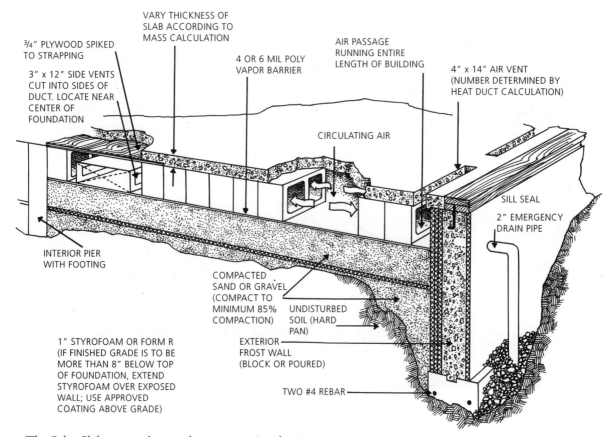

VARY THICKNESS OF SLAB ACCORDING TO MASS CALCULATION

¾" PLYWOOD SPIKED TO STRAPPING

3" x 12" SIDE VENTS CUT INTO SIDES OF DUCT. LOCATE NEAR CENTER OF FOUNDATION

4 OR 6 MIL POLY VAPOR BARRIER

AIR PASSAGE RUNNING ENTIRE LENGTH OF BUILDING

4" x 14" AIR VENT (NUMBER DETERMINED BY HEAT DUCT CALCULATION)

CIRCULATING AIR

SILL SEAL

2" EMERGENCY DRAIN PIPE

INTERIOR PIER WITH FOOTING

COMPACTED SAND OR GRAVEL (COMPACT TO MINIMUM 85% COMPACTION)

UNDISTURBED SOIL (HARD PAN)

1" STYROFOAM OR FORM R (IF FINISHED GRADE IS TO BE MORE THAN 8" BELOW TOP OF FOUNDATION, EXTEND STYROFOAM OVER EXPOSED WALL; USE APPROVED COATING ABOVE GRADE)

EXTERIOR FROST WALL (BLOCK OR POURED)

TWO #4 REBAR

The Solar Slab concrete heat exchanger: a section drawing.

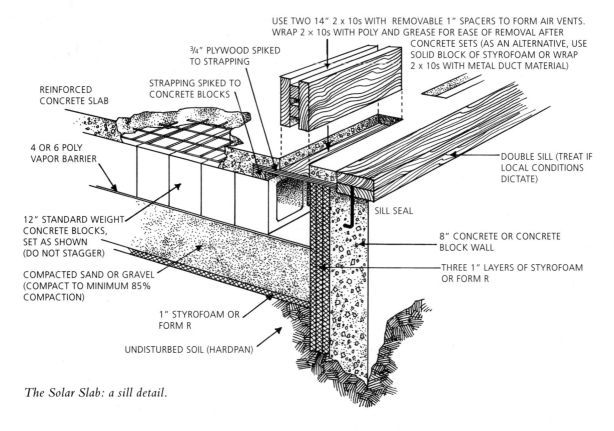

USE TWO 14" 2 x 10s WITH REMOVABLE 1" SPACERS TO FORM AIR VENTS. WRAP 2 x 10s WITH POLY AND GREASE FOR EASE OF REMOVAL AFTER CONCRETE SETS (AS AN ALTERNATIVE, USE SOLID BLOCK OF STYROFOAM OR WRAP 2 x 10s WITH METAL DUCT MATERIAL)

3/4" PLYWOOD SPIKED TO STRAPPING

REINFORCED CONCRETE SLAB

STRAPPING SPIKED TO CONCRETE BLOCKS

4 OR 6 POLY VAPOR BARRIER

DOUBLE SILL (TREAT IF LOCAL CONDITIONS DICTATE)

12" STANDARD WEIGHT CONCRETE BLOCKS, SET AS SHOWN (DO NOT STAGGER)

SILL SEAL

8" CONCRETE OR CONCRETE BLOCK WALL

COMPACTED SAND OR GRAVEL (COMPACT TO MINIMUM 85% COMPACTION)

THREE 1" LAYERS OF STYROFOAM OR FORM R

1" STYROFOAM OR FORM R

UNDISTURBED SOIL (HARDPAN)

The Solar Slab: a sill detail.

the concrete blocks that we would have used to build the cellar wall, and place them under the concrete slab. Instead of arranging them with their holes vertical, let's lay them on their sides with the holes lining up horizontally to form air passages running north to south. When the concrete is poured over these blocks, it will bond to the blocks and make a huge concrete "radiator"—the radiator's "fins" are the ribs in the concrete blocks (see the illustrations on pages 29 and above).

If this combination of poured concrete slab over horizontally laid blocks is ventilated by air holes along the north and south walls, air will naturally circulate through this concrete radiator when the sun is out. Remember, we oriented our new home with the long axis of the building running east to west. When the sun is out in winter, the south wall will be warmer than the north wall. As heat is transferred into the home by the south glass or by heat transfer through the wall, air that is next to or alongside the south wall will rise. Warmed air will then be pulled out of the ventilated slab, and the cooler air along the north wall will drop into the holes along the north wall. This thermosiphoning effect will naturally continue to pull air through the Solar Slab.

For the Solar Slab to effectively heat the home, it must be thermally accessible to the living space. It is therefore not cost-effective or thermally practical to utilize the lower level for a basement-storage area instead of as a living space.

STORAGE OF TRAPPED SOLAR HEAT

As heat from the sun "drives" the thermosiphoning, heat in the home, which has been trapped as in a greenhouse, will be taken up via the ribs as warm air passes through the concrete blocks, which in turn are thermally bonded to the concrete slab. Heat from the sun comes to us as light or short wave energy. Since glass is transparent to light, sunlight passes through glass and strikes objects within the interior of the home. As soon as it strikes an object, for instance the floor covering above the slab, light changes form—to long-wave energy or heat. In a highly insulated solar home, this heat will now be trapped. The temperature of the ventilated slab will rise as the trapped heat is absorbed by the concrete. Since concrete has almost no R-value it has little resistance or ability to stop the transfer of heat. Any heat transfered to the ventilated slab anywhere in the building will migrate evenly throughout the array of concrete blocks and poured slab.

We will explore this benefit further when we discuss the use of a woodburning stove as backup heat. The heat storage benefit is free, provided you are willing to trade a full basement for a Solar Slab.

The solar home, properly designed, can achieve thermal balance every day. The energy produced by the east-, south-, and west-facing glass will be either consumed directly by the heat demand of the home, or absorbed by the first floor heat sink as the heat comes into the home. If the heat comes in too fast to be absorbed by the mass, the home overheats. Overheating can be a major problem in passive solar design, and in many respects, passive solar design presents a significant cooling challenge.

THE OLD NEW ENGLANDERS' SALTBOX

One of the designs my company offered, the Green Mountain Homes' 28-foot by 38-foot Saltbox, will be used to explain the way the Solar Slab relates to the functionality of a solar home. For illustrative purposes, we will situate this solar home in Hartford, Connecticut, north latitude 41 degrees 5 minutes (41°5'). The floorplans and a cross section for the Saltbox 38 are shown in chapter 5.

Many of the plans and calculations in this book use a basic house design known as a saltbox. While designers and builders of solar homes can adopt a wide variety of house styles and construction techniques, the saltbox is useful as a model, since its design has a classic simplicity. The solar home shown here was built in 1978 in Virginia. Note use of deciduous trees for summer shading.

We will present detailed solar calculations in chapter 6, but in order to help explain how the system works we need briefly to examine the Solar Slab, which as you recall is comprised of a 4-inch concrete slab bonded to 12-inch concrete blocks. We can calculate that a standard concrete block is about 50 percent concrete, or the equivalent of 6 inches of solid concrete. Therefore, the 4-inch slab and 12-inch concrete block are the equivalent of 6 inches + 4 inches = 10 inches of solid concrete. Discounting air passages along the north and south walls and the amount of concrete blocks displaced by ductwork, for a 28 by 38 foundation the volume of concrete equals 754 cubic feet.

Assume that the Solar Slab temperature is 60 degrees at 7:00 AM and the daytime rise in Solar Slab temperature is 8 degrees. The Solar Slab temperature at 5:00 PM is then 68 degrees Fahrenheit. Picture what this means: The entire first floor of the living space is now up to 68 degrees; that's 754 cubic feet of concrete at 140 pounds per cubic foot, which is 105,560 pounds or 52¾ tons inside the house, covered with the floor covering of your choice, sitting there at almost 68 degrees.

Surely you have experienced sitting on a sun-warmed rock after sundown. It's nice and warm, and takes a long time to cool off. Remember, the design goal is keeping the furnace off, or requiring it to do very little work. The heat stored in the first floor of the living space, and dispersed evenly throughout the first floor, has to be beneficial to the heating and comfort of the home.

In chapter 6, the thermal balance calculation will show how extra heat provided by the sun is trapped by the greenhouse effect (the conversion of light energy to heat energy), stored, then released as needed from the Solar Slab.

Because the Solar Slab is an effective heat exchanger, with its fins of concrete, the sun's heat is stored in the Solar Slab at the time it enters the house and strikes the floor covering over the slab.

The surface area inside the blocks calculates to be 366 square inches while the top surface is 119 square inches ($7\frac{5}{8}$ inches x $15\frac{5}{8}$ inches). The ratio of square feet of surface area within the blocks below the floor surface to square feet of floor is $366 \div 119 = 3$. This means that air passing through the blocks is exposed to three times more surface area than if the air had simply passed over a flat surface. This ratio plus the roughness of the surface inside the blocks make the Solar Slab an effective heat exchanger.

KEEP THE HOME COMFORTABLE ALL DAY

In a building in which the solar design components have been properly sized and located, while the windows and patio doors are collecting solar energy, the temperature of the home will hold steady at between 68 and 70 degrees, and will not overheat. If the glass area is too large for the heat storage capacity of the mass, the house temperature will rise to uncomfortable levels, and the occupants will be forced to open windows to ventilate, thereby losing the benefits of both immediate comfort and storage of the sun's free heat for use later in the evening. Greenhouses are examples of spaces that overheat during the day and get very cold at night. On the other hand, too much thermal mass and not enough glass to collect heat will result in a chilly, cave-like space that will never come up to the comfortable temperature.

The home must have a proper balance between the square footage of its glass solar collectors and the dimensions of its effective thermal storage mass. A prevalent mistake in solar design is using too much glass. The thought pattern seems to be that if some south glazing is good, a lot more is better. As we discussed above, overglazing will cause overheating and detrimental negative temperature swings at night. In fact, in some cases, the cost to heat the overglazed home at night will exceed the benefit derived on sunny days. This consideration is especially important in the northeast, where we have about 50 percent sunshine in the winter and long cold winter nights. The good news in the northeast is that our heat season is so long and severe that almost

SUNNY DAY IN WINTER

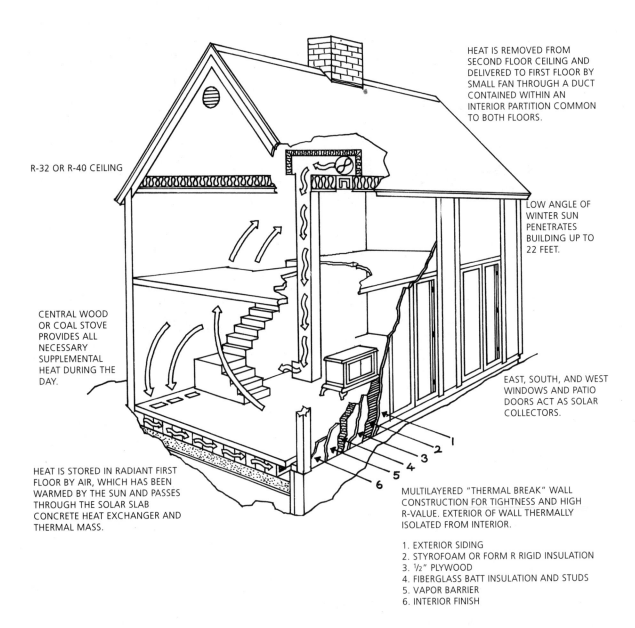

HEAT IS REMOVED FROM SECOND FLOOR CEILING AND DELIVERED TO FIRST FLOOR BY SMALL FAN THROUGH A DUCT CONTAINED WITHIN AN INTERIOR PARTITION COMMON TO BOTH FLOORS.

R-32 OR R-40 CEILING

LOW ANGLE OF WINTER SUN PENETRATES BUILDING UP TO 22 FEET.

CENTRAL WOOD OR COAL STOVE PROVIDES ALL NECESSARY SUPPLEMENTAL HEAT DURING THE DAY.

EAST, SOUTH, AND WEST WINDOWS AND PATIO DOORS ACT AS SOLAR COLLECTORS.

HEAT IS STORED IN RADIANT FIRST FLOOR BY AIR, WHICH HAS BEEN WARMED BY THE SUN AND PASSES THROUGH THE SOLAR SLAB CONCRETE HEAT EXCHANGER AND THERMAL MASS.

MULTILAYERED "THERMAL BREAK" WALL CONSTRUCTION FOR TIGHTNESS AND HIGH R-VALUE. EXTERIOR OF WALL THERMALLY ISOLATED FROM INTERIOR.

1. EXTERIOR SIDING
2. STYROFOAM OR FORM R RIGID INSULATION
3. ½" PLYWOOD
4. FIBERGLASS BATT INSULATION AND STUDS
5. VAPOR BARRIER
6. INTERIOR FINISH

How does the Solar Slab work? Here is a sequence of illustrations showing its operation in three modes. First, a sunny day in winter. Heat from the sun and when necessary a small backup woodstove is stored in the thermal mass of the radiant floor as sun-warmed air is drawn by vents through channels made by aligned concrete blocks beneath the poured slab and the home's finish flooring.

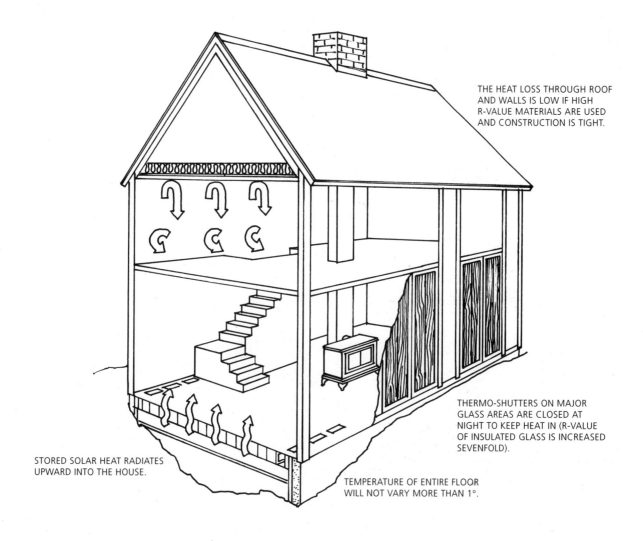

COLD WINTER NIGHT

THE HEAT LOSS THROUGH ROOF
AND WALLS IS LOW IF HIGH
R-VALUE MATERIALS ARE USED
AND CONSTRUCTION IS TIGHT.

THERMO-SHUTTERS ON MAJOR
GLASS AREAS ARE CLOSED AT
NIGHT TO KEEP HEAT IN (R-VALUE
OF INSULATED GLASS IS INCREASED
SEVENFOLD).

STORED SOLAR HEAT RADIATES
UPWARD INTO THE HOUSE.

TEMPERATURE OF ENTIRE FLOOR
WILL NOT VARY MORE THAN 1°.

*On a cold winter night, solar heat stored in the home's slab during the day
radiates upwards into the living space. The temperature of the entire floor will
not vary more than 1 degree. A small wood or coal stove will normally provide
adequate supplemental heat, and a small conventional furnace will double as an
air mover for the solar heat exchanger, as well as providing backup heat (see
chapter 7). Nighttime window insulation prevents the loss of heat through the
largest of the windows and patio doors.*

SUMMER COOLING

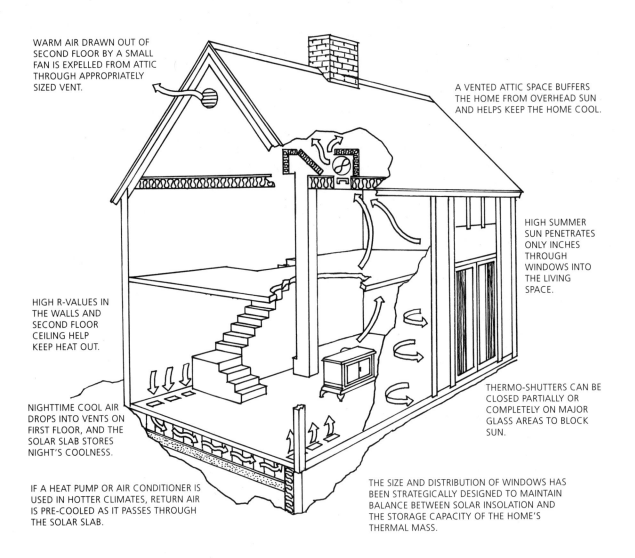

WARM AIR DRAWN OUT OF SECOND FLOOR BY A SMALL FAN IS EXPELLED FROM ATTIC THROUGH APPROPRIATELY SIZED VENT.

A VENTED ATTIC SPACE BUFFERS THE HOME FROM OVERHEAD SUN AND HELPS KEEP THE HOME COOL.

HIGH SUMMER SUN PENETRATES ONLY INCHES THROUGH WINDOWS INTO THE LIVING SPACE.

HIGH R-VALUES IN THE WALLS AND SECOND FLOOR CEILING HELP KEEP HEAT OUT.

NIGHTTIME COOL AIR DROPS INTO VENTS ON FIRST FLOOR, AND THE SOLAR SLAB STORES NIGHT'S COOLNESS.

THERMO-SHUTTERS CAN BE CLOSED PARTIALLY OR COMPLETELY ON MAJOR GLASS AREAS TO BLOCK SUN.

IF A HEAT PUMP OR AIR CONDITIONER IS USED IN HOTTER CLIMATES, RETURN AIR IS PRE-COOLED AS IT PASSES THROUGH THE SOLAR SLAB.

THE SIZE AND DISTRIBUTION OF WINDOWS HAS BEEN STRATEGICALLY DESIGNED TO MAINTAIN BALANCE BETWEEN SOLAR INSOLATION AND THE STORAGE CAPACITY OF THE HOME'S THERMAL MASS.

During a sunny summer day, because of proper siting, glazing, and sizing of thermal mass, the Solar Slab will aid in cooling the house, as excess solar heat is absorbed during the warm hours of the day. Before the home can overheat, the day has ended (this is called "thermal lag"). The same attic fan used in winter to redirect heat from the second floor ceiling can be used in summer to vent warm air out through the attic vents. In air conditioning areas, air-to-air heat pumps can also be used in tandem with the Solar Slab.

any measure we take to utilize the sun's free heat can result in significant cost and energy savings.

Let's return to the objective of keeping the furnace off. The furnace was off all day as the solar home collected and stored heat. During the evening, the occupants will need very little supplemental heat to maintain 68 to 72 degrees until 10:00 PM (bedtime), because the entire first floor of the house was 68 degrees at 5:00 PM. Basically, the backup heat is only heating the difference between the Solar Slab temperature and the desired room temperature. If 68 feels comfortable, then no backup heat is needed at all. As the Solar Slab gives up its heat to the first floor living space, the Solar Slab temperature will start to decline. The first floor room temperature at 7:00 AM will be the same as the Solar Slab temperature. Stored heat has been given up to the house through the night, and the Solar Slab is now ready to absorb the next day's free solar heat. This solar home will stay ready to instantaneously accept any solar heat available. If the sun comes out for just a few minutes between clouds, that heat will be collected, as there are no sensors that have to react to turn pumps on.

In addition, this solar home will absorb excess heat from cooking, lights, and yes, even the heat given off by human bodies. A particularly nice way to heat a solar home is to throw a party and invite lots of people over on a cold winter day! Remember, heat travels from warm bodies to cold bodies. We are each a small furnace, running at 98.6 degrees.

THE THERMAL FLYWHEEL

Do you remember the old John Deere tractors that had an external heavy-metal flywheel? The tractor's small engine slowly got the huge flywheel spinning. Once up to speed, very little energy was needed to keep the tractor moving. That is called mechanical inertia. A body in motion doesn't want to stop. Likewise, the Solar Slab provides thermal inertia to the home so that the home "wants" or tends to stay at a steady temperature, using very little purchased fuel in the process. With this kind of thermal inertia built into the solar home, we can downsize the backup heater, and instead size equipment for less than worst-case conditions.

Why haven't other people used this building technique? The answer most likely lies in the difficulty of trying to calculate the effect of a "room temperature heat sink." Some would say that this approach seems to violate conventional heating theories.

My approach to the problem of heating a home with the sun was to make my best engineering calculations, and then build and monitor a prototype. This represented both a professional and financial risk on my part, but it was well worth it. I was sure that my approach would work, but what I didn't know was how well. By measuring all energy entering the test building, and keeping careful records of the Solar Slab temperatures, we were able to verify the effectiveness of the design.

A PATENTED DESIGN

As I started to make heat loss and solar heat gain calculations in 1975, I became more and more convinced that I was on to something un-usual, and decided to protect my invention by applying for a U.S. Patent. In order to receive a patent one must prove that the idea or design is original. One of the unique aspects of the Solar Slab design is that the maximum achievable temperature is room temperature. Conventional thinking says that room temperature storage will be at best neutral, or at worst, will result in a drain of heat from the room. Remember the key concept of temperature difference (in engineer's jargon, "Delta T"), and the laws of heat transfer—heat will only flow from hot to cold.

The Monitoring Effort

As explained in chapter 1, Professor A.O. Converse, of the Thayer School of Engineering at Dartmouth College led a team that inde-pendently monitored our prototype, and he and I co-authored several papers which were presented at various solar conferences. His work culminated with the "Final Report Monitoring Studies of Green Mountain Home's Hybrid Systems," December 8, 1978. Page 7 of this report states in part, "We certainly conclude that the purchased energy requirements were quite low and the percent solar is well above 40 percent." New Mexico's Sandia Laboratories published their report on Green Mountain Homes in July, 1979 (its reference number is *SAND 79 - 0824*).

The monitoring effort with the Thayer School was centered around a Green Mountain Homes Model N-38 in Royalton, Vermont (see the floorplan on page 61). Professor Converse and I had a unique oppor-tunity to install instruments in the superstructure of the N-38 during construction. We also placed measuring devices in an "X" pattern within the Solar Slab and installed vertical probes in the gravel layer under the concrete blocks and inside and outside of the footings.

The first principle of good solar design is siting a home with a southern exposure and utilizing the natural features of the site, including trees that provide shelter from harsher weather that tends to come from the north.

A passive solar home will to a great extent heat and cool itself, with minimal use of conventional HVAC equipment, and with no additional conventional expenses over the cost of a comparably sized non-solar, fossil-fuel dependent house.

A solar home uses thermal mass — a material that readily absorbs heat — to collect and store the warmth of the sun during the day. This thermal mass will then radiate heat back into a home's living space during the cooler nighttime hours. This book describes a technique for constructing a Solar Slab, using ordinary concrete blocks and a poured slab, which transforms the conventional house foundation into a particularly effective thermal mass.

*Because of improvements in the standards for wall framing, windows, and insulation,
even conventional houses are now far more energy-efficient than our ancestors' homes.
As a result, it has never been easier to build a solar house.*

Above: Air grilles located in the first riser of the stairway discharge warm air collected at the second floor ceiling.

Right: Thermo-shutter designed to insulate windows during the cooler night (or shade the windows during times of intense sun) can be decorated to harmonize with the room decor.

Interior of the solar home shown on the first page of the color section. The airtight wood/coal stove provides the only backup heat needed by this 3,500-square-foot home, and also provides domestic hot water.

In a building that is tightly constructed and well insulated, you will need to be sure to provide for an adequate exchange of fresh air. You might want to consider including a solar cat in your household: not only will a cat infallibly follow the path of the sunlight over the course of the day, but with its frequent trips in and out through the door, the cat will help insure a comfortable exchange of air.

Three solar homes, all warm and comfortable even in the depths of winter. Note in the bottom picture how the snow lays very evenly on the roof. Proper insulation and venting of the roof allows the snow to melt away slowly without causing "tell-tale" icicles or creating ice-dam problems.

In addition, we also installed a device to measure the incoming solar energy (insolation).

All energy consumed by the building was documented. Meters measured the electricity consumed by the furnace and the second floor blower as well as the electricity used for all other purposes. A fuel meter was installed to measure the number of gallons of oil consumed by the furnace.

Solar Principle # 3

Provide effective thermal mass to store free solar heat in the daytime for nighttime use.

When sunlight strikes surfaces, the solar energy is converted from light to heat. Design a home's thermal mass to effectively absorb the warmth of sunlight as it enters the building in winter, thereby avoiding overheating. Achieve thermal balance by sizing the storage capacity of the thermal mass to provide for the heating needs of the building through the night. In summer, a properly sized thermal mass will serve to cool the building because of "thermal lag" — that is, excess heat will be absorbed during the daylight hours, and by the time the mass has heated up, the day is over and that stored heat can be discharged by opening windows to increase circulation during the night.

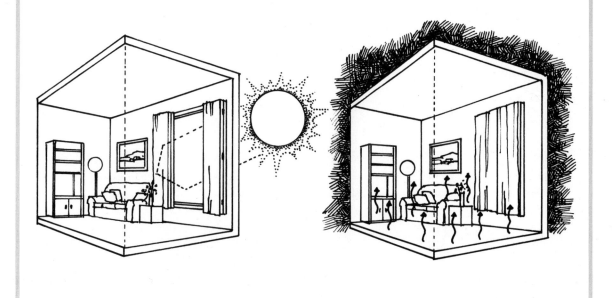

As evidenced in the Thayer report, the home was very energy-efficient and compared favorably with several active solar homes which were also being monitored by Converse and his colleagues at that time.

The efficiency of our design had exceeded my expectations, and the monitoring verified information that we had predicted in the U.S. Patent application. The ongoing independent monitoring of the prototype and the knowledge gained by working with solar homes located over a wide area with diverse design requirements allowed us to continually refine and improve our design methods.

PARTIAL RESULTS OF THE INFORMATION MONITORING EFFORT

1. The temperature was consistent and evenly distributed throughout the concrete slab and concrete blocks, with any difference in temperature being within one degree. This observation helped in the design of back up heating systems. That thermal consistency is particularly beneficial to the woodburning home; since the heat from the woodstove "migrates" evenly throughout the first floor, the design of a home that uses a woodstove as backup heat is essentially the same as designing for solar. The engineering problem is the same in the sense that the woodstove is an uncontrolled centralized source of heat that needs to be distributed evenly throughout the building and stored, if necessary, for use after the stove finishes its burn.

2. More than 100 percent insolation was measured on sunny winter days. This was attributed to the reflection up and into the building from snow cover on the south patio. This factor saves some of the homeowner's energy, because the south patio can be left unshovelled, allowing the snow cover to reflect the sun's heat and light into the building.

3. The temperature outside the footings (4 feet in the ground) reached a maximum of 68 degrees Fahrenheit in September, and slowly decayed to a minimum of 45 degrees in February. The huge reservoir of heat at 45 degrees or better in the ground below the gravel layer is transferred into the home when it is unoccupied and unheated. This effect is described in chapter 7.

4. A 12-degree temperature drop was measured as the air passed through the Solar Slab in summer. This indicated that the Solar Slab was indeed absorbing energy. This heat transfer and absorption was later incorporated into the design of air-to-air heat pumps for summer air conditioning.

5. We learned that the solar heating system's electrical energy usage, though small in magnitude, was a relatively significant part of the total usage because of the low overall heat demand of the solar home. Through trial and error, the second floor blower was reduced in size from the original $1/3$ horsepower squirrel-cage type to an inline $1/40$ horsepower duct fan, thereby almost eliminating it as a significant energy user.

Everyone's Legacy

U.S. patent law is very different from most of our other laws in that it discriminates; that is, it grants exclusive use of the invention to the inventor for seventeen years. We don't have many laws that obstruct free trade to the extent that our patent law does. In an effort to remedy this obvious conflict, the law gives the invention to the "People of the United States" after seventeen years. This book, hopefully, makes this gift more meaningful, as it is an attempt to explain to lay people as well as professional builders how best to utilize this invention to heat and cool homes yet to be built.

INSULATION, VENTING, AND FRESH AIR

4

As explained in chapter 1, insulation standards have increased dramatically since 1973. The quantities and types of insulation needed to facilitate solar heating of a home are no longer considered unusual or "alternative." As house construction becomes tighter and insulation standards rise, the danger of causing water damage through condensation increases. And by sealing fresh-air vents to the outside, we risk jeopardizing the indoor air quality. We will need to be very careful not to "over-do a good thing" by completely sealing up a home. Our homes need to have adequate fresh air. Just as overglazing will cause overheating problems, we can cause air quality and maintenance problems by not providing proper ventilation for the well-insulated and tightly constructed solar home.

WHAT IS VAPOR?

Vapor control is probably one of the most misunderstood principles in home design. In order to properly design a highly insulated solar home, we must first understand how to control vapor. We have all seen water condense on the outside surface of a glass filled with ice water on a hot summer day. The warm, moist summer air is full of water in the form of vapor—a gas. When this warm, moisture-laden air strikes the cold surface of the ice water glass, the water vapor changes from a gas to a liquid, and drops of water appear on the outside surface of the glass. The conditions existed for condensation to occur. These conditions are a combination of temperature, moisture content, and vapor pressure. Similarly, under certain conditions dew will form on the late evening or early morning summer grass, when chilled air makes contact with warm blades of grass and water vapor condenses to liquid droplets.

In winter, our homes are full of warm air, which has moisture in it. With the outside temperature being very cold, the conditions for condensation will sometimes occur within the wall and/or roof cavities. If moisture-laden air is allowed to enter the wall or roof cavity, and if it condenses there, the result will be water damage, just as if a leaky roof or burst pipe had flooded an area that is supposed to stay dry. First, this condensing water vapor will ruin the effectiveness of fiberglass insulation, and then it will cause rot and mildew. The irony is that the more insulation that's placed in the walls and roof, the greater the danger of creating the conditions for condensation within a wall or roof cavity.

WE NEED FRESH AIR

The remedies for such vapor problems are providing good fresh air make-up to the home, and providing positive vapor barriers in the walls and roof. We should maintain the fresh air replenishment of our homes at no less than two-thirds of an airchange per hour; that is, two-thirds of the entire air volume of your home should be replaced each hour. The ways in which this can be accomplished include the measures enumerated on page 46.

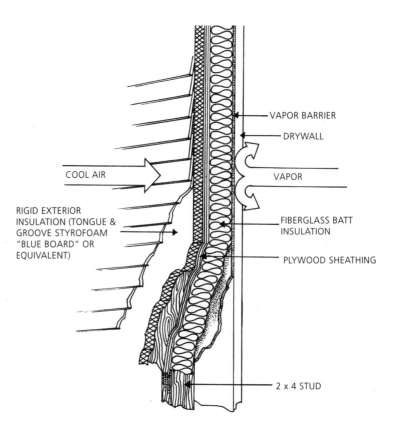

COOL AIR

VAPOR BARRIER

DRYWALL

VAPOR

RIGID EXTERIOR INSULATION (TONGUE & GROOVE STYROFOAM "BLUE BOARD" OR EQUIVALENT)

FIBERGLASS BATT INSULATION

PLYWOOD SHEATHING

2 x 4 STUD

Water vapor will migrate toward cooler areas, and without proper use of a well-sealed vapor barrier on the living-space side of the walls, insulation will gradually collect moisture, rendering it eventually useless.

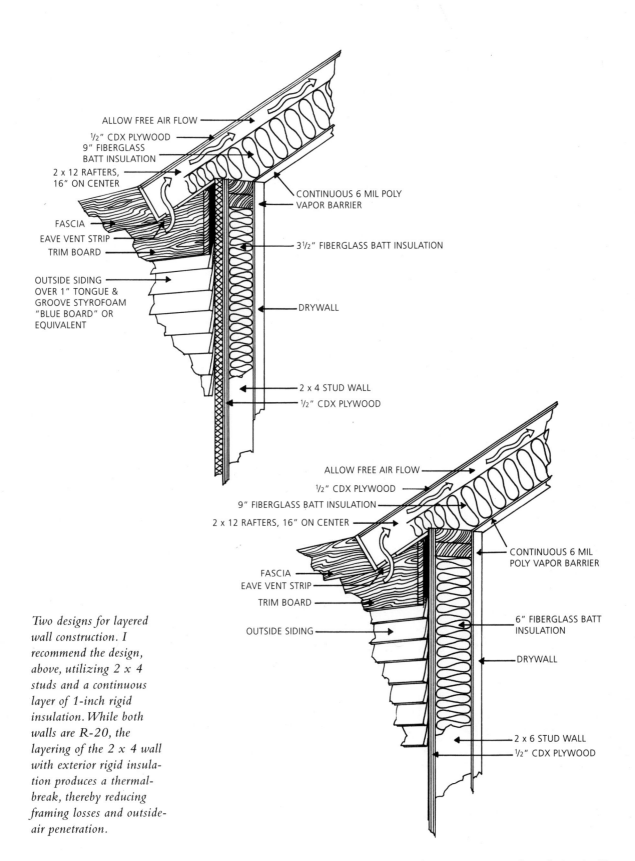

ALLOW FREE AIR FLOW

½" CDX PLYWOOD

9" FIBERGLASS
BATT INSULATION

2 x 12 RAFTERS,
16" ON CENTER

CONTINUOUS 6 MIL POLY
VAPOR BARRIER

FASCIA

EAVE VENT STRIP

TRIM BOARD

3½" FIBERGLASS BATT INSULATION

OUTSIDE SIDING
OVER 1" TONGUE &
GROOVE STYROFOAM
"BLUE BOARD" OR
EQUIVALENT

DRYWALL

2 x 4 STUD WALL

½" CDX PLYWOOD

ALLOW FREE AIR FLOW

½" CDX PLYWOOD

9" FIBERGLASS BATT INSULATION

2 x 12 RAFTERS, 16" ON CENTER

CONTINUOUS 6 MIL
POLY VAPOR BARRIER

FASCIA

EAVE VENT STRIP

TRIM BOARD

6" FIBERGLASS BATT
INSULATION

OUTSIDE SIDING

DRYWALL

2 x 6 STUD WALL

½" CDX PLYWOOD

Two designs for layered wall construction. I recommend the design, above, utilizing 2 x 4 studs and a continuous layer of 1-inch rigid insulation. While both walls are R-20, the layering of the 2 x 4 wall with exterior rigid insulation produces a thermal-break, thereby reducing framing losses and outside-air penetration.

1. Provide ventilation in all bathrooms. Fans should be vented directly to the outside.
2. Where possible, provide ventilation in the kitchen. Fans that just recirculate and filter kitchen air are not as good as fans that are ducted to the outside (see the drawing on page 133).
3. Be sure to vent a clothes dryer directly to the outside.
4. Don't be concerned about the use of a woodstove. It will pull fresh air into your home.
5. When it comes to daily comfort, use your best judgment, and don't be preoccupied with saving energy to the point that you don't open windows to allow fresh air into your home if the house feels stuffy or stale.

Let there be no misunderstanding about where the fresh air make-up is coming from. The walls and roof of your home should be very tightly constructed as shown in the details on pages 44 and 45. Fresh air will enter your home through controlled or deliberate openings, as previously described, not through gaps in the insulation or poorly sealed windows and doors. The amount of fresh air intake can be measured by independent testing agencies at a nominal cost. This service is provided in some cases at no cost by state agencies. One such testing method is called the "Blower Door Test," where a fan is installed in an exterior door, and the rest of the house is closed up. By running the fan and measuring the overall volume of air, the number of air changes can be determined. If the rate is too low, you will need to increase the amount of fresh air intentionally introduced, possibly by adding an air-exchange or ventilator system. If the rate is too high, you can reduce infiltration by improving insulation, adding weather-stripping, or sealing gaps around doors and windows.

POSITIVE VAPOR BARRIERS

In heating situations, the rule is that a vapor barrier must be placed toward the heat, in other words on the heated or interior side of the structure. In normal wall and roof construction, the vapor barrier is placed right behind the drywall—between the drywall and the studs. This vapor barrier should be "positive" in the sense of being a discrete membrane, not incidental to the batt insulation, and it should be carefully lapped and sealed. Positive vapor control means the placement of a separate vapor barrier such as the 6-mil "poly" shown in the 2 x 4 stud wall detail on page 45, which shows an R-20 wall and an R-32 roof section. In chapter 6 we will calculate these R-values (the R-value represents the resistance to heat transfer, therefore the higher the R-value, the less heat this material will transfer).

The preferred wall design shown on page 45 is the 2 x 4 stud wall with batt insulation and a layer of Styrofoam outside the exterior wall sheathing. This layering makes a tight wall and provides a continuous layer of rigid insulation outside the 1/2-inch plywood sheathing. Layering the wall construction in this manner reduces heat loss which occurs through the framing members ("bridging losses" are heat losses that result from studs transmitting cold directly into the home). It is all but impossible for outside air to penetrate a wall that has been layered in this way, since the seams between pieces of rigid insulation and the seams of the plywood will not coincide.

Although I don't recommend doing so, the exterior layer of rigid insulation may be eliminated by the substitution of 2 x 6 studs with 6-inch batt insulation; however, with larger studs bridging losses will be more significant, and these additional losses should be considered when the framing lumber is in direct thermal contact between the inside and the outside of the wall unit. Although 2 x 6 framing has become standard, in most cases it isn't structurally necessary to use 2 x 6s; a wall constructed of 2 x 6s 16 inches on center is probably overbuilt, and the bridging losses will be greater with 2 x 6s and no exterior rigid insulation. The use of an exterior house wrap is important with 2 x 6 wall construction to seal cracks and construction joints. Exterior house wraps (such as Tyvek or Typar) are designed to stop the wind but allow moisture to pass through (so that moisture will not be trapped inside the wall, but can exit to the exterior side). House wraps are not vapor barriers. House wrap is not needed with the 2 x 4 stud wall, since the outside tongue-and-groove Styrofoam serves as both additional insulation and a seal against penetration.

When selecting rigid exterior wall insulation, be sure to purchase closed-cell, extruded polystyrene insulation such as Dow Chemical's Styrofoam "Blue Board," or U.S. Gypsum's Formula R. Less expensive open-celled alternatives are susceptible to insect damage, and degradation in R-value over time.

Note the placement of the roof insulation and the roof venting details in the drawing on page 45. An ongoing free flow of air should be maintained from the eave to a continuous ridge vent. This flow of air above the insulation will keep the roof plywood from getting warm, helping to prevent "ice dams." It will also keep the roof cooler in the summer. In high snow areas, a "cold roof" is often used, in which a separate vented roof is installed above the roof plywood. This design is useful where double protection from moisture and cold is needed. The "cold" roof is added on top of the vented roof construction. The original roof is covered with heavy felt or tarpaper, and the top of the cold roof is typically covered with a metal roof to shed snow. I recently noticed that all new construction at Sun Valley, Idaho, is built this way.

Remember that damp insulation loses its ability to block the loss of heat, and wet insulation is worthless. Pay particular attention to the continuous interior vapor barrier shown in the wall and roof details. Placing unfaced batt fiberglass insulation and then applying a continuous and distinct vapor barrier is a better solution than relying on foil-faced or kraft-faced fiberglass for vapor control. Positive vapor control will stop water vapor from migrating into the wall or roof insulation cavity.

It is not uncommon for a newly constructed and tightly insulated home to have excess moisture content in the air during the first winter. This is due to the gradual stabilization of moisture content of all the materials used inside the home. As these materials dry, the moisture content of the air will slowly decrease. If there is excess moisture in the air, water vapor will condense on the coldest surface available—the windows. This is entirely predictable in the first few weeks of the first winter. The "cure" is to open a couple of windows and ventilate the home. If, however, this condensation persists, it means that there is a bigger problem, and the source of the excess moisture should be investigated.

A client once called me, sure that his ski house was "self destructing." A ¼-inch layer of ice had formed over some of the window surfaces, and water was dripping off the windows. The temperature was about 10 degrees outside. Upon inspection, a dryer vent was found to be venting to the inside of the house. As his clothes were dried, moisture was being pumped into the home. Since the home was properly constructed and had positive vapor control, the water vapor had only one place to go—the windows. The homeowner was instructed to "crank up" his woodstove and open a second floor window at each gable end to let the house vent. In a matter of hours, the house began to stabilize.

Another homeowner installed the batt insulation in the ceiling of his home but had never managed to install the vapor barrier. He was living in and finishing the construction of his home at the same time. After six weeks of the heating season, the ceiling insulation was completely saturated with moisture, rendering it useless. All of this soggy fiberglass had to be removed and replaced; this time he installed fiberglass insulation properly protected with a positive vapor barrier.

An old-time Vermont builder once told of installing a board ceiling in the second floor of a new home. Since he didn't believe in vapor barriers, the insulation was placed with no vapor barrier between it and the square-edged board ceiling. Halfway through the first winter, the boards were all water stained. Both the boards and the insulation had to replaced at his expense. His rationale had been that he always used batt ceiling insulation with no vapor barrier on top of drywall so

Solar Principle # 4

Insulate thoroughly and use well-sealed vapor barriers.

Build tightly constructed, properly insulated walls and roofs. Carefully install and seal discrete vapor barriers on the living-space side of walls, ceilings, and/or roofs. Incorporate an air-lock entrance.

that the ceiling could "breathe." Inadvertently, he was creating a dry-wall vapor barrier. Drywall with two coats of latex paint makes a fairly effective vapor barrier; however, when square-edged boards were substituted for the drywall, moisture traveled through the joints, and the dew point was reached within the ceiling insulation layer, causing the water problem.

R-VALUES

R-values have been mentioned several times. In order to specify the correct insulation levels for a passive solar home, we will need to understand what R-values are, how they are calculated, and how you can use the information derived from the calculations. All materials transfer heat at different rates, and R-value is the measure of the resistance of a given material to the transfer of heat. As explained in chapter 3, concrete transfers heat at a rapid rate, while wool sweaters with air trapped in their weave transfer heat more slowly. Appendix 3 shows a list of R-values for various materials.

"U-values" are the inverse or reciprocal of R-values. U-values are expressed in Btus per hour per square foot per degree Fahrenheit. Btu stands for British thermal unit, and is the amount of heat necessary to raise the temperature of one pound of water one degree Fahrenheit (in this book, for the sake of clarity, we will use the nomenclature "Btus" in text and equations when referring to these units in plural; true ASHRAE aficionados will note this departure from engineers' normal practice).

The heat loss of a home is calculated by first determining the U-values for the walls, windows, and roof. Individual heat losses for specific areas are determined by multiplying square feet of surface area by the U-value. Then a calculation is made of the amount of energy needed to reheat the fresh air that is coming into and escaping from the building during each hour. The total of these losses represents the total theoretical loss of the building. This kind of calculation will be demonstrated and explained in chapter 6.

NIGHTTIME WINDOW INSULATION

Notice in the floorplans shown in chapters 5 and 8 that thermo-shutters are shown on some of the windows and patio doors. In the three-bedroom plan (see page 57), the thermo-shutters are used on three south-facing patio doors as well as one window each in the east-facing dining/family room and west-facing master bedroom, on the first

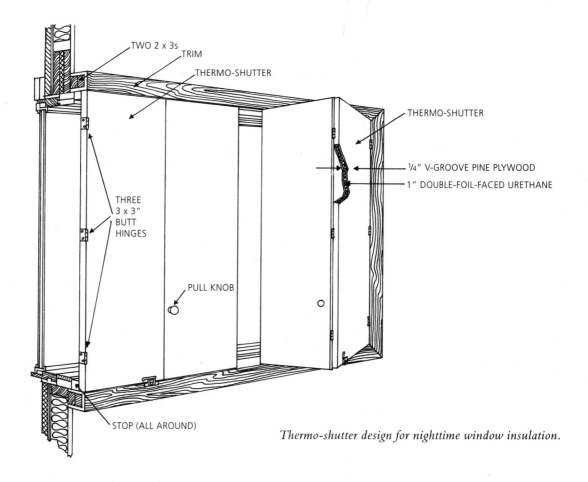

TWO 2 x 3s

TRIM

THERMO-SHUTTER

THERMO-SHUTTER

¼" V-GROOVE PINE PLYWOOD

1" DOUBLE-FOIL-FACED URETHANE

THREE 3 x 3" BUTT HINGES

PULL KNOB

STOP (ALL AROUND)

Thermo-shutter design for nighttime window insulation.

floor, and on two windows in the east- and west-facing bedrooms on the second floor. The combined area of these windows represents a total of 203 square feet of glass.

Insulating the windows and patio doors at night (especially the largest windows) will measurably improve their performance as solar collectors. A single pane of glass has an R-value of 1, meaning that single-glazed glass is essentially only keeping the wind out! The window companies have now developed better-insulated glass. High-performance glazing has selective coatings on various surfaces of the sheets of glass, and the air between the sheets of glass is replaced by gasses that are more effective insulators. And yet, although high-performance glass is better than ordinary glass, the R-value of even dual-pane glass pales when compared to an R-21.36 wall. Remember, insulated dual-pane glass has an R-value of 1.92, whereas the wall is 21.36/1.92, or 11 times better. While architecturally attractive glass makes an excellent solar collector while the sun is out, the winter nights are long and cold, turning windows and patio doors into thermal losers at night.

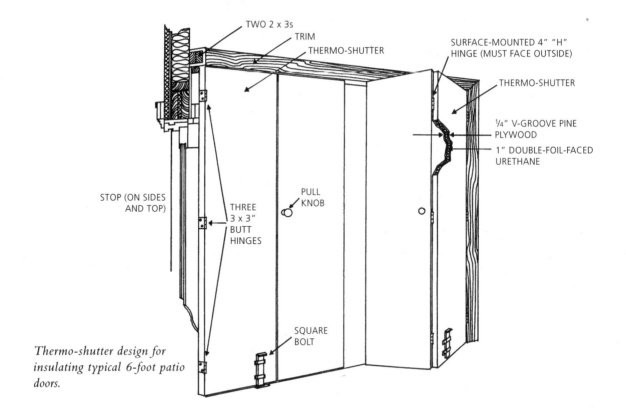

TWO 2 x 3s

TRIM

THERMO-SHUTTER

SURFACE-MOUNTED 4″ "H" HINGE (MUST FACE OUTSIDE)

THERMO-SHUTTER

¼″ V-GROOVE PINE PLYWOOD

1″ DOUBLE-FOIL-FACED URETHANE

STOP (ON SIDES AND TOP)

THREE 3 x 3″ BUTT HINGES

PULL KNOB

SQUARE BOLT

Thermo-shutter design for insulating typical 6-foot patio doors.

In addition to transmitting heat out of the home's airspace through thin panes of glass, uninsulated windows actually draw heat out of you. Have you ever noticed that it seems much colder to sit next to a patio door at night versus sitting next to a nicely insulated wall?

There's more bad news. Warm air from the room will be drawn toward the glass, and as this warm air is cooled by the colder glass surface, it flows toward the floor, allowing more warm air to be drawn to the cooling glass. This is the same kind of reverse thermosiphoning effect that can take place at night with the Trombe wall described in chapter 2.

Most heating system designers locate heat grilles in front of windows and patio doors to provide a "bath" of warm air across the glass surface. This increases the inside surface temperature of the glass, which increases the temperature difference across the glass, which in turn increases the heat loss of the glass. One error compounds another, and so on.

As you have probably deduced, the solution to this problem is to add nighttime insulation to the windows. The illustrations on pages 51 and 52 show thermo-shutter details for a typical six-foot patio door and six-foot-wide window grouping. Note that the interior insulation of the thermo-shutter is 1 inch of foil-faced urethane. The interior foil face will reflect heat back into the room, even though it is sealed inside the thermo-shutter. With the thermo-shutter closed you may now comfortably sit next to a patio door on a cold night. The thermo-shutter is providing added insulation as well as reflecting heat back into the room. The stop shown on the details allows the thermo-shutters to fit tightly, which eliminates reverse thermosiphoning at night.

The photograph below shows how the thermo-shutters may be decorated with fabric, which may be changed seasonally. Construction of thermo-shutters takes the skill of a qualified finish carpenter. You could hire a cabinet shop to make them.

Thermo-shutters have a year-round benefit, as they may also be closed to keep out the sun. They are most beneficial in summertime on east- and west-facing windows since the sun enters more directly into the living space in the morning and afternoon. The outside foil face of the insulation contained within the wood veneers will reflect the sun's summer heat back out the window.

Other Options for Window Insulation

There are commercial products made of fabric on the market that can be used to add insulation to windows and patio doors. Make sure that any product bought for this purpose provides both added insulation and a tight fit along the top or bottom edge (ideally both) to stop the nighttime reverse air flow.

Detail of thermo-shutter showing use of curtains as decorative finish. When in the open position, the folded-back shutters are no more obtrusive than curtains along the sides of a window or glass door. Likewise, when closed, the window will appear to be covered by curtains, yet the insulation value of the layered shutter is far superior to that of curtains alone.

5

BASIC LAYOUTS
AND FLOOR PLANS

A New England-style "saltbox" house (known to Green Mountain Homes customers as the Saltbox 38) will be used in the first part of this chapter to illustrate and explain energy-saving floor plan considerations (see pages 56 and 57). Then we will consider the unique features of two economical "starter" homes. In chapters 6 and 7 you will find an explanation of how to calculate your home's future solar gain and its backup heating needs. As emphasized consistently in this book, the more thoroughly and carefully you consider your space, energy, and heating and cooling requirements while planning your home, the more smoothly the construction process will go, and the happier you will be when you move in.

Assuming that you have now spent some time on your new solar home site, you will have begun to get a feel for the route of the sun throughout the day. We should lay out the home's rooms in relation to the patterns of the sun; that is, morning areas and activities should be planned for the east side of the home, and evening activities generally on the west side. Referring to the floor plans shown for the Saltbox 38, you will see that the kitchen is on the east side. This means that you will often start your day with the sun beaming into your east-facing windows.

If you are a morning person, you may want to occupy the second-floor east bedroom, as it will see the sun first. Even if the rest of your home is not up to temperature in the early morning, the east side will be collecting solar energy from the earliest sunlight, and you may not need any supplemental energy simply as a result of locating yourself on the sunny side of your home in the morning. If your backup heating system is controlled by a thermostat, locate this on an east-facing wall exposed to the morning sun. If it is going to be a bright and

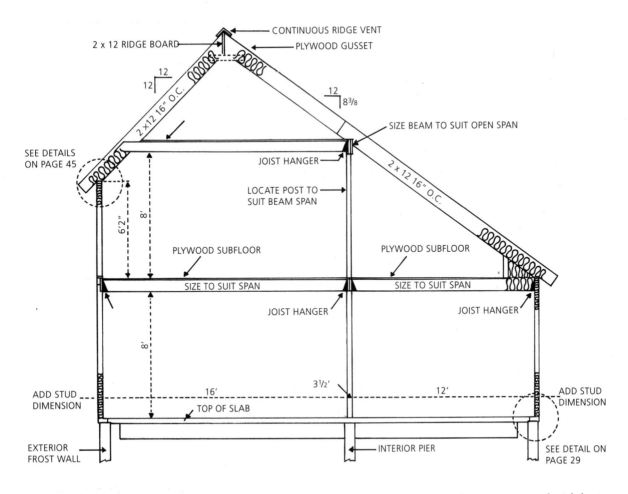

CONTINUOUS RIDGE VENT

2 x 12 RIDGE BOARD

PLYWOOD GUSSET

2 x 12 16" O.C.

12 / 12

12 / 8³⁄₈

SIZE BEAM TO SUIT OPEN SPAN

SEE DETAILS ON PAGE 45

JOIST HANGER

LOCATE POST TO SUIT BEAM SPAN

2 x 12 16" O.C.

6'2"

8'

PLYWOOD SUBFLOOR

PLYWOOD SUBFLOOR

SIZE TO SUIT SPAN

SIZE TO SUIT SPAN

JOIST HANGER

JOIST HANGER

8'

16'

3¹⁄₂'

12'

ADD STUD DIMENSION

ADD STUD DIMENSION

TOP OF SLAB

EXTERIOR FROST WALL

INTERIOR PIER

SEE DETAIL ON PAGE 29

Typical saltbox design: a cross-section. (Do not use for construction. Dimensions are given to correspond with heat loss calculations in chapter 6).

sunny solar day, the sun will strike the thermostat and "trick" it into not turning on the backup heat. If the sun stays out for the day, and as it migrates from east to west around your home, free solar energy will heat your living spaces, with any excess energy being stored in the Solar Slab for use later in the evening. You are satisfying the goal of keeping the furnace turned off just by room placement.

Notice in the saltbox floor plan that the living room is in the middle of the south side. The living room will be up to temperature slightly later than the dining/family room, as the sun and normal living habits migrate from east to west in the home. Later, as the days grow longer, you will be able to view sunsets through the west-facing bedroom windows.

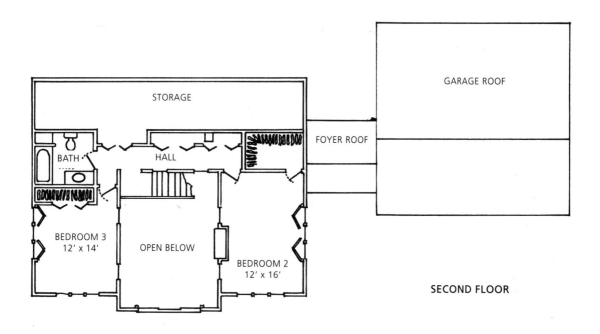

SECOND FLOOR

Sample floor plans for the Saltbox 38 used as the basis for the solar design calculations in chapter 6. Thermo-shutters are used on larger windows and patio doors.

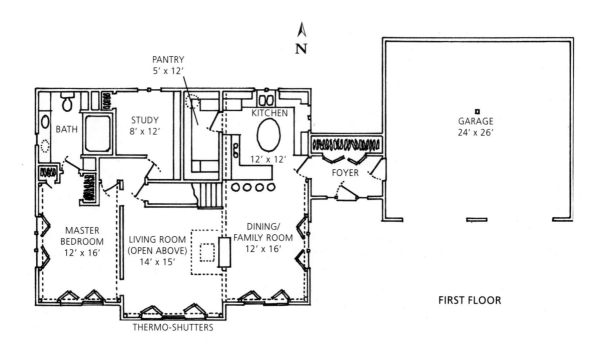

FIRST FLOOR

WOODSTOVES FOR BACKUP HEAT

The woodburning stove and chimney are located central to, and in close proximity with, the most lived-in areas of the home—the dining/family room and living room. The woodstove will radiate heat in all directions from its open, centralized location.

This also allows maximum safety for the interior chimney. An interior chimney stays warm as the hot gases are escaping up the chimney. This will minimize the build-up of creosote, provided that seasoned, dry hardwood is used for burning.

Since there is no basement, the space under the stairs can be used for utilities such as the domestic water heater and ventilation or air-circulation equipment. Keep waterlines in the interior partitions of the home, not in exterior walls. This will guard against possible freeze-ups.

You may also consider installing a domestic hot-water tempering tank, with water pipes and control wires running between the tempering tank and the woodstove, as many stoves have hot-water jackets

Solar Principle # 5

Utilize windows as solar collectors and cooling devices.

This idea sounds obvious, but many people overlook the obvious and spend large amounts of money purchasing, fueling, and maintaining furnaces and air-conditioners to address needs that high-quality windows can also address. Vertical, south-facing glass is especially effective for collecting solar heat in the winter when a home needs additional heat, whereas the same windows will let in much less heat in summer, because the sun's angle is more horizontal in winter and steeper in summer. Provide insulated window and patio door coverings to decrease nighttime heat loss in winter, and to control solar gain in spring, summer, and fall. Windows that open can be used to release excess heat and direct cooling breezes into the house.

that can be used to heat water in winter. The woodstove will heat the water in the tempering tank which in turn will feed pre-heated water to the conventional hot water heater. A simple drain-down external solar collector can be added to the system to pre-heat the water with sunlight in spring, summer, and fall.

FACE THE LONG DIMENSION OF YOUR HOME SOUTH

The 38-foot house dimension is lined up east to west; that is, the ridge of the home runs east to west. By facing the long, sloping roof to the north, you will orient the high side of the home with its majority of surface to the sunny south, and the other facade, with its reduced surface area, will face to the sunless north.

Two-story homes are more energy efficient, because they have double the living space under one roof. Heat rises, so the second floor, at least thermally, comes almost free. Two-story home construction costs are also less per square foot, since double use is made of one concrete base and one roof.

Floor plans for the N-38-X discussed in chapter 6. This house has three bedrooms and two baths, and every room is sunny: there is no dark "north side." Thermo-shutters are indicated on the larger windows and patio doors.

FIRST FLOOR

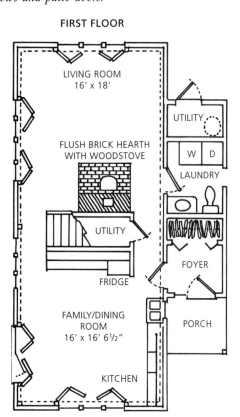

SECOND FLOOR

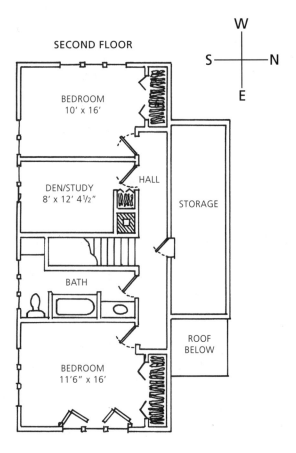

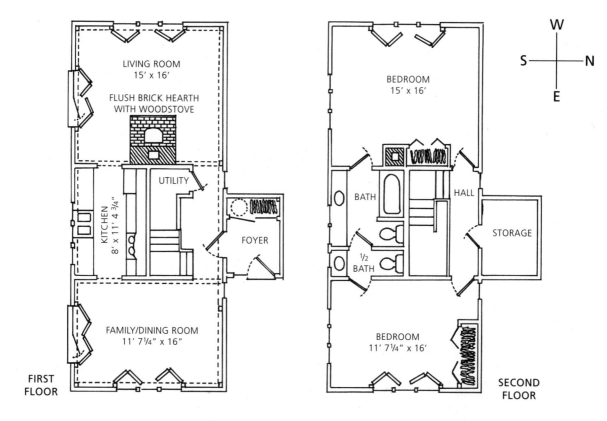

FIRST
FLOOR

SECOND
FLOOR

Note the concentration of windows and patio doors on the east, south, and west elevations. There are only two small windows facing north on the Saltbox 38.

Since there is no full basement, storage has been provided on the second floor under the north-sloping roof. In addition, there is attic storage space in the east and west sections of the building.

For this layout, the ideal location for the garage and air lock entry is on the northeast side of the home. Try to locate garage doors on the south elevation to allow the sun to help remove snow and ice. East or west locations for garage doors are next best, while the least desirable location for a garage door is north. Remember that most of what is carried into and out of a home involves the kitchen. The northeast garage location and air lock entrance are the most convenient for carrying groceries into the kitchen.

These same principles are also illustrated in the smaller, more economical N-38 "starter" home shown in the illustrations above. Note that there are no north rooms in this home, as every room in this 16-foot-wide house has a south exposure. The N-38 was the prototype built first and used by Green Mountain Homes to demonstrate the Solar Slab design.

Floor plan for the prototype Green Mountain Homes N-38 that was used for the monitoring study discussed in chapter 3.

HOW TO DO
THE SOLAR DESIGN
CALCULATIONS

6

Let's assume that you have found a good solar building site. Using a popular Green Mountain Homes saltbox design as a representative plan, we will move into the more technical portion of the design process by conducting what an engineer would call a "thermal study" of the planned solar home. I will demonstrate with the specifications for a "Saltbox 38" the calculations essential for solar design. Subsequently, in chapter 8, I will explain how to use the worksheets included in this book to do your own thermal study incorporating the specifications for your particular design and site.

For the sake of discussion, let's plan on locating our examples of this Saltbox 38 in Hartford, Connecticut. This is not the most obvious locale, perhaps, for a solar home, but Connecticut is perfectly suitable. And if solar heating will work in frosty New England, it will work wherever you are planning to build your home. Another way to say this is that Western and Southwestern states with high elevations, clear skies, and high annual percentages of sunshine tend to be associated with solar home design, but obviously many people desiring solar homes live elsewhere.

CALCULATE R-VALUES FIRST

The illustration on page 56 shows the Saltbox cross-section, and the one on page 45 shows wall and roof insulation. I recommend a 2 x 4 stud wall with a layer of 1-inch Styrofoam outside the exterior plywood sheathing. We first need to calculate the heat loss of the building. Step one of this calculation involves determining the wall and roof U-values. Remember from chapter 4 that U is the reciprocal of

TABLE 6–1
LOCATION: HARTFORD, CONNECTICUT
NORTH LATITUDE 41°5′
(SEE APPENDIX 4 FOR SOURCE)
WINTER DESIGN TEMPERATURE: 0°F

Square footage of glass is:

South	=	162
East	=	64
West	=	35
North	=	10
Total	=	271 sq. ft.

R, and expressed as Btu/hr • ft² • °F. The R-value of the wall or roof is the sum of the individual R-values of the various elements that make up the total.

The total wall and roof R-value for the Saltbox 38 is given below.

TABLE 6–2
TOTAL WALL R-VALUE

Item	R
15 MPH wind (outside)	0.17
1-inch rough sawn cedar outside siding	1.25
1-inch tongue & groove foamboard insulation	5.00
½-inch exterior plywood	0.62
3 ½-inch fiberglass batt insulation	13.00
6 mil poly	Negligible
½-inch drywall	0.64
still airspace (inside)	0.68
Total R-value =	21.36
Total U-value = 1/21.36 =	0.0468

TOTAL ROOF R-VALUE

Item	R
15 MPH wind (outside)	0.17
325# asphalt roof shingles	0.44
15# felt paper	0.06
½-inch exterior plywood	0.62
9-inch fiberglass batt insulation	30.00
6 mil poly	Negligible
½-inch drywall	0.64
still airspace (inside)	0.68
Total R-value =	32.61
Total U-value = 1/32.61 =	0.0307

We will use insulated dual-pane windows and patio doors and assume the manufacturer's published overall R-value is 1.92 (so that means that the U-value will be 1/1.92 = 0.5208).

REHEATING THE FRESH AIR
COMING IN

The thermal "cost" to reheat the recommended ⅔ air change per hour discussed in chapter 4 will comprise the infiltration portion of the total heat loss. There are several ways to calculate infiltration losses; we will use the air change method and assume the total air infiltration from all sources is ⅔ air change per hour. This assumption is based on data derived from the formal monitoring conducted on the prototype N–38 in Royalton, Vermont. This figure includes losses from cracks around windows and doors, the amount of air lost by entering and exiting the building, and the air expelled out of the building by fans in the bathrooms.

Experienced technicians can conduct tests to determine the number of air changes per hour. If for some reason the home has less than a ⅔ air change per hour, fresh air should be introduced to keep the airspace fresh and safe.

According to the 1972 ASHRAE *Handbook of Fundamentals*, the heat required to heat one cubic foot of air one degree is the product of the air's specific heat times its density, or

$$H = c \times d$$

where:

H = heat required to raise 1 cubic foot of air 1 degree Fahrenheit
c = specific heat of air (0.24 Btus per pound per degree Fahrenheit)
d = density of air (0.075 pounds per cubic foot)

If

$$H = 0.24 \text{ Btus per pound} \times \text{degree} \times 0.075 \text{ pounds per ft}^3$$

then

$$H = 0.018 \text{ Btus/ft}^3 \cdot °F$$

To obtain our infiltration loss we will use the following formula:

$$I = V \times H \times Q$$

where:

I = infiltration loss
V = volume of house (in cubic feet)
H = heat removed (Btus/ft³ • °F)
Q = volume of air change (air changes per hour)

If

$$I = V(\text{cubic feet}) \times H \ (\text{Btus/ft}^3 \cdot °F) \times Q \ (\text{air changes per hour})$$

then

$$I = \text{Btus/hr} \cdot °F$$

We now have all the information we need to calculate the total heat loss of the Saltbox 38. Referring to the Saltbox 38 floor plan, elevations and cross-section (see chapter 5), the total heat loss can be calculated as shown in Table 6–3.

TABLE 6–3 AREA OF EXTERIOR HEATED WALLS (in square feet)		
South 15' × 38'	=	570 sq.ft.
North 9' × 38'	=	342
East 29' × 9' + (½ × 29') × 16'	=	493
West	=	493
		———
Total:		1,898 sq.ft.

Subtracting the square feet of glass from the above total wall area, the net wall area is:

1,898 total square feet of wall area − 271 square feet of glass = 1,627 square feet of unglazed wall area

Estimated Atmospheric clearness numbers in United States for nonindustrial localities. The clearness number changes from winter to summer in certain locations. See page 70 for more on atmospheric clarity.

The total heat loss for the walls, glazing, and roof is the sum of the products of the square feet of area multiplied by the respective U-values as shown on the following page.

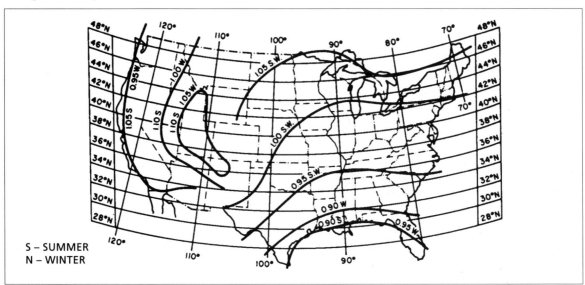

S – SUMMER
N – WINTER

A. Net Wall Loss = Heated Wall Area (1,627 square feet) × U-value of Heated Wall (0.0468 Btus/hr • ft^2 • °F) = 76.14 Btus/hr • °F

B. Roof Loss = Roof Area (38 feet × 40 feet = 1,520 square feet) × U-value of roof (.0307 Btus/hr • ft^2 • °F) = 46.67 Btus/hr • ft^2 • °F

The house's Infiltration Loss, calculated using the air change method of analysis is predicted as follows:

C. Infiltration loss = Total Volume of Living Space × Heat Removed × Air Changes per Hour

Total Volume = (8 feet × 28 feet × 38 feet) + (19.67 feet × 8 feet × 38 feet) = 14,492 cubic feet

Infiltration loss = 14,492 ft^3 × 0.018 Btus/ft^3 • °F × ⅔ air changes per hour = 174.77 Btus/hr • °F

D. Total Heat Loss through Glazing = Area of Glass × U-value

The total area of glazing is shown in Table 6–4 (use your window manufacturer's literature to obtain the square footage of glass area per window, in your particular case). In our sample Saltbox, the heat loss through glass will be:

271 square feet of glass × 0.5208 Btus/hr • ft^2 • °F (U-value of glass) = 141.14 Btus/hr • °F

TABLE 6–4 AREA OF GLASS (in square feet)	
South	162
East	64
West	35
North	10
	———
Total	271

The house's total heat loss is summarized in Table 6–5.

TABLE 6–5 TOTAL HEAT LOSS		
ITEM	HEAT LOSS BTUS/HR • °F	% OF TOTAL HEAT LOSS
Walls	76.14	17
Roof	46.67	11
Infiltration	174.77	40
Windows & patio doors	141.14	32
	—————	
	Total = 438.72 Btus/hr • °F	

Since this house has no basement, basement losses are not indicated in Table 6–5. Due to the highly insulated perimeter of the Solar Slab and the small area exposed above grade, the Solar Slab perimeter heat loss is insignificant, and also not indicated in the table. If the Solar Slab perimeter loss were to be calculated, it would amount to 2 percent of the total heat loss. This loss should be included if, for some site or design reason, it would amount to more than 2 percent.

Another heat loss factor to consider is the heat transmitted through the framing; this is also referred to as bridging loss. Since the outside wall on this sample Saltbox is constructed as I've recommended, with a continuous exterior layer of rigid insulation, and since 2 x 12s were used as roof rafters, bridging losses were deemed to be insignificant, and were therefore omitted in the wall and roof R-value determinations. In most contemporary houses, tightly constructed and well-insulated, these bridging losses will be likewise insignificant, and may be ignored in heat loss calculations.

If, on the other hand, your framing represents more than 10 percent of the wall area, the framing loss should be included in your own calculations. This might occur in certain forms of post-and-beam or log-wall construction. Should you wish to adjust your calculations for framing or bridging losses, one method is to adjust the U-value. For example, in a 2 x 6 wall with the 2 x 6s 16 inches on center, the 2 x 6s account for about 10 percent of the wall area. At 24 inches on center, they account for about 6 percent of the wall area. The following example shows how to adjust the U-value for a 2 x 6 wall 24 inches on center, and a 2 x 12 roof 16 inches on center:

Average U-value of Wall = (Framing Area % of Total Wall Area × Framing Material's U-value) + (Insulation Area % of Total Wall Area × Insulated Wall U-value)

Average U-value of Wall = (0.06 × 0.1478★) + (0.94 × 0.0468) = 0.0529 Btus/hr • ft² • °F

Average U-value of Roof = (0.10 × 0.0723★) + (0.90 × 0.0307) = 0.0349 Btus/hr • ft² • °F

★ The U-value for a 2 x 6 is 0.1478 and for a 2 x 12 is 0.0723, assuming kiln-dried hemlock-fir or spruce-pine-fir

In our Connecticut example, the outside temperature used as the basis for calculation is 0 degrees; this is referred to as the "outside winter design temperature," and you can find a table with representative outside winter design temperatures in appendix 4. Assuming the inside temperature to be 72 degree Fahrenheit, the theoretical hourly heat loss of the Saltbox 38 in Hartford, Connecticut, is:

438.72 Btus/hr × °F difference (72 degrees inside − 0 degrees outside) = 31,588 Btus/hr

CALCULATING SOLAR GAIN

Next we need to calculate the solar gain, the heat input attributable to sunshine. The percentage of sunshine in Hartford, Connecticut, for the heating season is shown in Table 6–6.

One should never assume that there is not enough sun in a given location to justify building a solar house. It might be surprising to many people that the average insolation for the nine-month heating

TABLE 6–6 ANNUAL PERCENTAGE OF SUN	
Month	**Percentage Sun**
September	57
October	55
November	46
December	46
January	46
February	55
March	56
April	54
May	57

season in Hartford, Connecticut is 52.4 percent, meaning that the daylight hours are sunny more than 50 percent of the time on average in this location. Your new home should be designed to take advantage of whatever natural solar benefits are available. It is reasonable to assume that the economical percentage of solar heat attainable approximates the percent sunshine in a given location. Therefore, when designed properly, this home in Connecticut should receive about half of its heat free from the sun. If so, how can a solar house *not* work in Hartford, Connecticut?

Remembering that the Saltbox 38 used in this chapter has 162 square feet of south-facing glass, 64 square feet of east-facing glass, and 35 square feet of west-facing glass, we will calculate the predicted monthly insolation using appendix 2, Solar Intensity and Solar Heat Gain Factors (SHGF), for north latitude 40 degrees, from the 1993 ASHRAE *Handbook of Fundamentals*. The table lists half-day totals, and reads from top to bottom for sunrise to solar noon, and bottom to top for solar noon to sunset. We will ignore the sun's contribution of heat into the house's west glass in the morning, and likewise we will ignore the afternoon values for east glass, making the east-side SHGF equal to the west-side SHGF. Since the home faces true south, we will double the south-side SHGF half-day totals. The heat gain per square foot of glass on a given orientation is the product of:

Solar Heat Gain Factors (SHGF) × Shade Coefficient (SC)

In the case of our saltbox, the SC is the reduction in solar gain due to sunlight being reflected off each sheet of glass. (Shade Coefficient is the ASHRAE term. For our purposes, "reflection coefficient" would be a more descriptive term.) Again from the 1993 ASHRAE *Handbook*, we find that the SC for ½-inch insulated glass is 0.88. The SHGF also assumes atmospheric clarity of 1.00 (see the map on page 66). If your location is high in elevation and has dry and clear atmosphere, the SHGF may be increased up to 15 percent. Conversely, if the location is hazy and humid, the SHGF should be reduced. To illustrate the calculation, I will use the figures for the September Solar Heat Gains.

From appendix 2, and using the SHGF for 40 degrees north latitude, the September SHGF half-day totals are:

East	=	787 (reading down the table)
South	=	672
West	=	787 (reading up the table)

TABLE 6–7 SOLAR HEAT GAIN FACTORS FOR 40 DEGREES NORTH LATITUDE					
Month	% Sun	Days	East	South	West
Sep	57	30	787	1,344	787
Oct	55	31	623	1,582	623
Nov	46	30	445	1,596	445
Dec	46	31	374	1,114	374
Jan	46	31	452	1,626	452
Feb	55	28	648	1,642	648
Mar	56	31	832	1,388	832
Apr	54	30	957	976	957
May	57	31	1,024	716	1,024

The potential solar gain (expressed in Btus per square foot per day) for east-, west-, and south-facing glass are shown in Table 6–7 (remember that south is multiplied by 2, in order to indicate two half-day subtotals).

Multiply each column by the square footage of glass on each elevation, then by the number of days in each month, and finally by the percent sunshine. The totals for each elevation are tabulated in Table 6-8 in millions of Btus. Let's use September as a sample calculation.

East = 787 SHGF × 64 square feet × 30 days × 57% sunshine
= 0.86 million Btus

South = 1,344 SHGF × 162 square feet × 30 days × 57% sunshine
= 3.72 million Btus

West = 787 SHGF × 35 square feet × 30 × 57% sunshine
= 0.47 million Btus

The totals in Table 6–8 need to be adjusted for the heat reflected back from the window due to dual glass. Calculate the loss by multiplying the above monthly totals by a Shade Coefficient of 0.88 (the SC of ½-inch insulated glass).

TABLE 6–8
COMBINED SHGF FOR ALL ELEVATIONS
(in millions Btus)

Month	East		South		West		Total (millions Btus)
Sep	0.86	+	3.72	+	0.47	=	5.05
Oct	0.66	+	4.37	+	0.37	=	5.40
Nov	0.39	+	3.57	+	0.21	=	4.17
Dec	0.34	+	3.58	+	0.19	=	4.11
Jan	0.41	+	3.75	+	0.22	=	4.38
Feb	0.63	+	4.09	+	0.35	=	5.07
Mar	0.92	+	3.90	+	0.50	=	5.32
Apr	0.99	+	2.56	+	0.54	=	4.09
May	1.15	+	2.05	+	0.63	=	3.83

TABLE 6–9
MONTHLY SHGF ADJUSTED BY SHADE COEFFICIENT
(in millions Btuss)

Month	SC		Monthly Total		Net Total
Sep	0.88	×	5.05	=	4.44
Oct	0.88	×	5.40	=	4.75
Nov	0.88	×	4.17	=	3.67
Dec	0.88	×	4.11	=	3.62
Jan	0.88	×	4.38	=	3.85
Feb	0.88	×	5.07	=	4.46
Mar	0.88	×	5.32	=	4.68
Apr	0.88	×	4.09	=	3.60
May	0.88	×	3.83	=	3.37

CALCULATING HEAT LOAD

Degree days are a measure of the heat required for a building, and degree day data from the 1981 ASHRAE *Handbook of Fundamentals* will be used in this chapter (see appendix 5). A degree day is defined as the difference between the median outdoor temperature and 65 degrees for a 24-hour period. The standard assumption is that the inside design temperature is 72 degrees, of which 7 degrees will be derived from sources other than the furnace. These sources include heat from lighting and cooking, the body heat of people, and so forth. Degree day tables are tabulated with an outside base temperature of 65 degrees. For example, if the outdoor median temperature was 64 degrees for the 24-hour time period, then that day had 1 degree day. The local power company keeps accurate track of degree days for its heat load calculations, and is usually a good source for this information. Oil and propane companies use degree days as a guide to tell them how frequently to make deliveries. The National Oceanic and Atmospheric Administration (NOAA) also tabulates this and other valuable weather data. The nearest engineering or earth sciences library will most probably have this data on microfiche. Ask for the five-year average to obtain a good approximation of your heat load. The degree day data obtained from other sources may differ slightly from the data contained in this book, since this kind of information is routinely updated. Slight differences will not materially affect your solar prediction calculations. Remember that we are dealing with a "fuzzy" (transient) problem, and solar predictions at best will be an informed approximation.

Knowing the calculated heat loss of our building, the degree days for our location, and the solar gains for our location, we are now ready to tabulate this information and derive our solar performance prediction.

Let's first calculate heat load per month. See Table 6–10 for a summary by month of the building's projected heat load.

TABLE 6–10				
HOUSEHOLD MONTHLY HEAT LOAD				
MONTH	**HEAT LOSS OF HOME**		**DEGREE DAY**	**MONTHLY HEAT LOSS (millions Btus)**
Sep	10,529*	×	117**	= 1.23
Oct	"	×	394	= 4.15
Nov	"	×	714	= 7.52
Dec	"	×	1,101	= 11.59
Jan	"	×	1,190	= 12.53
Feb	"	×	1,042	= 10.97
Mar	"	×	908	= 9.56
Apr	"	×	519	= 5.46
May	"	×	205	= 2.16
			Total	= 65.17

★ 438.72 Btus/hr • °F × 24 hrs/day = 10,529 Btus/°F • day
★★ See appendix 4

The Performance Summary for the home is shown in Table 6–11.

			DIFFERENCE: NOT
MONTH	HEAT LOAD	SOLAR SUPPLIED	SOLAR SUPPLIED
Sep	1.23	4.44	0
Oct	4.15	4.75	0
Nov	7.52	3.67	3.84
Dec	11.59	3.62	7.97
Jan	12.53	3.85	8.68
Feb	10.97	4.46	6.51
Mar	9.56	4.68	4.88
Apr	5.46	3.60	1.85
May	2.16	3.37	0
	Total = 65.17		Total = 33.73

TABLE 6–11
PERFORMANCE SUMMARY
(in millions of Btus)

The Difference: Not Solar Supplied in Table 6-11 is the purchased fuel that will be needed per year. Note that in September, October, and May, the home is receiving more solar heat than needed, and in that case the windows are probably open, releasing the extra heat. In the table, when the "Solar Supplied" number exceeds the "Heat Load" number, zero is used for that month in the "Difference" column.

In this example the calculation process is as follows:

Total Purchased Fuel = 33,730,000 Btus

Total Heat Demand = 65,170,000 Btus

Percentage of Purchased Fuel = 33,700,000 Btus ÷ 65,170,000 Btus × 100 = 52% Not Solar Supplied

Percentage supplied by Solar = 100% − 52% = 48% Solar Supplied

The above calculation assumes that the home is faced true south. In our example, Hartford, Connecticut has a westerly magnetic deviation from true north of 12 degrees (see appendix 7 for an isogonic map, which indicates magnetic declinations). That means that once we have established our north–south compass line, the north–south axis of our solar home should be rotated clockwise 12 degrees.

HEAT LOSS REDUCTION DUE TO
WINDOW INSULATION

In chapter 4 we discussed the benefits of providing supplementary window insulation using thermo-shutters or some other form of nighttime insulation on at least some of the home's glazing. Let's now calculate the difference in performance assuming that we are going to install thermo-shutters on 203 square feet of window and patio glass. This example further assumes that the thermo-shutters will be closed at night during the heating season.

Utilizing the same technique demonstrated earlier in this chapter, we calculate the R-value of the thermo-shutter to be 7.76. The total R-value of the window or patio door with the thermo-shutter closed is shown in Table 6–12.

TABLE 6–12 TOTAL R- AND U-VALUES FOR INSULATED GLAZING	
ITEM	R-VALUE
15 MPH wind (outside)	0.17
Dual-glazed glass	1.92
Dead airspace*	0.80
Thermo-shutter	7.76
Still airspace **	0.68
Total R-value =	11.33
Total U-value =	0.0883

★ Between glass and thermo-shutter
★★ Inside surface of the thermo-shutter

Assuming that the thermo-shutters are closed for sixteen hours per night and open for eight hours during the day, the thermo-shutter credit will be calculated as follows:

Square feet of thermo-shuttered glass × (U-value of glass − U-value of thermo-shutter) × Number of hours with thermo-shutters in closed position

203 square feet × (0.5208 Btus/hr • ft^2 • °F − 0.0883 Btus/hr • ft^2 • °F) × 16 hours/day

= 1,405 Btus/°F • day

Applying the above thermo-shutter credit to our previously calculated total heat loss, the new predicted heat loss total will be:

10,529 Btus/°F • day − 1,405 Btus/°F • day = 9,124 Btus/°F • day

Using this revised heat loss calculation, we now recalculate the monthly heat load as shown in Table 6–13.

		TABLE 6–13		
	MONTHLY HEAT LOAD WITH WINDOW INSULATION			
	(in millions Btus)			
MONTH	HEAT LOSS OF HOME		DEGREE DAYS	MONTHLY HEAT LOSS
Sep	9,124	× 117	=	1.07
Oct	"	× 394	=	3.59
Nov	"	× 714	=	6.51
Dec	"	× 1,101	=	10.05
Jan	"	× 1,190	=	10.86
Feb	"	× 1,042	=	9.51
Mar	"	× 908	=	8.28
Apr	"	× 519	=	4.73
May	"	× 205	=	1.87
		Total	=	56.47*

* The previous total without thermo-shutters was 65.17 million Btus. The thermo-shutter reduction in total heat load is 65.17 − 56.47 = 8.70 million Btus for the nine-month heating season.

Table 6–14 shows the home's total heat load in relation to the portion that is supplied by solar and not supplied by solar.

Now the totals can be summarized as follows:

Total Purchased Fuel = 26,060,000 Btus

Total Heat Demand = 56,470,000 Btus

Percentage of Purchased Fuel = 26,060,000 Btus ÷ 56,470,000 Btus × 100 = 46%

Percentage Supplied by Solar = 100 − 46 = 54%

TABLE 6–14
PERFORMANCE SUMMARY
(in millions Btus)

Month	Heat Load	Solar-Supplied	Difference: Not Solar-Supplied
Sep	1.07	4.44	0
Oct	3.59	4.75	0
Nov	6.51	3.67	2.84
Dec	10.05	3.62	6.43
Jan	10.86	3.85	7.01
Feb	9.51	4.46	5.05
Mar	8.28	4.68	3.60
Apr	4.73	3.60	1.13
May	1.87	3.37	0
	Total 56.47		Total 26.06

As you can see, adding thermo-shutters lowers the total heat require-ment of the home and increases the percentage supplied by solar. The overall effect of using thermo-shutters is summarized in Table 6–15.

TABLE 6–15
NET EFFECT OF USING WINDOW INSULATION
(as percentage of total heat load)

	WITHOUT THERMO-SHUTTERS	WITH THERMO-SHUTTERS
Total Heat Load	65,170,000 Btus/year	56,470,000 Btus/year
Purchased Energy	33,730,000 Btus/year	26,060,000 Btus/year
% Supplied by Solar	48%	54%

From the performance summaries in this chapter, we can see that about two-thirds of our purchased energy is required to meet heating needs in December, January, and February. It is in these months that nighttime window and patio door insulation is the most beneficial. These months have the longest nights and shortest days, making it less inconvenient to cover our glass, since we can't see out anyway. There are also non-numerical benefits provided by nighttime window and patio door insulation. Many people find that a home with window insulation psychologically "feels" cozier and more secure.

DID WE KEEP THE FURNACE OFF?

The performance summary tabulations are based on monthly averages and don't tell us when and if the furnace runs, or what the living space and Solar Slab temperatures are. Have we met our design goal of keeping the furnace off?

February is a high-intensity solar month, making it a good one in which to check the living space and Solar Slab temperatures. We need to make sure that the home is in thermal balance and not overheating. In the following discussion, we will continue with and refine the concepts introduced in chapter 3.

Let's assume that the Solar Slab is comprised of 4 inches of concrete slab bonded to 12-inch concrete blocks, as illustrated on pages 29 and 30. Since the Solar Slab is inside the perimeter-foundation-wall insulation, and contains ductwork that displaces some of the concrete blocks, we will reduce the volume of theoretical concrete mass by 15 percent.

Remembering from chapter 3 that a concrete block is about 50 percent solid concrete, the volume of concrete in our Solar Slab is calculated as follows:

Volume of concrete = foundation dimensions × depth of concrete × % of theoretical concrete volume that is functional thermal mass

In the sample Saltbox, let's define these variables in this way:

Depth of concrete = ½ of concrete block height (½ × 12 inches)+ slab thickness (4 inches) = 10 inches (or 0.833 feet)

Volume of concrete =
(28 feet × 38 feet × 0.833 feet) × 85% = 754 cubic feet

The adjusted predicted heat loss with thermo-shutters will be:

9,124 Btus/°F • day ÷ 24 hr/day = 380 Btus/hr • °F

Let's see if the furnace needs to run. Our start time will be 10:00 PM, and we will assume the following circumstances:

1. The automatic thermostat has switched to its set-back position of 55 degrees, and our occupants have retired for the night.
2. The 10:00 PM Solar Slab temperature is 68 degrees, because the preceding day was sunny.
3. The overnight outside temperature is 10 degrees.

Let's calculate what the 7:00 AM Solar Slab temperature will be. Appendix 2 shows that in February, our solar day starts at 7:00 AM and ends at 5:00 PM.

We also need to estimate what the average inside temperature will be overnight. Using our 10:00 PM start temperature of 68 degrees, and assuming a 7:00 AM morning temperature of 60 degrees, the average overnight living space temperature is then 64 degrees. Our Delta T (temperature difference between inside and outside) will be calculated this way:

$$\text{Delta T} = \text{inside temperature } (64°) - \text{outside temperature } (10°)$$
$$= 54 \text{ degrees Fahrenheit}$$

Likening the Solar Slab to a battery, we will next see how much of a "charge" (measured in degrees) we will lose overnight. We will need to calculate the Solar Slab Thermal Capacity (SSTC). The SSTC is the product of the volume of concrete multiplied by the capacity of concrete to hold heat.

As explained above, the measure of a material's capacity to hold heat is called "specific heat," which is the ratio of the amount of heat required to raise a quantity of a given material one degree to that required to raise an equal mass of water one degree. The heat storage capacity of the Solar Slab is about 30 Btus per cubic foot per degree. This figure is derived as follows. The specific heat of 12-inch standard weight concrete blocks is about 0.22 Btus per pound per degree Fahrenheit. The specific heat of poured concrete is between 0.19 and 0.24 Btus per pound per degree Fahrenheit. Using 0.215 for the combination of concrete slab and concrete blocks, and 140 pounds per cubic foot as their combined weight, the heat capacity of the sample Solar Slab is calculated as follows:

$$0.215 \text{ Btus/pound} \cdot °F \times 140 \text{ pounds/ft}^3 = 30.1 \text{ Btus/ft}^3 \cdot °F$$

The SSTC equals

$$754 \text{ ft}^3 \text{ of concrete} \times 30 \text{ Btus/ft}^3 \cdot °F$$
$$= 22,620 \text{ Btus/degree of change}$$

The 10:00 PM to 7:00 AM heat loss will be:

$$380 \text{ Btus/hr} \cdot °F \times 54° \times 9 \text{ hours} = 184,680 \text{ Btus}$$

Since there is a positive temperature difference between the Solar Slab and the living space, the Solar Slab will supply the necessary overnight heat. Dividing the 10:00 PM to 7:00 AM heat loss by the SSTC, we find how many degrees the Solar Slab lost overnight:

$$184,680 \text{ Btus} \div 22,620 \text{ Btus per degree} = 8.2 \text{ degrees}$$

Our "battery" lost 8 degrees of "charge." Subtracting the overnight temperature loss of 8 degrees from the 10:00 PM Solar Slab temperature of 68 degrees, we find that the 7:00 AM Solar Slab temperature would be $68 - 8 = 60$ degrees.

The set-back on an automatic thermostat lowers the temperature at which the thermostat calls for heat, and does so at a time which the resident specifies. In this example the set-back, overnight temperature is 55 degrees between 10 PM and 7:00 AM. That is, the house temperature must go below 55 degrees before the thermostat will switch on the furnace. Since the Solar Slab temperature will not decay to less than 60 degrees in this example, in actuality there will be no requirement for the furnace to operate to maintain a comfortable overnight temperature, even though the ambient or outside temperature may be severely cold.

This is a situation where even the most skeptical person will agree that the Solar Slab is yielding heat from its stored state back into the living space.

Since the thermostat was set to turn on the furnace at 55 degrees, the furnace did not operate from 10:00 PM to 7:00 AM because the minimum overnight living space temperature was 60 degrees.

Next let's assume that the daytime heat setting is 68 degrees, and as suggested in chapter 5, we have located the thermostat on an east-facing interior wall. Let's further assume that we have another sunny day. At 7:00 AM we are having breakfast in our sunny east side dining/family area, and the sun is warming us and also striking the thermostat, which heats up and does not turn the furnace on. As the solar day progresses, the entire home rises in temperature to 68 degrees. As excess solar heat enters the home, and is stored in the Solar Slab, the living space temperature will probably increase to between 70 and 72 degrees. Since these temperatures are above the thermostat setting of 68 degrees, from 7:00 AM to 5:00 PM the furnace will not operate.

Using the information contained in appendix 2, from the 1993 ASHRAE *Handbook of Fundamentals*, the amount of solar energy or insolation available to vertical glass on February 21 at north latitude 40 degrees is as shown in Table 6–16.

TABLE 6–16
INSOLATION ON FEBRUARY 21 FOR NORTH LATITUDE 40

ELEVATION	SHGF (BTUS/SQUARE FEET OF GLASS)
East*	648 (half-day total, reading down the table)
South	821 × 2 = 1,642 (for full day)
West*	648 (half-day total, reading up the table)

* AM values for west glass and PM values for east glass are ignored; therefore, the East SHGF = West SHGF.

Because some of the sun's energy is reflected out of dual-glazed windows, the amount of heat passing through the insulated dual-glazed window is reduced by multiplying the above totals by 0.88, which you will recall is the Shade Coefficient (SC) for ½-inch insulated glass.

Our total solar gain for the day can be calculated as:

0.88 × (648 SHGF × 64 square feet of east-facing glass) + 0.88 × (1,642 SHGF × 162 square feet of south-facing glass) + 0.88 × (648 SHGF × 35 square feet of west-facing glass)= 290,537 Btus

The average outside winter temperature for Hartford, Connecticut, is 37 degrees Fahrenheit (see appendix 5). Let's assume that our sunny February 7:00 AM to 5:00 PM outside temperature is 40 degrees. Using 68 degrees as the inside temperature, the Delta T (temperature difference between inside and outside) will be

$$68° - 40° = 28°\text{ Fahrenheit}$$

The heat loss from 7:00 AM to 5:00 PM will therefore be:

$$380\text{ Btus/hr} \cdot °F × 28° × 10\text{ hr} = 106,400\text{ Btus}$$

Note: It is reasonable to use the reduced heat loss figure of 380 Btus per degree-hour, because the windows are heat gainers on sunny days. Also, the sun striking the south wall neutralizes it in terms of heat loss.

The amount of free solar heat available for storage during the 10-hour solar collection time period can be summarized as:

Total Insolation	290,537 Btus
Heat Loss	(106,400)
	————
Excess Available:	184,137 Btus to store

To find the daytime Solar Slab temperature increase, divide the above figure by the SSTC:

$$184,137\text{ Btus} ÷ 22,620\text{ Btus per degree} = 8.14\text{ degrees}$$

Our battery took on a daytime charge of 8 degrees. Adding the daytime Solar Slab temperature gain of 8 degrees to the 7:00 AM Solar Slab temperature of 60 degrees, we have a 5:00 PM Solar Slab temperature of 68 degrees. Since the temperature of the home will have quickly risen to 68 degrees even though the furnace had been "tricked" into not operating during breakfast, the furnace will have ended up not running all day.

From 5:00 PM to 10:00 PM the furnace may be needed to supplement the heat in the Solar Slab to keep the temperature at 68 degrees or higher, as required by the occupants.

Should the next day be sunless, the furnace will operate longer to keep the airspace up to temperature. In chapter 7 we will discuss how the Solar Slab assists the furnace even on sunless days.

IS THE HOME
IN THERMAL BALANCE?

The above 24-hour analysis demonstrated how the furnace was off for long periods of time, and showed that the Solar Slab's 24-hour temperature swing or variation was about 8 degrees. Using this methodology for design calculations, a home incorporating a Solar Slab should

be designed to keep the Solar Slab temperature swing within a range of about 10 degrees or less.

TABLE 6–17 THERMAL SUMMARY FOR SOLAR SLAB (24-hour period)		
TIME PERIOD	BTUS GAIN (LOSS)	TEMPERATURE GAIN (LOSS)
10:00 PM to 7:00 AM	(184,680)	(8 degrees)
7:00 AM to 5:00 PM	184,137	8 degrees
5:00 PM to 10:00 PM	No gain or loss	No gain or loss

Table 6–17 gives the thermal summary for the Solar Slab for the 24-hour period described above.

Thermal balance has been achieved because the overnight loss in heat is about equal to the amount of heat that the east-, south- and west-facing glass was able to collect in excess of the amount of heat needed by the home during the day while the sun was out. This excess heat was absorbed by and later given back by the Solar Slab. The Solar Slab daily gain was approximately equal to the nighttime loss.

In our example of a Saltbox 38 in Hartford, Connecticut on a sunny February 21, the amount of energy collected by the windows and the patio doors, the heat demands of the home, and the size of the thermal

An example of a smaller, one-story solar home, in which every room is sunny.

mass are all in proper proportion. This home is not overheating and the daily temperature swing was within comfortable limits.

What was the cost to heat this solar home for the 24-hour period described above? Let's assume that the furnace fires at 0.85 gallons of oil per hour. The furnace will probably have run for about 1.5 hours in the evening and possibly .5 hours in the early morning. In that 24-hour period, the furnace ran about 2 hours, consuming

2 hours × 0.85 gallons per hour = 1.70 gallons of oil

At $1.00 per gallon, the residents will have paid $1.70 for their fuel for that February day and night. The vast majority of the heat they used was free, simply harvested from the sky.

INSURING COMFORT: SOME BASIC GUIDELINES

It is difficult to make a general rule that dictates the amount of glass and the amount of thermal mass that a solar home will need to perform optimally throughout the year. Try not to use too much of a good thing. That is, don't overglaze. Make sure that the thermal mass is sized to allow no more than a 8-degree temperature swing from its warmest to coolest state. The occupants will feel comfortable with a temperature swing in the Solar Slab from a low of 62 to high of 70 degrees, and uncomfortable if it is colder in the morning than 62 or hotter in the afternoon than 70.

Typically, a poured slab will be 4 inches thick in a larger home, and up to 7 inches thick in a smaller home such as the N-38-X shown on page 60, which was another model offered by Green Mountain Homes. The N-38-X represents a small house with 1,408 square feet of living space, whereas the Saltbox 38 represents a larger home of 1,895 square feet (see photo on page 84).

Attempts have been made to produce ratios that will dictate the ideal relationship of glass to mass, or glass to wall area, or glass to floor area. Again, considering the wide variations in regional climatic conditions and in the specific characteristics of local building sites, general rules are difficult to create and apply. There really is no substitute for good solar design and good judgment. As can be seen in the example above, the amount of glass on each elevation and the size of the thermal mass are interrelated, and such relationships are dependent on location, the heat loss of the building, and other factors.

The Saltbox 38 we have been using as an example is designed according to the following ratios of glazing to insulated wall area, considering the glass area on the east, west, and south as a percentage of insulated wall area:

261 square feet of glass ÷ 1,898 square feet of insulated wall area × 100 = 14%

Using 8 degrees as the design temperature "swing" in the Solar Slab, the smaller home shown on page 60 will be used to illustrate a procedure to determine the appropriate thickness of the poured slab.

The specifications for this representative N–38–X (sample location: Middlebury, Vermont) are:

Footprint (dimensions of Solar Slab) = 16 feet × 38 feet
    = 608 square feet

East- and west-facing glass = 44 square feet each

South-facing glass = 122 square feet

East-, west-, and south-facing glass area ÷ insulated wall area
    = 210 square feet ÷ 1,720 square feet × 100 = 12%

Area of glazing insulated with thermo-shutters = 80 square feet

Total heat loss for the house, with thermo-shutters in use
    = 295 Btus/hr • °F

Let's determine the thickness of the Solar Slab needed to keep the above solar home in thermal balance. Middlebury is approximately 44 degrees north latitude. Since appendix 2 lists the SHGF for 40 and 48 degrees north latitude, the SHGF will be interpolated for 44 degrees north latitude. Using a peak February day, and 8 degrees as our maximum desired Solar Slab temperature swing, the correct calculation is as follows:

Elevation	Solar Heat Gain Factor
East	594 Btus per square foot (half-day total, reading down the table)
South	817 × 2 = 1,634 Btus per square foot (full day)
West	594 Btus per square foot (half-day total, reading up the table)

Solar Principle # 6

Do not over-glaze.

Incorporate enough windows to provide plenty of daylight, but do not make the mistake of assuming that solar heating requires extraordinary allocations of wall space to glass. An over-glazed building, as shown below, will probably overheat. A highly insulated and well-constructed home with a proper number and distribution of high-quality windows does not need much energy to maintain comfortable temperatures year-round.

Using a Shade Coefficient of 0.88 (for ½-inch insulated glass), the total insolation for a peak February day is:

East = 44 ft² × 594 Btus /ft² × 0.88 = 23,000 Btus

South = 122 ft² × 1,634 Btus/ft² × 0.88 = 175,426 Btus

West = 44 ft² × 594 Btus/ft² × 0.88 = 23,000 Btus

Total: 221,426 Btu

Since the SHGF Tables assume a Clearness Number of 1.00, and since Middlebury is in snow country, the total insolation will actually be increased by 10 percent, because the low angle of the February sun will reflect heat upward from the snow cover. The new total, adjusted accordingly, is:

221,426 Btus × 1.10 = 243,569 Btus

The average outside winter temperature for Middlebury, Vermont, is about 30 degrees. Using 68 degrees as the average inside temperature, the Delta T or difference is:

68° − 30° = 38° Fahrenheit

The 7:00 AM to 5:00 PM heat loss will be:

295 Btus/hr • °F × 38 degrees × 10 hours = 112,100 Btus

The amount of free solar heat available for storage during the 10-hour solar collection time is:

Total Insolation	243,569 Btus
Heat Loss	(112,100 Btus)
Excess available to store:	131,469 Btus

The formula to determine the necessary thickness for this home's Solar Slab is:

Stored Btus = cubic feet of concrete × Btus per cubic foot per degree × maximum design Solar Slab temperature variation, or

131,469 Btus = x cubic feet of concrete × 30 Btus per cubic foot per degree × 8 degrees

This means that the correct figure in the equation for the cubic feet of concrete needed will be 548. The next calculation will involve dividing this cubic foot total by the square footage of the slab multiplied by 85 percent to account for the functional percentage of thermal mass in the overall slab (the figure 0.85 compensates for the portion of concrete block displaced by air passages and ducts):

$$548 \text{ cubic feet} \div (16 \text{ feet} \times 38 \text{ feet} \times 0.85)$$
$$= \text{thickness of Solar Slab (1.06 feet, or 13 inches)}$$

Since 12-inch concrete blocks are half solid, the slab thickness is 13 inches − 6 inches = 7 inches.

NO COOKBOOK RECIPES FOR SOLAR DESIGN

While writing this book I conducted a search of the design records for existing Green Mountain Homes in the hope of finding certain ratios or percentages that were common to all solar homes and that could be used to assist other designers. No obvious "cookbook recipe" emerged, except for two basic design parameters:

1. The square footage of east-, south-, and west-facing glass should be in the range of 10 to 20 percent of the total exterior heated wall area.
2. The peak solar-supplied February-day increase in Solar Slab temperature should be 8 degrees.

Is there a general rule about the ideal square footage of east- or west-facing glass as it relates to the square footage of south-facing glass? As mentioned earlier, east- and west-facing glass, though beneficial in late fall and early spring, must be used judiciously in locations where summer air conditioning is required. In northern New England, where air conditioning is never really necessary, the amount of east- or west-facing glass can be increased; however, in Maryland, where the expense of air conditioning is a factor, the amount of east- and west-facing glass should be less, in order to reduce morning and afternoon heat gain. The range of east- or west-facing glass as a percentage of south-facing glass in the homes we researched was from 25 percent to 75 percent, which is too high a spread to yield any general rule. Other factors influencing decisions about the amount of east- and west-facing glass are the floor plan or layout of the home, the location of shade trees, the direction of special views, the use of window insulation, the dominant weather conditions at the site, and most importantly, the desires and aesthetic preferences of the homeowner.

Our design philosophy and practice has been first to present ideal considerations to the people planning a house, and then to incorporate as many of these idealized factors as possible while carefully considering the clients' desires, needs, and particular site situation.

One way to solve a problem is to guess. (There's a fancier engineering term for the stratagem — convergence by trial and error). Then make the appropriate calculations and see what the results look like. Then repeat the calculations procedure with a better guess, until the variables converge toward the best result. The same method can be used to design a home with a Solar Slab.

SUMMARY OF THE DESIGN PROCEDURE

In summation, the sequence of steps in the solar design procedure are as follows:

1. Conduct a site analysis: in other words, really get to know this place where you may be spending many years. Make numerous visits at different times of day and in different seasons.
2. Begin to do progressively more refined drawings and floor plans for the home, keeping in mind the solar design principles presented in this book, and using the amount of glass suggested in this chapter for the east-, south-, and west-facing elevations. Keep the total square footage of the east-, south-, and west-facing glass between 10 to 20 percent of the total square footage of heated wall area.
3. Find the north latitude of the home site (see appendix 4).
4. Find the Outside Winter Design temperature for this location (again, see appendix 4).
5. Calculate the R-values for the walls, glass, and roof (see appendix 3).
6. Calculate the overall predicted heat loss of the home, taking a nighttime insulation credit if nighttime glass insulation will be used.
7. Find the degree day data for the specific home site (see appendix 5).
8. Find the insolation values for the home site (see appendix 2).
9. Find the percentage of sunshine for the home site (see appendix 6).
10. Tabulate in Btus the heat load, including the portion that will be solar-supplied and the difference, not solar-supplied.
11. Calculate the percentage of total heat load that will be supplied by solar.

12. Use the "converging guess" method to make several "runs," adjusting the variables and trying out different combinations, to see which design produces the best economy while satisfying the aesthetic and living-space requirements of the home's future residents.

13. Using a peak solar day in February, calculate the following:

    A. The predicted daytime excess solar energy: the amount of heat available to be stored for later.

    B. The necessary thickness of the Solar Slab based on an ideal daytime temperature swing of 8 degrees.

14. Check your overall results using common sense and good judgment—for which there is no substitute!

THE FOUNDATION
PLAN, AND BACKUP
HEATING AND COOLING

7

In this chapter we will complete the design process for the Connecticut Saltbox analyzed in chapter 6, concentrating on the foundation plan. Next, we will size backup heating and cooling systems for various fuels, and describe how to utilize these backup systems in conjunction with the Solar Slab.

As always, our goal is to keep the furnace or air conditioner off. To measure the effectiveness of a solar-assisted heating or cooling plan, it is necessary to predict annual fuel usage to determine the best size for the backup equipment. In chapter 6, the Saltbox 38 located in Hartford was found to be in thermal balance with approximately an 8-degree temperature variation in the Solar Slab; that is, on a representative February day, the early morning temperature of the Solar Slab would be about 60 degrees Fahrenheit, and this temperature would rise to about 68 degrees by the time the sun went down.

THE FOUNDATION PLAN

The final step in the design of our Saltbox 38 in Hartford, Connecticut, is the detailing of the foundation plan. The picture on page 92 shows what this plan should look like. Note that the plan is not to scale, is not dimensioned, and is not to be used for construction. This diagram is included to illustrate the following important design details:

1. *Orientation:* The "compass rose" is shown on the upper-left corner. The person who needs this information the most is the foundation contractor — even though that contractor may not be accustomed to thinking in solar terms. Remember our discussion in chapter 2 about the cost of positioning a home too far from the ideal orientation to true south. Be sure that the foundation is oriented exactly as

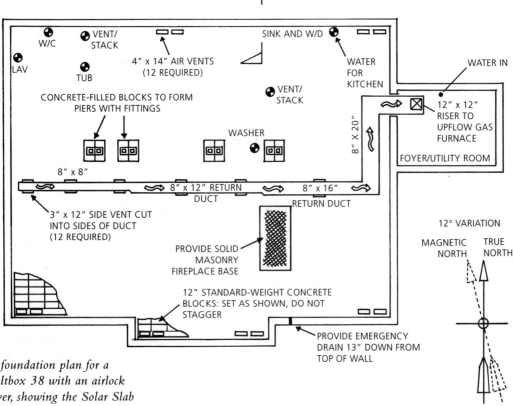

A foundation plan for a Saltbox 38 with an airlock foyer, showing the Solar Slab heat exchanger and the proper configuration of vents and piers. See the sill detail on page 30.

your site plan specifies, since the resulting foundation "footprint" will determine how the house subsequently built relates to the sun. Showing the cardinal directions on your foundation plan will help insure that the home will be oriented properly.

2. *Air Vents:* The minimum number of air vents for a home with a Solar Slab is eight — two air vents at each corner of the first floor. However, in this case they were not placed in the northwest corner because that's where the master bath is located. It is not a good idea to draw moisture-laden air or odors from a wet area such as a bathroom into the Solar Slab. See page 96 to see how to arrive at the total number of air vents needed.

3. *Central Return Duct:* The duct shown running down the middle of the base under the poured slab is included in all cases. It should always be used as the return-air duct: Do not reverse the air flow pattern shown on the control diagrams. By using the Solar Slab as part of the return-air duct system, the Solar Slab will constantly

assist the furnace by pre-heating the return air. Even if the home will be heated with a woodstove and emergency electric furnace, the return duct should be included and the air mover hooked up per the appropriate control diagram (see the illustration on page 110).

4. *Piers and Chimney Bases:* Solid masonry on undisturbed hardpack must be provided to insure that heavy column loads and chimney loads will not crack the slab.

5. *Miscellaneous:* Plumbing risers need to be properly placed. Cast iron is the material of choice, and should be placed in the layer of sand under the concrete blocks. Water pipes embedded in the Solar Slab should be "K" copper sleeved in heavy-duty PVC plastic to protect against the corrosive reaction between concrete and copper.

Note also that there is a drain shown through the south wall. This emergency drain will allow water to drain out of the Solar Slab at the bottom of the concrete blocks. One homeowner unfortunately had a fire on the second floor of his Green Mountain Home. The firemen quickly extinguished the blaze with a heavy dose of water. The water apparently ran down the stairs, found an air vent, then flowed into the Solar Slab and out the emergency drain. As a result, the damage was minimal. Another homeowner had a bird crash through his patio door glass. It happened during severe cold and the owner hadn't turned off the water supply. A nearby water pipe froze and burst. When the owner returned, water was flowing from the broken pipe into an air vent and out the emergency Solar Slab drain. Again, thanks to the drain, the damage was minimized.

BACKUP HEATING OPTIONS

Let's assume that the convential backup heat for the Connecticut saltbox will be an oil-fired furnace. Later in this chapter we will calculate the theoretical size of the oil furnace to be 45,000 Btus per hour.

The problem with small oil furnaces is that the oil burner nozzle orifice has a tendency to plug due to the impurities in fuel oil. A 45,000-Btus-per-hour oil-fired furnace would normally be used in a small house trailer. These units tend to be operationally troublesome. A 90,000 or 100,000+-Btus-per-hour furnace will run quite nicely due to the larger oil orifice size, but such units are too big for this house in this location.

The 45,000-Btus-per-hour load is probably too much for the fan-coil arrangement shown on page 110. Our best backup for this home would be a gas-fired furnace. Gas-fired furnaces are readily available in the smaller Btu ranges and are operationally quite reliable. For these reasons, the sample Saltbox 38 solar home in Hartford, Connecticut, will be equipped with an upflow gas-fired furnace and a gas-fired hot water heater located in a utility room created by extending the foyer (see the floor plan on page 108). This will keep the equipment out of the living space, isolated for safety and noise-abatement reasons. Feed ducts will be located in the super structure, and each room will have a heat outlet grille.

Later in this chapter, I will show you how to calculate that the net output of the propane gas furnace is 42,000 Btus per hour. The smallest commercially available upflow gas furnace normally will be rated at 40,000 Btus per hour. Adding duct loses to our theoretical 42,000 Btus per hour, we will need to go to the next commercially available size of 60,000 Btus per hour. Let us assume that the manufacturer's specifications for the furnace call for an 8 x 20-inch return duct with a blower size of 900 cubic feet per minute (CFM). As a guideline, assume the side vents cut into the sides of the central return duct in the Solar Slab have an air flow capacity of 75 CFM each. Dividing the total amount of air being moved by the furnace blower by 75 will yield the number of side vents needed. In this case, $900 \div 75 = 12$.

Likewise, the air vents that allow air into the Solar Slab, discussed in #2 above, should equal or exceed the number of side vents cut into the sides of the return duct. Again, assume that the 4 x 14-inch air vents will have an air flow of 75 CFM.

The 75 CFM assumption for side vents and air vents is conservative; that is, they have the capacity to allow more air flow. However, high air flows will be accompanied by noise. Low air flows will give you a quiet running system. Also, the air vents can be regulated to direct return air flows to various parts of the home. By conservatively sizing them, you provide operational flexibility. It's a lot easier to close off an air vent than to jackhammer an extra one after the concrete is poured. The Solar Slab needs to have free air flow. In this case, more is better than fewer.

Note also that the return duct is reduced in size the further it is placed from the blower. This manifolding will even out air flows within the Solar Slab when the air mover is operating.

CONVENTIONAL BACKUP HEAT

No matter how committed one is to conserving energy and not burning fossil fuels, some form of conventional backup heating must be installed. Many existing solar homes are heated only by the sun and a woodstove, and many homeowners are very comfortable utilizing alternative and renewable forms of energy. However, provisions should be made for a conventional back up heating system for the following reasons:

1. A home is probably the largest single financial expenditure a person will ever make, and the value of the home should be protected by providing for a conventional backup heating system. Resale value should be considered, as prospective buyers may not have the same enthusiasm for the use of alternative energy as the original owners.
2. Times change. A client of mine in Maine insisted that his home would be heated only by a "Russian woodstove" and the sun. He didn't want to consider a conventional backup system. As a concession, he agreed to wire the house for backup electric heat but not to install the heaters. During his lifetime, the sun and the woodstove kept the home very comfortable; but, this kind of self-reliance was "his thing." After his death, his wife asked to have the backup electric heaters installed.

Use the Furnace Blower Fan to Circulate Solar Heat

Since good circulation of air within the home and through the Solar Slab is an important part of an effective solar heating plan, the solar design described in this book is an ideal complement to a conventional warm-air heating system. This combination gives the homeowner the best of both worlds: the ease of operation and responsiveness of an on-demand warm-air system, and free solar heat when available.

The Solar Slab heating and cooling system operates in a similar fashion to an automobile cooling system. Imagine your car radiator, which works fine without the cooling fan while traveling at 60 miles per hour. This is the equivalent of air naturally flowing through the array of concrete blocks in the Solar Slab.

When stopped in traffic, a thermostat turns on the automobile radiator fan to ventilate the radiator mechanically. The fan pulls air through the radiator fins, which cools the water circulating through the engine. The Solar Slab operates in much the same way. As the sun's heat enters the home and is stored in the Solar Slab, the effectiveness of the Solar Slab during peak collection times can be increased by turning on a fan.

The most cost-effective way to provide mechanical assistance to the Solar Slab is to use the air mover or fan in the furnace. By using the Solar Slab in tandem with a conventional warm-air system as described in this chapter, you can assure that the furnace is always receiving solar-preheated air, making it more efficient. In addition, the fan can be used alone, without turning on the furnace's heater, simply to serve as an air mover for the circulation of solar heat.

How Big Should the Backup Furnace Be?

To size backup heating equipment and to estimate the amount of fuel consumed per heating season, you can use the following formulas:

Furnace Size =
(Heat Loss × Design Temperature) ÷ Combustion Efficiency

Fuel Consumed per Year =
Difference Not Solar Supplied ÷ Usable Btus of Selected Fuel

In our chapter 6 example, the thermal performance summary for the Saltbox 38 in Hartford, Connecticut was:

Heat Loss without thermo-shutters: 10,529 Btus/°F • day, or

10,529 ÷ 24 = 438.72 Btus/°F • hr

Purchased Energy per Year without thermo-shutters:
33,730,000 Btus

Purchased Energy per Year with thermo-shutters: 26,060,000 Btus

A gallon of #2 fuel oil contains approximately 140,000 Btus, and typically an oil furnace will operate at 70 percent efficiency. Therefore, a gallon of oil will yield 0.70 × 140,000 Btus, or 98,000 Btus per gallon. The subsequent calculation for a home without thermo-shutters would be:

Oil Furnace Size = 438.72 × 72 ÷ 0.70 = 45,125 Btus per hour

Say, 45,000 Btus per hour net delivery ("at the bonnet"). The predicted number of gallons of oil needed will be:

For a home without thermo-shutters: 33,730,000 ÷ 98,000
= 344 gallons

For a home with Thermo-Shutters: 26,060,000 ÷ 98,000
= 266 gallons

How Much Will the House Cost to Heat?

We have reached the moment of truth. As indicated in the calculation above, the predicted fuel usage of the Saltbox 38 example in Hartford, Connecticut, will be 266 gallons of oil per year, assuming the conscientious use of thermo-shutters. At today's oil price of about

$1.00 per gallon, that's $266.00 per year. Without the use of thermo-shutters, the cost would be $344.00 per year.

If oil-fired domestic hot water were also used, we could presume an average usage of 200 gallons of fuel oil per year. Adding that additional 200 gallon allowance for water heating to the worst-case (without thermo-shutters) fuel use prediction, we total 200 + 344 = 544 gallons per year. A 1,000-gallon storage tank filled in the summer would carry this home for the entire heating season with 456 gallons to spare.

Fuel

By investing in your winter's supply of oil or gas in July or August, you can buy your fuel at the lowest price for the year. As the price of fuel rises through the heating season, your summer fuel investment will be saving you more money than if you had kept that money in the bank and purchased fuel at the higher winter price.

Many readers of this book will want to heat their homes entirely with wood and sunlight. A well-designed home can be a multi-fuel home; that is, solar plus wood heat can do 100 percent of the job, or solar plus oil can do 100 percent of the job. In actual practice most solar homes use combinations of the conventional backup heat and renewable energy. This flexibility makes the best use of what's available, and gives us the ability to emphasize one type of backup heat or the other as local, regional, and world fuel markets fluctuate and/or our lifestyles change.

TABLE 7–1
IMPACT OF DESIGN MODIFICATIONS ON ANNUAL FUEL USE

Specification	Predicted Use (gallons of oil per year)	Savings (gallons of oil per year)
This book's standard wall R-20, roof R-32	266	
Increase wall thickness to R-32	231	35
Increase roof thickness to R-40	253	13
Reduce fresh air from ⅔ to ⅓ air change per hour	148	118

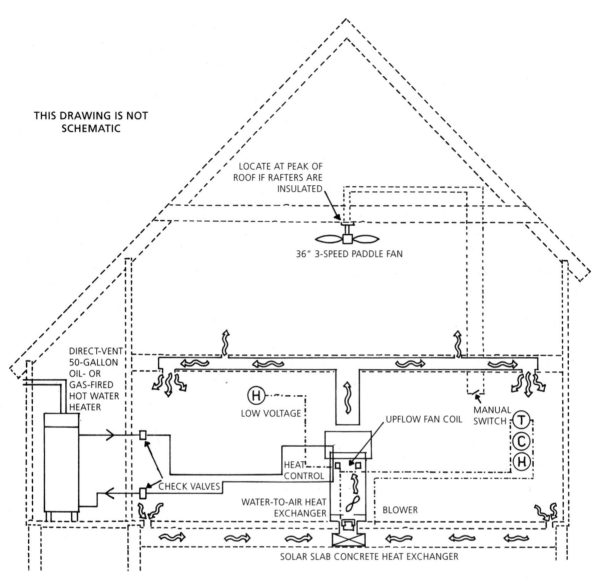

THIS DRAWING IS NOT
SCHEMATIC

LOCATE AT PEAK OF
ROOF IF RAFTERS ARE
INSULATED

36" 3-SPEED PADDLE FAN

DIRECT-VENT
50-GALLON
OIL- OR
GAS-FIRED
HOT WATER
HEATER

(H)
LOW VOLTAGE

UPFLOW FAN COIL

MANUAL
SWITCH

(T)
(C)
(H)

HEAT
CONTROL

CHECK VALVES

WATER-TO-AIR HEAT
EXCHANGER

BLOWER

SOLAR SLAB CONCRETE HEAT EXCHANGER

SEE PAGE 107 FOR EXPLANATION OF
HOW TO HOOK UP THE BACKUP
FURNACE. LEGENDS FOR THERMO-
STATS SHOWN ARE GIVEN ON PAGE
110.

Very often an efficient, highly insulated solar home will require only a very small backup furnace. Because small oil furnaces (less than 60,000 Btus per hour) present operational problems, instead you can use the hot water heater both to heat domestic water and to serve as the furnace. This diagram shows a fan coil combined with the water heater. The components for this system, which works well for houses requiring 40,000 Btus per hour or less, can be purchased separately or in a package such as that offered by Apollo Hydroheat System. The water heater used in this way should probably be oversized relative to the home's hot water needs, and should be an oil- or gas-fired quick-recovery unit.

Table 7–1 indicates the effect of modifying certain aspects of our standard solar design. As you see, making the walls or the roof thicker will produce insignificant savings. At $1.00 per gallon, the change in wall insulation amounted to savings of $35.00 per year and the roof change amounted to savings of $13.00 per year. The increased expense in labor and materials for framing more substantial walls and roof members, by contrast, is significant, and would not appear to be economically justified for the small savings produced.

Fresh Air

In any case, all walls, windows, openings, and roofs should be tightly constructed and fresh air should be introduced into the home only by controlled means, as discussed in chapter 4. The calculation in Table 7–1 shows significant savings for reducing the fresh air supply. However, while it is expensive to heat fresh outside air, the benefits of saving fuel by this means are not worth the health risks of living without adequate fresh air.

When any particular design change is considered, we must carefully weigh the incremental benefits versus additional costs and hazards that may result.

Other Fuels: Propane and Electric

The following efficiencies may be used to determine the size of a propane gas furnace or electric heater:

1. Propane gas heat at 75 percent efficiency × 91,500 Btus per gallon = 68,625 Btus per gallon.
2. Electric heat at 100 percent efficiency yields 3,415 Btus per kilowatt-hour

Using for total purchased energy with thermo-shutters a figure of 26,060,000 Btus and the same formula as above, the results would be:

1. Size of propane gas furnace = 42,000 Btus per hour with an annual consumption of 379 gallons
2. Size of electric heating system = 9.25 kilowatt-hours, with an annual consumption of 7,616 kilowatts

Propane has a higher furnace efficiency, but contains fewer Btus than fuel oil, so on a per-Btu basis, propane is more expensive. Yet propane has other advantages: it burns cleaner, no chimney is needed for the propane burner, and leaks cause less pollution. In some areas of the country, propane will be the more economical choice.

As for electric heat, the calculations are more complex since the generating source of this heat is elsewhere. Saying that electricity is 100 percent efficient for the end-user is misleading. Electric power is 100 percent usable once it enters the home, but to calculate its true efficiency, one ought to consider generating and transmission losses, which can be quite significant.

The calculation for the electric backup option determined that we would need 9.25 kilowatts per hour for the Saltbox 38 in Connecticut. If baseboard heaters are to be used, that will be the total amount of energy needed, because the heat is distributed among the rooms by the baseboard strip heaters. A second way to provide electric backup heat is to use an electric furnace, which includes an air mover similar to that of an oil or gas furnace.

If the home is going to have a woodstove, the conventional backup heating system will no doubt be used less often. Oil and gas furnaces are like automobiles. The more they are used, the better they run. If a gas or oil furnace is not used for long periods of time, the risk of the unit not starting, failing while in operation, or causing other damage is increased. By contrast, an electric furnace can sit idle for an indefinite period of time and still start instantly when needed. An electric unit also requires no annual tune-up, there is no fuel tank to worry about, and the cost of a chimney is avoided.

Heat Pumps

A third way to utilize electricity as backup heat is to use an air-to-air heat pump. Heat pumps use the refrigeration cycle to produce heat. The next time you pass by your refrigerator, put your hand near the floor: you will feel a flow of warm air when the refrigerator is running. A refrigerator operates by compressing a refrigerant (in the form of a gas), and then allowing the gas to expand. This process of compression and expansion absorbs and releases heat. The heat you felt near the floor is the heat that was extracted from the contents inside the refrigerator. A refrigerator is an example of a heat pump.

In a similar way, an air-to-air heat pump extracts heat from outside air and delivers the heat to the home. The air patterns in the home are similar to those in any other warm-air system; the advantage of a heat pump (over burning electricity in a coil) is indicated by a measure called "coefficient of performance" (COP). By using electricity to operate a heat pump, the amount of heat produced can be three times that of just burning up the same amount of the electricity in a coil or baseboard resistance heater. The coefficient of performance is dependent on the temperature of the outside air. In climates similar to Maryland or California, heat pumps perform very well. In cold climates such as Idaho or Vermont, they have little advantage.

In warm areas where air conditioning is used, a heat pump has an additional advantage as it can be reversed for summer cooling.

WOODSTOVES

Sizing a backup woodstove is less straightforward than sizing an oil or gas furnace. Selecting the correct size woodstove depends not only on the efficiency of the particular stove, but also on the quality and species of the wood to be used. Burning unseasoned softwoods yields much lower heat in Btus, and can also cause safety problems.

It is best to undersize a woodstove according to its manufacturer's specified "capacity," so that it will nearly always be burned hot. An oversized woodstove will overheat the living space, and it will therefore frequently be damped down by the house's occupants and left to smolder. As stove and chimney temperatures drop, incomplete combustion will create a buildup of creosote in the stove, stove pipe, and chimney, which can lead to a chimney fire or other undesirable consequences. A chimney fire can actually destroy the chimney's liner, necessitating a costly and time-consuming replacement, if the fire doesn't burn the whole house down in the process.

An undersized woodstove, conversely, will require a longer and hotter "burn" to heat the living space. The hotter stove will burn more efficiently, thereby minimizing creosote build up.

The woodstove location must be carefully planned to conform to all safety requirements. Woodstoves take considerable floorspace to provide for necessary clearances, and the location cannot be an afterthought. Provisions for woodstoves have to be carefully incorporated into the original design and layout of the home.

The chimney should be masonry, and located as close to the center of the building as possible. If alternative chimney materials are used, pay strict attention to the manufacturer's installation instructions and abide by all applicable safety regulations.

If thermo-shutters are used, the overall heat loss from the house at night will be reduced. In your calculations, credit should be taken for the use by averaging the heat loss with and without thermo-shutters. Again, for the model Saltbox 38 in Connecticut, the design temperature is 72 - 0 = 72 degrees Fahrenheit. The heat loss with thermo-shutters will be 380.17 Btus per hour per degree of difference between the inside and outside temperature, and without thermo-shutters is 438.72 Btus per hour per degree difference. (In order to average the heat loss with and without nighttime insulation, we'll add the two figures together and divide them in half.) Therefore, assuming an airtight stove with 85 percent efficiency, the calculation for sizing a backup woodstove to complement the Solar Slab is as follows:

$$\text{Size of Woodstove} = [\tfrac{1}{2} \times (438.72 \text{ Btus/hr} \cdot \text{degree difference} + \\ 380.17 \text{ Btus/hr} \cdot \text{degree difference}) \times 72] \div 0.85 \\ = 34{,}682 \text{ Btus/hr}$$

Let's call it 35,000 Btus per hour.

The amount of heat generated per cord of dry, seasoned firewood varies by species. We can use an average figure of 17,000,000 Btus per cord of dry hardwood. Determine the species available to you locally, and look up its caloric value. The quantity of wood needed annually can be estimated by dividing the purchased energy per year by the amount of heat available in a cord of firewood (in this case—dry, seasoned hardwood). Calculate the amount of firewood needed per year for a home without thermo-shutters, as follows:

$$33{,}730{,}000 \text{ Btus} \div 17{,}000{,}000 \text{ Btus per cord} = 2 \text{ cords}$$

Just to be safe, we will add another $\tfrac{1}{2}$ cord, making the predicted total 2.5 cords. Next, let's calculate the number of cords needed per year for a home *with* thermo-shutters:

$$26{,}060{,}000 \text{ Btus} \div 17{,}000{,}000 \text{ Btus per cord} = 1.5 \text{ cords}$$

Once again add a margin for error of $\tfrac{1}{2}$ cord, and the total is 2 cords.

We often see people cutting and splitting firewood in the fall, "getting ready for winter." The wood used for a given heating season should be a year or more old; that is, wood cut in one fall should be stacked to dry for a full calendar year before burning. To ensure that your wood is properly seasoned, split the logs, in lengths appropriate for your stove, and stack them under cover with adequate gaps for air circulation. If it isn't possible for whatever reason to get a full year ahead in your reservoir of firewood, be sure that your wood is cut, split, and stacked no later than the end of April for the following winter. Remembering the solar principles emphasized throughout this book, it is also best to store firewood in a shed with an open southern exposure, to facilitate drying.

There really is no substitute for the radiant heat derived from a woodstove, but as any fireman can attest, woodstoves require great caution in planning and constant vigilance in operation. Study one of the many books solely devoted to woodburning.

There once was a young woman in Vermont who got married and proudly invited her father to her new home, to show off the central oil-fired heating system with baseboard heaters, and with no woodstove anywhere to be seen. Her father entered the home on a cold winter's evening and started to roam from room to room. The daughter asked him if anything was wrong.

"No," he said as he continued to wander around the living room.

"Well, there must be something wrong. How come you keep wandering around?"

The father looked at her with a puzzled look and asked, "Whar do ya go to git warm?"

GEOTHERMAL HEAT

Through the monitoring program discussed in chapter 1, a minimum of 45 degrees Fahrenheit was measured below the gravel layer underlying the concrete blocks of the Solar Slab (see the illustrations on pages 29 and 30). Note that there is a 1-inch thick layer of Styrofoam insulation specified on top of the hardpan. This layer of insulation is placed there to prevent the possibility of a rapid loss of heat to the ground below the building, but it will allow a slow transfer of heat upward if conditions are suitable. These conditions will occur in an unoccupied and unheated home.

If the temperature in the unoccupied home is allowed to drop to the 45 to 50 degree range, the thermostat marked "H" shown below the thermostat marked "C" on page 110 will turn the blower on at 50 degrees and circulate air to extract ground or geothermal heat. Note that in this mode the normal "H" thermostat connected to the heat control is set at 45 degrees. It is important to purchase thermostats that read accurately down to 45 degrees in order for this mode to function properly.

As the unoccupied home loses heat, the Solar Slab will first give up the heat in its concrete block and slab layers. These layers are the active part of the Solar Slab; that is, they routinely take on and give off heat. The layers below the concrete blocks are more passive, as they will be slower to rise or drop in temperature.

A home that is unoccupied will first draw out the heat available in the active portion of the Solar Slab, and then will draw heat from the passive layers that underlie the concrete blocks. This underlying reservoir of heat is almost infinite. If the Solar Slab is not extracting heat fast enough from the lower levels, the circulating fan in the furnace will be turned on thermostatically, and the Solar Slab will act as a heat exchanger between the ground and the house. The cost of this heat extraction will be only the minor cost of running the furnace's blower. The theoretical minimum temperature to which a home with a Solar Slab will drop is the ground temperature under the Solar Slab, a temperature that is exceedingly stable.

USING THE SOLAR SLAB
FOR SUMMER COOLING

The natural solar and backup heating systems discussed in this book are all very helpful in controlling a home's inside temperature. But an important function of air conditioning is the reduction of the moisture content of the air. Unfortunately, in warm and humid regions a mechanical and energy-intensive air conditioner is needed to do this job.

In summer, air returning to the heat pump air mover will be precooled by the Solar Slab. While monitoring the performance of the Solar Slab in summer, we observed a 12-degree drop in temperature as the air entered and exited the vents for the Solar Slab. Just as we noted with furnaces for winter, this assistance allows the air conditioner to be downsized smaller than standard practice would suppose. For instance, by informal monitoring in Maryland, we found that the best cooling was achieved by having a slightly "undersized" air conditioner running steadily instead of a larger unit cycling on and off.

The cooling capacity of air conditioning equipment is measured in "tons of cooling." In days gone by, the White House was cooled by filling a huge room in the basement with ice, and then passing the living-space air over the ice so that cooled air was recirculated by ducts into the building's rooms. A ton of cooling is related to the cooling capacity of a ton of ice (12,000 Btus per hour). The term stuck. In our case, a credit of approximately ½ ton of cooling can be taken due to air returning through the Solar Slab.

The total cooling load for a home is the sum of "sensible heat" and "latent heat." Sensible heat is the heat that is gained by the same factors considered in a heat-loss calculation. Latent heat is the additional cooling load due to the necessity of reducing moisture in the air to be cooled. The calculation needed to properly size an air conditioner is complex and is not included in this book. That kind of precise evaluation is a job for a heating/ventilating engineer; however, a reasonable estimate of the proper size for a household air conditioner can be made by utilizing a rudimentary guideline.

To estimate the basic cooling load for a home, multiply by three the actual or projected volume in cubic feet of the conditioned airspace in the building. The resulting number will approximate the cooling load in Btus per hour. In our Saltbox 38 example, the conditioned airspace is 14,492 cubic feet; the cooling load approximation is 14,492 × 3 = 43,476 Btus per hour. One ton of cooling equals 12,000 Btus per hour. Therefore, the home's proper air conditioner size should be about 43,476 Btus per hour ÷ 12,000 Btus per hour (or one ton of cooling), which is 3.6 tons of cooling.

Applying a Solar Slab cooling credit of about ½ ton, the unit size comes out to approximately 3 tons. So this sample home in Connecticut will probably need about 3 tons of cooling, or an air conditioner with a capacity of 3 × 12,000 Btus per hour, or 36,000 Btus per hour.

The home's cooling load will almost always dictate duct size, as more air movement is needed to satisfy the cooling load than the heat load. It also costs more to cool air than to heat air. In this example, three tons of cooling will require a movement of about 400 cubic feet of air per minute per ton, or 1,200 CFM. As you will recall, the sample home's furnace air mover requirement was 900 CFM.

HOW TO HOOK UP THE BACKUP FURNACE OR AIR CONDITIONER

The diagram on page 110 shows how to install a backup gas-, oil-, or electric-fired furnace. The drawing is schematic relative to the actual locations in the building and the relative size of the equipment's components. Most warm-air systems have one or two central returns and a distributed feed system via ducts and grilles located throughout the house. This diagram shows a distributed return system. The distributed return is accomplished by locating intake grilles along the north and south walls. These are the same grilles needed for the natural flow of the Solar Slab. Do not locate intake grilles in utility rooms, bathrooms, or any other room which has either excess moisture or undesirable odors that could be introduced to the air circulation system. When the furnace blower is turned on, air is returned via the grilles located along the north and south walls. The air movement will be very slow, because of the distribution and oversizing of the return-air grilles, and as a result the floor surface will be almost draft-free. Once the return-air enters the air passage in the Solar Slab on the north- or south-facing wall, it will flow into the open channels in a row of blocks, and eventually return to the furnace air mover via the return duct placed near the center of the house along the east-west axis of the Solar Slab. Three-

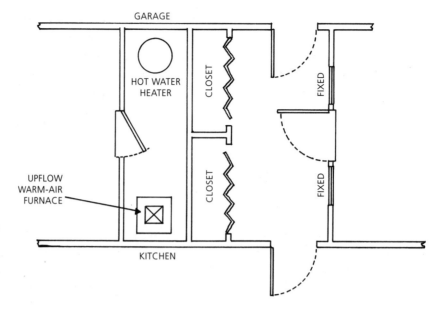

GARAGE

HOT WATER
HEATER

CLOSET

FIXED

UPFLOW
WARM-AIR
FURNACE

CLOSET

FIXED

KITCHEN

Layout for modified foyer for floor plan on page 57, showing the location of the furnace and hot water heater. This utility room will provide good sound isolation for the furnace while leaving the backup heat equipment accessible when necessary.

inch by twelve-inch vents cut into the sides of the return duct will allow the air to enter into the duct and return to the air mover. When the furnace gun or heat element is operating, the returning air will arrive carrying residual heat from the Solar Slab and provide warmer return air than would be the case if the air was returned directly from the airspace to the furnace's intake vents.

Note in the diagram that the thermostat marked "C" is a cool thermostat, which will turn the furnace's blower on if the home starts to overheat due to the accumulation of heat from the sun. In this situation, the furnace gun or heat element will remain off while only the blower runs to cycle air through the Solar Slab, in order to store the heat that actuated the cooling thermostat.

In summer, heat that was stored during the day, which helped cool the home, is expelled at night by simply allowing the home to ventilate through open windows or by mechanically expelling stored heat by running the furnace blower from midnight to 4:00 AM—the coolest part of the 24-hour summer day. In the diagram, the timer marked "T" controls this function.

The furnace is shown centered on top of the return duct for illustrative purposes only. It should be located outside the living space for noise abatement. One cost-saving idea is to locate an electric furnace inside the stair enclosure leading to the second floor, which allows for air distribution directly from this central location, thereby reducing or eliminating the feed-duct system. The disadvantage of this scheme is noise. In homes using a woodstove as the prime backup source of heat, this lower-cost siting of the furnace may be acceptable despite the proximity of a noisy blower to the living space, since the electric heat will be used very little or not at all. More likely, the backup furnace will be used while the occupants are away for extended periods, making the problem of noise from the blower inconsequential, since no one will be home to hear it.

Solar Principle # 7

Consider the contribution of solar energy (indicated by insolation values for your region) and natural processes (including breezes and shade) to the heating and cooling of the home, in order to avoid oversizing a backup heating system or air conditioner. A home that is oriented to true south, is tightly constructed and well insulated, and has operable windows for air circulation should not require large fossil-fuel burning equipment to maintain thermal comfort.

Size the conventional backup systems to suit the small, day-to-day heating and cooling needs of the home. Do not oversize backup oil or gas furnaces, as they are inefficient, cycling on and off, when not supplying heat at their full potential. Air conditioners are likewise expensive and wasteful when operated inefficiently.

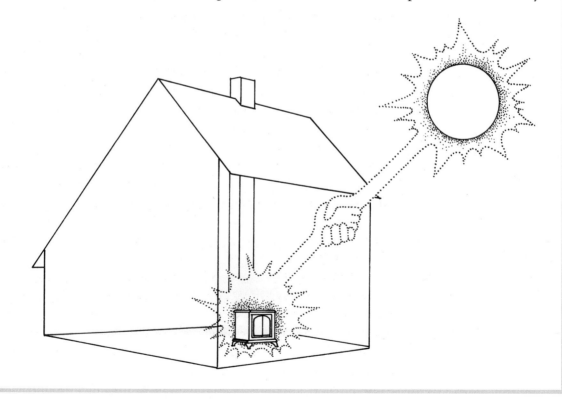

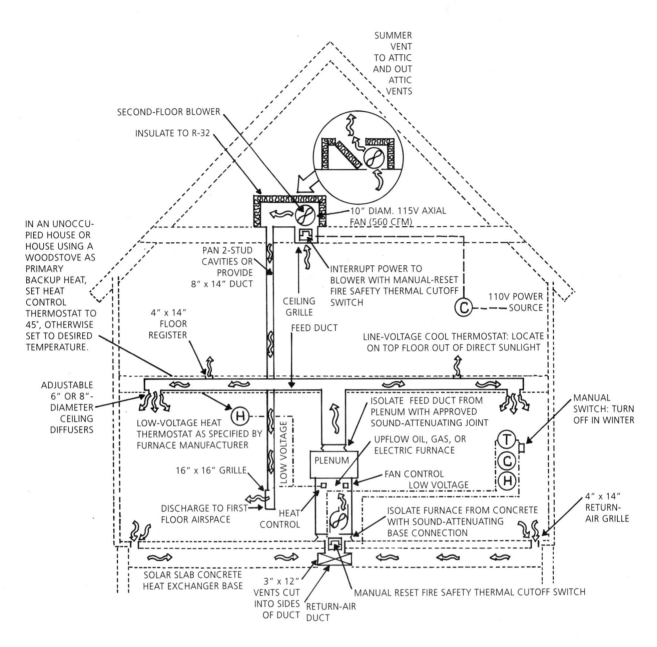

SUMMER
VENT
TO ATTIC
AND OUT
ATTIC
VENTS

SECOND-FLOOR BLOWER

INSULATE TO R-32

10" DIAM. 115V AXIAL
FAN (560 CFM)

IN AN UNOCCU-
PIED HOUSE OR
HOUSE USING A
WOODSTOVE AS
PRIMARY
BACKUP HEAT,
SET HEAT
CONTROL
THERMOSTAT TO
45°, OTHERWISE
SET TO DESIRED
TEMPERATURE.

PAN 2-STUD
CAVITIES OR
PROVIDE
8" x 14" DUCT

INTERRUPT POWER TO
BLOWER WITH MANUAL-RESET
FIRE SAFETY THERMAL CUTOFF
SWITCH

110V POWER
SOURCE

CEILING
GRILLE

FEED DUCT

4" x 14"
FLOOR
REGISTER

LINE-VOLTAGE COOL THERMOSTAT: LOCATE
ON TOP FLOOR OUT OF DIRECT SUNLIGHT

ADJUSTABLE
6" OR 8"-
DIAMETER
CEILING
DIFFUSERS

LOW-VOLTAGE HEAT
THERMOSTAT AS SPECIFIED BY
FURNACE MANUFACTURER

ISOLATE FEED DUCT FROM
PLENUM WITH APPROVED
SOUND-ATTENUATING JOINT

UPFLOW OIL, GAS, OR
ELECTRIC FURNACE

MANUAL
SWITCH: TURN
OFF IN WINTER

LOW VOLTAGE

PLENUM

FAN CONTROL
LOW VOLTAGE

16" x 16" GRILLE

4" x 14"
RETURN-
AIR GRILLE

DISCHARGE TO FIRST
FLOOR AIRSPACE

HEAT
CONTROL

ISOLATE FURNACE FROM CONCRETE
WITH SOUND-ATTENUATING
BASE CONNECTION

SOLAR SLAB CONCRETE
HEAT EXCHANGER BASE

3" x 12"
VENTS CUT
INTO SIDES
OF DUCT

RETURN-AIR
DUCT

MANUAL RESET FIRE SAFETY THERMAL CUTOFF SWITCH

(T) OPTIONAL 24-HOUR TIMER, SET TO ENERGIZE BLOWER FROM 12
MIDNIGHT THROUGH 4 AM IN SUMMER TO PRE-COOL SOLAR SLAB WITH
COOL NIGHT AIR

(C) LOW-VOLTAGE COOL THERMOSTAT: SET INITIALLY AT 74°, ADJUSTED TO
SUIT RESIDENTS AFTER HOME IS OCCUPIED. THIS THERMOSTAT WILL
ALLOW FURNACE BLOWER TO MECHANICALLY AID IN STORAGE OF SOLAR
HEAT BY CIRCULATING SUN-WARMED AIR THROUGH THE SOLAR SLAB
BASE.

(H) LOW-VOLTAGE HEAT THERMOSTAT, SET TO 50°. FREEZE-UP PROTECTION.
THIS THERMOSTAT WILL ALLOW FURNACE BLOWER TO MECHANICALLY
EXTRACT HEAT STORED IN SOLAR SLAB. LOCATE ON FIRST FLOOR (LOCATE
OPTIONAL SECOND THERMOSTAT ON SECOND FLOOR).

*Heat control diagram used to
show the relationship between
the Solar Slab and oil, gas, or
electric backup heat equipment. This drawing is
schematic.*

Again, the picture on page 108 shows how the airlock foyer can be modified to locate the furnace and domestic hot water heater outside the living space. In this configuration, with properly designed ductwork, the operation of the warm–air system will be almost silent.

Recirculate Warm Air from the Second Floor

The last item on page 110 to be discussed is the second-floor ceiling blower. In winter this small blower takes warm air that rises to the second-floor ceiling, and delivers it back to the first floor. In houses with woodstoves, it is advantageous to locate the exit grille behind the woodstove to direct warm air away from the woodstove while it is operating.

In summer, the second-floor fan enclosure can be vented to the outside as shown. The energy consumed by a small axial fan is a very reasonable expense for the winter heating and summer cooling assistance provided by this small blower.

LET THE LAWS OF NATURE
WORK FOR YOU

Let's review the design we have been discussing. Over 50 tons of effective thermal mass have been built into the home. This has been coupled with the correct amount of east, south, and west glass to collect solar heat. In addition, the home has been highly insulated in a manner which protects the occupants from undesirable side effects from poor air quality.

The physics, or laws of nature, which have been built into the design will work on your behalf twenty-four hours per day for the life of the building. There is no predicted maintenance of the basic solar heating and cooling system. The various backup heat schemes and their associated equipment are merely refinements on this fundamentally natural solar design. None of the refinements, including the use of thermo-shutters, should be interpreted as necessary to permit the system to work as it will work naturally.

Just as modern day automobile engineers have been able to increase horsepower and fuel mileage without increasing the size of the engine, backup heating and cooling equipment can "push" the natural system to make it perform better. All of the backup schemes described here make double use of the backup equipment; that is, this equipment will function as a supplementary heater or air conditioner, and in addition, the same equipment can be used to provide mechanical assistance to the natural solar collection and distribution system.

A SIDEHILL VARIATION, AND SOLAR DESIGN WORKSHEETS

8

Humans discovered long ago that the world is not flat. So it goes with house sites. As the easy-access lots are sold off, we find ourselves gradually moving up hillsides to build our homes. Our example of how to utilize a hillside site will be a Green Mountain Homes Sidehill "C-32," the floor plan for which is shown on page 114.

The design of the Solar Slab for the sidehill situation is illustrated on page 134. The most notable difference between the Solar Slab for a flat lot and the sidehill adaptation is the inclusion of the north side concrete wall in the home's thermal mass.

This is accomplished by placing three 1-inch layers of rigid insulation on the outside of the wall as shown in the diagram. Also note the extra 1-inch layer of Styrofoam under the flat portion of the Solar Slab (making a total of two 1-inch layers of rigid insulation in the sidehill slab). The north side's usual 4-inch x 14-inch air vents have been extended upward to the first floor and the south air vents are placed along the south wall on the lower level.

This sidehill design utilizes the lower level for living space. Remember that for the Solar Slab to be effective, it has to be in thermal contact with the living space. It is not cost-effective — nor thermally effective — to utilize the lower level for a basement/storage area.

LET'S TRY SUNNY WYOMING FOR THE SIDEHILL SITE

For the sake of discussion and calculation, we will locate our model C-32 Sidehill in Cheyenne, Wyoming, and analyze it using the method developed in chapter 6 and the worksheets included in this chapter and in appendix 1. I will show you how I would use these worksheets

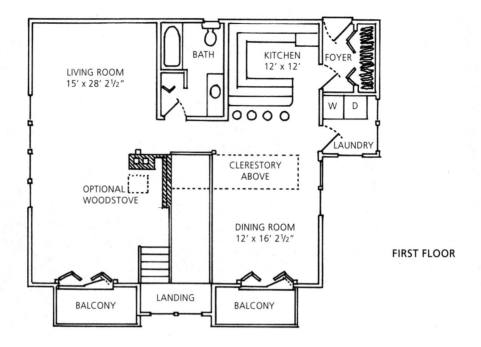

FIRST FLOOR

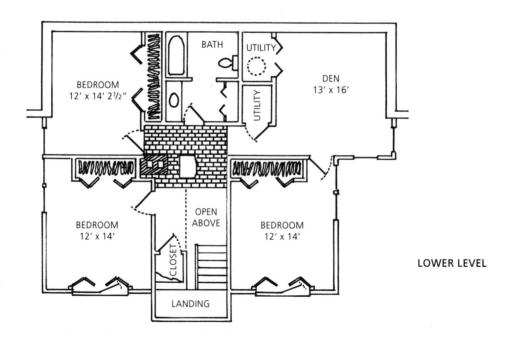

LOWER LEVEL

A floor plan for a sidehill version of the C-32 saltbox design. Construction against a sidehill permits use of the "bermed" back wall as part of the home's thermal mass.

Another sidehill variation.

to do design calculations for the Wyoming house, and you can photo-copy the blank worksheets in the appendix to use in your own planning process.

Let's fill in as much information as we can on Worksheet #1.

You can start with lines 1 through 19.

Line 2: Obtain from appendix 4.

Line 3: Obtain from appendix 7.

Lines 4, 5, 6, 7, 8, 9, 10, 14, 16, 17, and 18: Obtain from your own house drawings.

Line 11: Obtain from the manufacturer's literature for your proposed window and patio doors.

For line 12: 0.88 is the Shade Coefficient for ½-inch dual-glazed glass. Enter the correct Shade Coefficient for your glass.

Line 19: Obtain from appendix 4.

Line 25 can now be entered on Worksheet 1A. The Standard Clearness Number is 1.00. Since Cheyenne's elevation is 6,126 feet above sea level, and Cheyenne has a dry clear atmosphere, we can judgmentally increase the clearness factor by 10 percent. Therefore, our clearness number is 1.10.

Using Worksheet 2, we will next calculate U-values.

Worksheet 1-A

1. House Location: <u>Cheyenne, Wyoming (sidehill site)</u>
2. Latitude: <u>North 41°1'</u>
3. Magnetic Deviation: <u>3° east</u>
4. House Alignment: <u>True south</u>
5. Area (in square feet) of east-facing glass: <u>52</u>
6. Area (in square feet) of west-facing glass: <u>55</u>
7. Area (in square feet) of south-facing glass: <u>184</u>
8. Area (in square feet) of north-facing glass: <u>2</u>
9. Total area (in square feet) of glass: <u>293</u>
10. Area (in square feet) of glass with nighttime insulation: <u>160</u> (using thermo-shutters)
11. Manufacturer's U-value of window glass: <u>0.5208</u>   Patio glass: <u>0.5208</u>
12. Shade Coefficient of glass: <u>0.88</u>
13. U-value of glass with nighttime insulation:
14. Area (in square feet) of exterior (heated) walls: <u>1,816</u>
15. Net area (in square feet) of exterior (heated) walls: Subtract line 9 from line 14 = <u>1,523</u>
16. Area (in square feet) of heated lower living-space concrete wall (in sidehill design): <u>464</u>
17. Area (in square feet) of insulated flat ceiling (or angled ceiling if house has a cathedral ceiling): <u>1,120</u>
18. Volume (in cubic feet) of the heated airspace of the house: <u>17,024</u>
19. Outside Winter Design Temperature: <u>– 15° F</u>
20. U-value of total framed wall area:
21. U-value of total roof/ceiling area:
22. U-value of total lower living-space concrete wall:
23. Total heat loss from home without nighttime insulation for glass (excluding lower concrete wall):
24. Total heat loss from home with nighttime insulation for glass (excluding lower concrete wall):
25. Clearness number: <u>1.10</u>
26. Recommended size of furnace:
27. Total requirement (in kilowatt-hours) of electric backup heat:
28. Recommended size of woodstove:
29. Estimated annual fuel consumption:
30. Required thickness of poured concrete for Solar Slab:

The individual R-values called for can be obtained from appendix 3, except for the window insulation R-value. Obtain the R-value of your nighttime insulation device by using the manufacturer's specs or, if you make your own device, calculate it by adding up R-values for the materials used to get a cumulative total (as shown in chapter 4). In the Wyoming model calculations, we'll use the R-value for thermo-shutters.

The wall and roof sections will be the preferred design described in chapter 4 (2 x 4s with rigid exterior insulation), shown on page 45.

In the north wall detail shown on page 134, we will assume that the exposed interior concrete on the lower level will be covered on the inside with 1-inch Styrofoam, with ½-inch drywall screwed to 1-inch strapping placed 16 inches on center across the Styrofoam insulation. A 6 mil vapor barrier should be placed behind the drywall, similar to the placement of the vapor barrier on the framed wall drawing (page 44).

We can now fill in lines 13, 20, 21, and 22 on Worksheet #1.

Worksheet 1-B	
13. U-value of glass with nighttime insulation:	0.0883
20. U-value of total framed wall area:	0.0468
21. U-value of total roof/ceiling area:	0.0307
22. U-value of total lower living-space concrete wall:	0.0456

We now have enough information to fill in Worksheet #3, House Heat Loss. Next, taking the information from Worksheet #3, fill in lines 23 and 24 on Worksheet #1.

Worksheet 1-C	
23. Total heat loss from home without nighttime insulation for glass (excluding lower concrete wall):	11, 126 Btus
24. Total heat loss from home with nighttime insulation for glass (excluding lower concrete wall):	10,019 Btus

Worksheet 2
R- and U-value Calculation

A. FRAMED WALL: R-VALUE

1. 15 MPH wind (outside)	0.17
2. Exterior siding: 1-inch rough-sawn cedar boards	1.25
3. Rigid insulation: 1-inch Styrofoam	5.00
4. Exterior house wrap	N/A
5. Exterior sheathing: ½-inch CDX plywood	0.62
6. Fiberglass insulation: 3 ½-inch fiberglass batt	13.00
7. Vapor barrier: 6 mil poly	negligible
8. Interior wall covering: ½-inch drywall	0.64
9. Still air (inside surface of wall)	0.68
Total R-value:	21.36

U-value of wall =1/R = 0.0468 Btus/hr • ft² • °F

(Increase U-value if framing or bridging loss is significant): not significant

B. ROOF OR CEILING: R-VALUE

1. 15 MPH wind (outside)	0.17
2. Roofing material: 325# asphalt shingles	0.44
3. Felt roofing paper: 15#	0.06
4. Roof sheathing: ½-inch CDX plywood	0.62
5. Fiberglass insulation: 9-inch fiberglass batt	30.00
6. Vapor barrier : 6 mil poly	negligible
7. Inside roof or ceiling covering: ½-inch drywall	0.64
8. Still air (inside suface of roof or ceiling)	0.68
Total R-value:	32.61

U-value of roof or ceiling =1/R = 0.0307 Btus/hr • ft² • °F

(Increase U-value if roof or ceiling framing or bridging loss is significant): not significant

Worksheet 2
(continued)

C. GLASS WITH NIGHTTIME INSULATION

1. 15 MPH wind (outside)	0.17
2. Dual-glazed glass	1.92
3. Dead air space (between glass and thermo-shutter)	0.80
4. Insulating device: thermo-shutters	7.76
5. Still air (inside surface of insulating device)	0.68
Total R-value:	11.33

U-value of nighttime insulated glass (1 ÷ R): 0.0883 Btus/hr • ft^2 • °F

D. LOWER LIVING-SPACE CONCRETE WALL: R-VALUE

1. Exterior rigid insulation: 3-inch Styrofoam	15.00
2. Concrete: 8-inch x 0.075	0.60
3. Interior insulation: 1-inch	5.00
4. Vapor barrier: 6 mil poly	negligible
5. Interior wall covering: ½-inch drywall	0.64
6. Still air (inside surface of wall)	0.68
Total R-value:	21.92

U-value of lower living-space concrete wall = 1/R = 0.0456 Btus/hr • ft^2 • °F

Worksheet 3
House Heat Loss Calculation

1. EXTERIOR WALL HEAT LOSS

Area of exterior walls (from Worksheet 1, line 15) × framed wall U-value
(from Worksheet 2, section A)

<u>1,523</u> square feet × <u>0.0468</u> Btus/hr • ft^2 • °F = <u>71.28</u> Btus/hr • °F

2. ROOF OR CEILING LOSS

Area of roof or ceiling (from Worksheet 1, line 17) × roof or ceiling U-value
(from Worksheet 2, section B)

<u>1,120</u> square feet × <u>0.0307</u> Btus/hr • ft^2 • °F = <u>34.38</u> Btus/hr • °F

3. INFILTRATION LOSS USING VOLUME METHOD

Volume of heated space (from Worksheet 1, line 18) × specific heat of air × air changes per hour

<u>17,024</u> cubic feet × 0.018 Btus/ft^3 • °F × <u>.67</u> air changes/hr = <u>205.31</u> Btus/hr • °F

4. HEAT LOSS THROUGH GLASS (WITHOUT NIGHT-TIME WINDOW INSULATION)

Area of window and patio door glass (from Worksheet 1, line 9) × U-value of glass
(from Worksheet 2, section C)

<u>293</u> square feet × <u>0.5208</u> Btus/hr • ft^2 • °F = <u>152.60</u> Btus/hr • °F

5. TOTAL HEAT LOSS:

Walls	<u>71.28</u> Btus/hr • °F
Roof or Ceiling	<u>34.38</u> Btus/hr • °F
Infiltration	<u>205.31</u> Btus/hr • °F
Glass	<u>152.60</u> Btus/hr • °F
Wall framing or bridging loss (if significant)	<u>N/A</u>

Roof and/or ceiling framing or bridging loss (if significant) <u>N/A</u> Btus/hr • °F

Solar Slab perimeter loss (if significant) <u>N/A</u> Btus/hr • °F

Combined total rate of heat loss= <u>463.57</u> Btus/hr • °F

For a total of the house's predicted Heat Loss Without Nighttime Glass Insulation, multiply the above combined total rate of heat loss by 24 hours per day:

<u>463.57</u> Btus/hr • °F × 24 hr/day = <u>11,126</u> Btus/°F • day

6. REDUCTION OF HEAT LOSS DUE TO NIGHTTIME GLASS INSULATION
(applicable only if nighttime insulation used)

The Heat Loss Credit for insulated glass can be calculated as follows:

Area of glass with nighttime insulation (from Worksheet 1, line 10) × [U-value of glass without nighttime insulation (from Worksheet 1, line 11) – U-value of glass with nighttime insulation (from Worksheet 2, section C)] × number of hours that nighttime insulation will be used

<u>160</u> square feet × (<u>0.5208</u> Btus/hr • ft^2 • °F – <u>0.0883</u> Btus/hr • ft^2 • °F) × <u>16</u> hours per day = <u>1,107</u> Btus/°F • day

Using the Heat Loss Credit just derived, the Total Heat Loss With Nighttime Insulation is calculated as follows:

Heat Loss Without Nighttime Glass Insulation (from section 5, above) – the Heat Loss Credit

<u>11,126</u> Btus/°F • day – <u>1,107</u> Btus/°F • day = <u>10,019</u> Btus/°F • day

7. ADDITIONAL HEAT LOSS IN SIDEHILL DESIGN

In a sidehill situation, the heat loss through the lower living-space concrete wall is a constant. For simplicity, let's call this the "Lower Concrete Wall Loss" or LCWL, which can be calculated as follows:

(continued on next page)

**Worksheet 3
(continued)**

Area of lower living-space concrete wall (from Worksheet 1, line 16) × U-value of lower living-space concrete wall (from Worksheet 1, line 22) × difference between inside and outside temperatures (or 65 degrees − 45 degrees)

<u>464</u> square feet × <u>0.0456</u> Btus/hr • ft² • °F X 20 degrees = <u>423</u> Btus/hour

8. DESIGN CHECK

Calculate the total area of the east-, west-, and south-facing glass as a percentage of the gross upper and lower heated wall area:

<u>(52 + 55 + 184)</u> square feet of E, W, and S glass (from Worksheet 1, lines 5, 6, and 7) ÷ <u>(1,816 + 464)</u> square feet of wall (from Worksheet 1, lines 14 and 16) × 100 = 291/2280 × 100 = <u>13</u> percent

The resulting percentage should be between 10 and 20 percent. <u>Yes</u>

Worksheet #4 will be next. Solar Heat Gain Factors shown in appendix 2 for north latitude 40 degrees are the closest to Cheyenne's location at 41 degrees 1' north latitude. You'll see in the ASHRAE table that listings are 8 degrees apart in latitude. Cheyenne happens to be close to 40 degrees north latitude, but if you encounter a design situation which is halfway between the SHGFs given in the appendix 2 tables, you may interpolate between the two. That is, if a house is to be located at or near 44 degrees north latitude, then use the average of the half-day SHGFs given for 40 degrees and 48 degrees north latitude. Remember that the SHGFs are read up and down on these tables, as described in chapter 6.

Moving on to Worksheet 5, we'll calculate the monthly heat load for the C-32 Sidehill house.

Using appendix 5, fill in the degree days for each month for your location, in our case Cheyenne. Then calculate the monthly loss due to the lower concrete living-space (heated) wall by multiplying the LCWL (From Worksheet 3) by 24 hours per day and then by the number of days per month.

Worksheet 4
Solar–Supplied Heat Gain

1. Using appendix 6, enter the percent sunshine for your home site:

MONTH	% SUNSHINE
September	69
October	69
November	65
December	63
January	65
February	66
March	64
April	61
May	59

2. From appendix 2, enter the east, south, and west half-day totals of Solar Heat Gain Factors for your home site latitude. (Read the table from top to bottom for sunrise to noon and from bottom to top for noon to sunset.) Assuming that your home faces south, multiply the south half-day total SHGF by 2. Ignore the west SHGFs for the AM and likewise ignore the east SHGFs for the PM (therefore, the east SHGF will equal the west SHGF).

MONTH	EAST	SOUTH (x2)	WEST
September	787	1344	787
October	623	1582	623
November	445	1596	445
December	374	1550	374
January	452	1626	452
February	648	1642	648
March	832	1388	832
April	957	976	957
May	1024	716	1024

Multiply the SHGFs given above by the area (in square feet) of glass on each elevation, and obtain a total for each month (square feet × Btus per square foot × days per month) = Btus per month

(continued next page)

Worksheet 4
(continued)

Month	Days	52 Square feet of East Glass × East SHGF × Days per Month		184 Square feet of South Glass × South SHGF × Days per Month		55 Square feet of West Glass × West SHGF × Days per Month		Total (in millions of Btus)
Sep	30	1.23	+	7.42	+	1.30	=	9.95
Oct	31	1.00	+	9.02	+	1.06	=	11.08
Nov	30	0.69	+	8.81	+	0.73	=	10.23
Dec	31	0.60	+	8.84	+	0.64	=	10.08
Jan	31	0.73	+	9.27	+	0.77	=	10.77
Feb	28	0.95	+	8.46	+	1.01	=	10.42
Mar	31	1.34	+	7.92	+	1.42	=	10.68
Apr	30	1.49	+	5.39	+	1.58	=	8.46
May	31	1.65	+	4.08	+	1.75	=	7.48

Tabulate the Solar Heat Gain for each month. Multiply the percentage of sunshine × the monthly total Btus × the Shade Factor × the Clearness Number:

Month	% Sunshine (as decimal)		Total Btus/month (from above)		Shade Factor		Clearness Number		Total (millions of Btus)
Sept	0.69	×	9.95	×	0.88	×	1.10	=	6.65
Oct	0.69	×	11.08	×	0.88	×	1.10	=	7.40
Nov	0.65	×	10.23	×	0.88	×	1.10	=	6.44
Dec	0.63	×	10.08	×	0.88	×	1.10	=	6.15
Jan	0.65	×	10.77	×	0.88	×	1.10	=	6.78
Feb	0.66	×	10.42	×	0.88	×	1.10	=	6.66
Mar	0.64	×	10.68	×	0.88	×	1.10	=	6.62
Apr	0.61	×	8.46	×	0.88	×	1.10	=	5.00
May	0.59	×	7.48	×	0.88	×	1.10	=	4.27

To digress for a moment, let's see what the loss across the lower concrete wall would be, if the wall were left uninsulated similar to the way many full basement cellar walls have been left. The R-value for an uninsulated 8-inch concrete wall is 0.60, as shown on Worksheet #2, section D.

$$U = 1/R = 1.6667$$

The loss for this 464 square feet of concrete wall then would be: square feet of concrete × U-value × difference between interior and exterior temperatures, or

$$464 \times 1.6667 \times (65 - 45)\star = 15,467 \text{ Btus/hour}$$

★ From Worksheet #3

The loss for the 464 square feet of insulated concrete wall in the Sidehill example would be 423 Btus per hour (see Worksheet #3), which means that an uninsulated wall would lose 36½ times more heat than an insulated wall. As you can see, badly designed full basements can be big losers of heat.

This calculation also helps explain the benefit of earth berming. As our figures clearly demonstrate, the temperature difference across the lower concrete wall is a constant, due to the relatively warm (and stable) temperature of the earth. The earth's temperature in this example was conservatively assumed to be 45 degrees.

We are now ready to summarize our calculations on Worksheet #6.

From the totals on Worksheet #6, we can see that this solar home in Wyoming will derive 67 percent of its heat *free*, from the sun.

The next worksheet will show us how to size the conventional backup oil-fired furnace and woodstove, plus it will show the estimated annual fuel consumption, using the methods of analysis presented in chapter 7.

For this example, oil was chosen to be the conventional backup fuel source. Note that the figure for heat loss without thermo-shutters was used to size the oil furnace. This approach is a little conservative, but experience has shown that to be reasonable. The possibility exists that window and/or patio door insulation devices may never get installed despite the best of initial intentions; or they might be removed, by the second owner of a home.

Worksheet 5
House Heat Load Calculation

Using appendix 5, enter the monthly degree days for your house location.

Monthly Heat Load (in Btus) = Total House Loss (in Btus/°F • day) × degree days + lower sidehill concrete wall loss or LCWL (from Worksheet 3, line 7) <u>423</u> Btus per hour × 24 hours × days per month

If this is a sidehill design, first calculate the monthly heat loss through the lower concrete wall (MCWL) as follows:

Month	LCWL (in Btus)		Hours per day		Days per month		MCWL (millions of Btus)
Sep	423	×	24 hours	×	30 Days	=	0.30
Oct	423	×	24 hours	×	31 Days	=	0.32
Nov	423	×	24 hours	×	30 Days	=	0.30
Dec	423	×	24 hours	×	31 Days	=	0.32
Jan	423	×	24 hours	×	31 Days	=	0.32
Feb	423	×	24 hours	×	28 Days	=	0.28
Mar	423	×	24 hours	×	31 Days	=	0.32
Apr	423	×	24 hours	×	30 Days	=	0.30
May	423	×	24 hours	×	31 Days	=	0.32

Month	Total House Heat Loss (in Btus)		Degree Days		MCWL		Monthly Heat Load (millions of Btus)
Sep	10,019	×	219	+	0.30	=	2.49
Oct	"	×	543	+	0.32	=	5.76
Nov	"	×	909	+	0.30	=	9.41
Dec	"	×	1,085	+	0.32	=	11.19
Jan	"	×	1,212	+	0.32	=	12.46
Feb	"	×	1,042	+	0.28	=	10.72
Mar	"	×	1,026	+	0.32	=	10.60
Apr	"	×	702	+	0.30	=	7.33
May	"	×	423	+	0.32	=	4.56
					Total	=	74.52

From Worksheets 4 and 5, enter the total monthly heat load and the figure for solar-supplied heat. Subtract the monthly solar-supplied figure from the total heat load. If the difference is less than "0," enter "0" in the last column.

Month	HEAT LOAD (millions Btus) FROM WORKSHEET 5	SOLAR SUPPLIED (millions Btus) FROM WORKSHEET 4	DIFFERENCE: NOT SOLAR SUPPLIED (millions Btus)
Sep	2.49	6.65	0
Oct	5.76	7.40	0
Nov	9.41	6.44	2.97
Dec	11.19	6.15	5.04
Jan	12.46	6.78	5.68
Feb	10.72	6.66	4.06
Mar	10.60	6.62	3.98
Apr	7.33	5.00	2.33
May	4.56	4.27	0.29
	Total = 74.52		Total = 24.35

Difference: Not Solar Supplied = Btus to be supplied by purchased fuel

Totals are:

A. Total Purchased Fuel (from column 3, above)   24,350,000 Btus

B. Total Heat Load (from column 1, above)   74,520,000 Btus

C. % Purchased Fuel (A ÷ B × 100)   24,350,000 ÷ 74,520,000 x 100 = 33%

D. % Solar (100 − C)   100 - 33 = 67%

The woodstove calculation shows a method to undersize the choice of stove, as recommended in chapter 7. It is better to have an undersized woodstove burning hot rather than an oversized woodstove smoldering and creating creosote.

So, now we can fill in lines 26, 27, 28, and 29 on Worksheet #1, as shown in Worksheet #1D.

Congratulations, you have reached the last worksheet! It is time to put your solar home in thermal balance by sizing the Solar Slab to absorb the excess free solar energy available while keeping the home within comfortable temperatures during peak solar-collection times.

Worksheet 7
Backup Heat and Annual Fuel Usage Calculation

1. NET AVAILABLE BTUS FOR VARIOUS FUELS

A. #2 fuel oil: (theoretical heat energy = 140,000 Btus per gallon). Assuming 70% combustion efficiency, the net heat will be 0.70 × 140,000= 98,000 Btus per gallon.

B. Propane gas: (theoretical heat energy = 91,500 Btus per gallon). Assuming 75% combustion efficiency, the net heat will be 0.75 × 91,500 = 68,625 Btus per gallon.

C. Electricity (theoretical heat energy = net heat in this case): 3,415 Btus per kilowatt-hour.

D. Split and dry hardwood: Average net heat energy is 17,000,000 Btus per cord (a cord is 128 cubic feet).

2. FOR COMBUSTION EFFICIENCY IN STEP 2, BELOW, USE THE FOLLOWING VALUES:

Oil furnace: .70

Propane gas furnace: .75

Electric resistance heaters or electric furnace: 1.00

Woodstove: .85

3. SIZING THE CONVENTIONAL BACKUP HEAT EQUIPMENT

The appropriate furnace size (in Btus per hour) can be calculated as follows:

Step 1.

Total Heat Loss (from Worksheet 3, line 5*) 11,126 Btus/°F • day ÷ 24 hr/day × (72 – –15 Outside Winter Design Temperature**) 87 degrees + Sidehill Lower Concrete Wall Loss***

571 Btus per hour

= 40,903 Btus per hour

*Use Total Heat Loss without taking nighttime insulation credit
** Outside Winter Design Temperature from Worksheet #1, line 9
***Area of lower concrete wall (Worksheet 1, line 16) 464 square feet x U-value of lower concrete wall (0.0456 Btus/hr • ft² • °F) × (72 – 45 Degrees) = 571 Btus per hour

Step 2.

The answer from Step 1 40,903 Btus per hour ÷ combustion efficiency (as a decimal, from section 2, above) = 40,903 Btus per hour ÷ .70 = 58,433 Btus per hour

Rounded for simplicity to the nearest thousand: Furnace Size = 60,000 Btus per hour****

**** Btus per hour net at bonnet. Increase slightly for duct and other losses.

4. SIZING A WOODSTOVE

The recommended woodstove size can be calculated as follows:

Step 1.

Take the average of Heat Loss (from Worksheet 3, lines 5 and 6) (11,126 Btus/hr + 10,019 Btus/hr) ÷ 2 ÷ 24 hours per day × (72 − −15 Outside Winter Design Temperature) 87 degrees + sidehill LCWL (from section 1, above) 571 Btus per hour = 38,896 Btus per hour

Step 2.

Answer from Step 1 38,896 Btus per hour ÷ .85 (combustion efficiency from section 2, above) = 45,760 Btus per hour

Rounded for simplicity the nearest thousand:
Woodstove size = 46,000 Btus per hour

5. ANNUAL FUEL CONSUMPTION

Total Purchased Fuel (from Worksheet 6, line A) ÷ net available heat energy in Btus per gallon, kilowatt-hour, or cord (from section 1, above) = annual fuel consumption in Btus*

*Monthly totals can also be obtained using the same method working with Worksheet 6, column 1.

SUMMARY:

Annual Purchased Oil Consumption (if 100% source of backup heat):
24,350,000 Btus ÷ 98,000 Btus per gallon = 248 gallons of oil

Annual Electricity Consumption (if 100% source of backup heat):
24,350,000 Btus ÷ 3,415 Btus per kilowatt-hour = 7,130 kilowatt-hours

Annual Firewood Consumption (if 100% source of backup heat):
24,350,000 Btus ÷ 17,000,000 Btus per cord + 0.5 cord (to be conservative) = 1.9 cords

To calculate the cost of these various sources of backup heat, simply multiply your totals for this section by the present rate in your area for 1 gallon, 1 kilowatt-hour, or 1 cord of split and dried hardwood firewood.

Worksheet #8 follows the same procedure described in chapter 6. The figure for House Heat Loss with thermo-shutters was used as a way to compensate for the fact that the home's windows during the 10 hours described were collectors of energy, not losers of energy. Further, the heat loss through a wall is directly proportional to the difference in temperature between the inside and the outside of the wall. During that 10-hour collection period, the sun was warming the exterior of the wall, thereby stopping the flow of heat outward. For this reason, a house will always benefit from having the most wall area on the south side, even if there are no windows!

Note also that the lower concrete wall is not included in the thermal mass calculation because it will not respond to daily temperature differences in the same manner as the horizontal Solar Slab. Its benefit, however, can easily be seen by the overall reduction in heating load, since the amount of heat lost through the lower living-space wall into the earth is so small.

You made it. Enter 6 inches for line 30 on Worksheet #1.

The C-32 Sidehill in my example is theoretically located in sunny Cheyenne, Wyoming. As a comparison, let's relocate the Sidehill design to Ann Arbor, Michigan. Making the same kind of solar analysis for a sidehill house in Michigan, the calculations show it to be 40 percent solar heated with a predicted oil usage of 431 gallons per year, whereas the same design in Cheyenne yielded 67 percent solar with a predicted need for 248 gallons of oil per year.

Needless to say, Ann Arbor, Michigan, and Hartford, Connecticut are not the usual places one would pick to illustrate the efficacy of

Worksheet 8
Sizing the Solar Slab

1. DETERMINING THE TOTAL INSOLATION FOR YOUR HOUSE ON A SUNNY DAY IN FEBRUARY

A. Insolation for a representative February day*:

East-facing glass <u>52</u> square feet × East SHGF ½-day total <u>648</u> Btus per square feet + South-facing glass <u>184</u> square feet × South SHGF ½-day total × 2 <u>1,642</u> Btus per square feet + West-facing glass <u>55</u> square feet × West SHGF ½-day total <u>648</u> Btus per square feet = <u>371,464</u> Btus

*Obtain your Solar Heat Gain Factors (SHGFs) for February from Worksheet 4, part 2.

B. Peak Insolation for February day:

Multiply result from A (from above) <u>371,464</u> Btus × Shade Factor (as a decimal) <u>0.88</u> × Clearness Number (as a decimal) <u>1.10</u> = <u>359,577</u> Btus

2. DETERMINING THE PREDICTED HEAT LOSS OF THE HOUSE (WHILE COLLECTING THE BTUS INDICATED IN SECTION 1, ABOVE)

A. Calculate the heat loss from 7:00 AM to 5:00 PM as follows:

<u>10,019</u> Btus/hr • °F (from Worksheet 3, lines 6 or 5, if no nighttime glass insulation is used) ÷ 24 hours per day <u>417.5</u> Btus/°F • day × [68 – average Outdoor Winter Design Temperature for house location (from appendix 5) <u>34</u> degrees] × 10 hours = <u>141,936</u> Btus

B. If using a sidehill design, add the Lower Concrete Wall Loss (from Worksheet 3, line 7) <u>423</u> Btus per hour × 10 hours = <u>4,230</u> Btus, which is the 10-hour heat loss in Btus

C. Then add A + B = <u>146,166</u> Btus

3. DETERMINING THE EXCESS AVAILABLE HEAT TO STORE IN THE SOLAR SLAB:

Total from section 1, above <u>359,577</u> Btus – Total from section 2, above <u>146,166</u> Btus = <u>213,411</u> Btus

(continued on next page)

4. DETERMINING THE VOLUME OF THE SOLAR SLAB

Total from section 3, above <u>213,411</u> Btus ÷ 30 Btus/ft^3 • °F* ÷ 8 degrees** = <u>889</u> cubic feet

*Specific Heat of Solar Slab (combination of 12-inch concrete blocks and poured concrete over blocks)
**Desired Maximum Temperature Difference

5. DETERMINING THE APPROPRIATE SLAB THICKNESS (MINIMUM 4 INCHES)

T = total thickness in feet
l   = length in feet
w = width in feet
t   = thickness of poured concrete over 12-inch blocks

A. T = Total Volume (from section 4, above) <u>889</u> cubic feet ÷ [0.85 × area of 1st-floor Solar Slab 1,008 square feet (using outside dimensions)] = <u>1.04</u> feet or 12.4 inches

B. t = T (from A, above) 12.4 inches – 6 inches* = <u>6.4</u> inches. Use 6 inches.

*12-inch blocks are approximately ½-solid concrete

solar design. Western states with high elevations, clear skies, and high percent sunshine are more apt to be used for solar home design examples. And yet many people desiring solar homes live elsewhere.

All too frequently we hear someone say, "Solar won't work here." How can solar energy not work? We all live in solar locations; although in some locales, as gardeners know, more sunlight is available for greater portions of the year. Does that mean that because your site is not the perfect solar location that you shouldn't take advantage of the sun's capacities for heating and cooling? The basic premises for a good solar home are simply the premises of good home design:

1. Make the most of what's available to you in terms of both your environment and the materials that you are planning to use in your home construction.
2. Let the tendencies of nature work for you and not against you.

3. Work toward the goal of keeping the conventional furnace and air conditioner switched off, and also try to minimize your reliance upon alternative backup fuels such as wood. Only sunlight is free.

A 2,085-square-foot home burning 431 gallons of oil per year in Ann Arbor, Michigan, doesn't sound as good as the same kind of home burning 248 gallons of oil per year in Cheyenne, Wyoming, which is a colder place. And yet, if you live in Michigan, then you did the best you could with the solar energy available to you. That 431 gallons of

Solar Principle # 8

Provide fresh air to the home without compromising thermal integrity.

To maintain a high level of indoor air quality, a well-insulated and tightly constructed home needs a continual supply of fresh air equivalent to replacing no less than ⅔ of the building's total volume of air every hour. This exchange of air should occur through intended openings, for instance an exterior-wall fan in both the kitchen and bathroom, rather than through leakage around poorly sealed doors and windows.

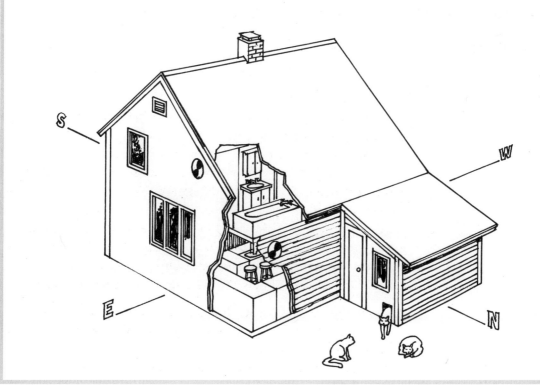

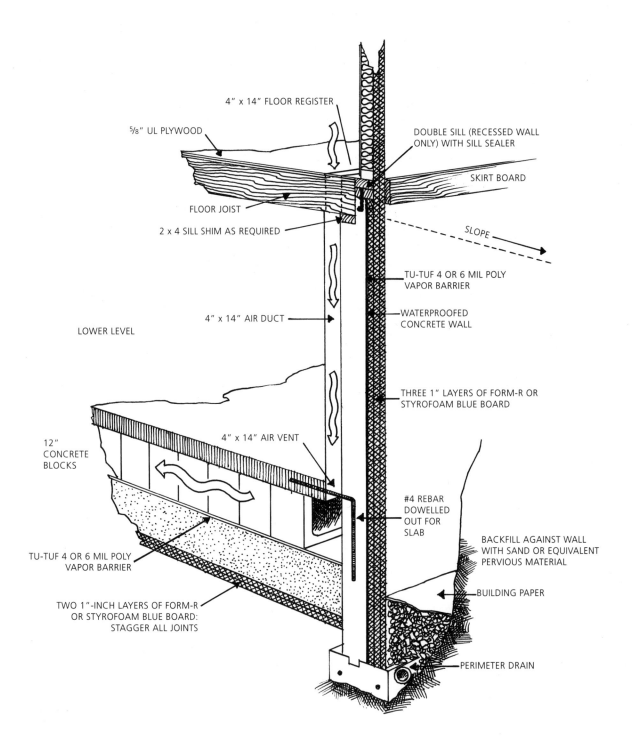

4" x 14" FLOOR REGISTER

⁵⁄₈" UL PLYWOOD

DOUBLE SILL (RECESSED WALL ONLY) WITH SILL SEALER

SKIRT BOARD

FLOOR JOIST

2 x 4 SILL SHIM AS REQUIRED

SLOPE

TU-TUF 4 OR 6 MIL POLY VAPOR BARRIER

WATERPROOFED CONCRETE WALL

4" x 14" AIR DUCT

LOWER LEVEL

THREE 1" LAYERS OF FORM-R OR STYROFOAM BLUE BOARD

12" CONCRETE BLOCKS

4" x 14" AIR VENT

#4 REBAR DOWELLED OUT FOR SLAB

BACKFILL AGAINST WALL WITH SAND OR EQUIVALENT PERVIOUS MATERIAL

TU-TUF 4 OR 6 MIL POLY VAPOR BARRIER

BUILDING PAPER

TWO 1"-INCH LAYERS OF FORM-R OR STYROFOAM BLUE BOARD: STAGGER ALL JOINTS

PERIMETER DRAIN

Sidehill modification of the basic plan, showing a detail of the north wall footings, drainage, and connection to the Solar Slab.

oil a year bought in the summer as an advance, one-time purchase at $1.00 a gallon will mean only about $431.00 per year for heating; plus your solar home is bright and cheerful.

Too often people wishing to heat with alternative fuels spend spring, summer, and fall getting ready for winter. Remember, cutting and stacking two cords of wood is a lot easier than cutting and stacking eight. And in addition to reducing your annual heating load, a highly insulated home with proper vapor barriers and stained natural sidings will minimize the need for periodic summertime exterior painting, staining, and weatherstripping. Furthermore, when it snows, a properly designed roof will not cause ice jams and water dams.

A natural solar home when properly designed, sited, and built will make life a lot easier by working for you, day in and day out, instead of requiring you to be constantly working for it.

9

SUNSPACES AND SPECIAL DESIGN CONSIDERATIONS

It is easier to understand a concept if one can point to an example and say, "Aha, that's what makes it work." Sunspaces and greenhouses satisfy conventional expectations about solar design in that they reach high daytime temperatures, and anyone can understand why. Just as a car left with its windows closed in a hot summer parking lot will become an oven, so the sunspace will build up high temperatures, which will allow a positive transfer of heat from areas that are warm to areas that are cooler, for instance from the 90-degree sunspace to the 70-degree interior of the house. Sunspaces are overglazed on purpose, and designed to overheat.

It might seem that a sunspace that is gathering enough heat to become 90 degrees Fahrenheit on a cold, 15-degree but sunny winter day would be beneficial to the home. And yes, it can be beneficial. However, the same overglazed sunspace that accumulated all that heat during the cold but sunny day will need lots of added heat when the sun goes down to prevent it from freezing, which means that the sunspace or greenhouse will tend to draw heat from the rest of the house as its flow of solar heat reverses course, back out through the glazing.

It is not uncommon for a sunspace to soar in temperature to 90-plus degrees during the day, and then "struggle" to maintain 32 degrees at night. The large nighttime loss is due, of course, to the overglazing. As you will remember from our calculations in chapter 6, even the most energy-retentive thermal-pane glass has only a fraction of the insulation capacity or R-value of unglazed wall.

THE COST OF "ADD-ON" SOLAR

In order to analyze any benefits that may come from a feature such as a sunspace, one has to calculate the daytime heat gains and factor these against nighttime losses. For the sunspace to be a net benefit, you will also need to provide for an effective means of transferring the solar heat from the sunspace into the house.

In making these sunspace heat gain and loss calculations, one must also remember that the sunspace is taking up wall space on the south-facing elevation. Ideally, it will be located in front of a patio door that can be closed at night. This will isolate the sunspace thermally from the primary living space. And we have seen in our previous design examples that a patio door is already an effective solar collector. Adding a sunspace in front of a south-facing patio door amounts to putting a solar collector in front of a solar collector. And yet a sunspace placed in front of a patio door will shade the living space, making the room darker than it would be without the sunspace.

Tilted Glass—A Liability

Most readers will be able to picture the typical sunspace or greenhouse design, in which south-facing glass is tilted so that the angle of winter sun is more perpendicular to the panes of glass. Tilted glass is a more effective solar collector than vertical glass. In February at 48 degrees north latitude, tilted glass will be approximately 20 to 30 percent more effective than vertical glass. However, in summer, tilted glass will continue to be more perpendicular to the sun's rays than vertical glass, and will continue to take in heat. The common problem of summertime overheating in sunspaces may be easier to explain than solve.

Because of gravity, providing window insulation for tilted glass is a more complicated problem than providing the same kind of covering for vertical glass. Special rails or attachments will be needed to hold the window insulation snugly against the sloping glass. In addition, on tilted glass nighttime condensation will drip on to window coverings, causing stains and possible degradation of the insulating material.

Through our monitoring process of a prototype home with a sunspace in Royalton, Vermont, we found that there was no discernible difference in overall thermal performance of the home with or without the added sunspace. The sunspace, however, did not take heat from the home, or was thermally neutral. That is, any daytime heat derived from the sunspace was "paid" back at night to maintain minimum temperatures.

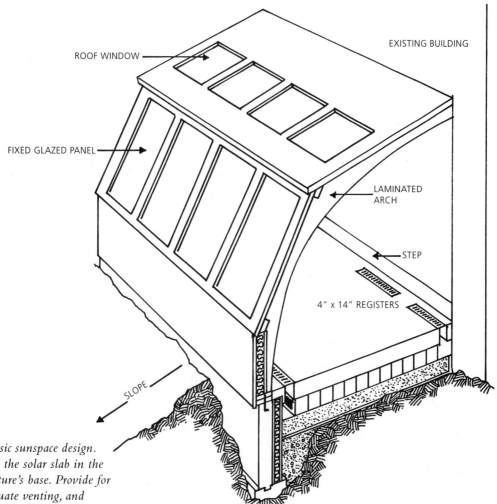

ROOF WINDOW

EXISTING BUILDING

FIXED GLAZED PANEL

LAMINATED ARCH

STEP

4" x 14" REGISTERS

SLOPE

A basic sunspace design. Note the solar slab in the structure's base. Provide for adequate venting, and consider isolating the added-on sunspace thermally from the rest of the house, to prevent the sunspace glazing from drawing the home's heat out on cold winter nights.

The figure above shows a representative four-panel sunspace. Assuming that the east and west elevations of the sunspace have 40 square feet of glass per side, this sunspace has the following specifications:

East glass	40 square feet
South glass	200 square feet
West glass	40 square feet
Wall area, unglazed	330 square feet
Roof area	91 square feet
Volume	1,300 cubic feet

The net performance of a sunspace can be improved by thermally isolating it. For example, by placing the sunspace outside of a sliding glass door and closing this door at night and on sunless days, you can mini-

TABLE 9-1 PERFORMANCE SUMMARY FOR 4-PANEL SUNSPACE*	
BURLINGTON, VERMONT HEAT LOAD: NOT SOLAR SUPPLIED (in millions Btus)	
Nov	1.42
Dec	3.72
Jan	3.11
Feb	1.25
HARTFORD, CONNECTICUT HEAT LOAD: NOT SOLAR SUPPLIED (in millions Btus)	
Nov	0
Dec	0
Jan	0
Feb	0

*Using the methodology developed in this book, and adjusting Solar Heat Gain Factors for tilted glass

mize the amount of heat that the home needs to "pay back" during times when the sunspace is not collecting solar heat. You will also need to provide supplementary heat to the interior of the sunspace to maintain minimum temperatures at night and on overcast days.

Remember that about two-thirds of the fuel needed for a solar home will be consumed in December, January, and February. As you can see from Table 9–1, a sunspace located in Burlington, Vermont, needed additional heat in those months, so it added an energy burden to the house at the time of year when energy loads and expenses are already greatest. In Hartford, Connecticut, a comparable sunspace was close to breaking even in terms of costs and benefits, even in those three months. For the sunspace to yield a significant improvement in the performance of a solar home, it has to contribute positively in those three winter months. The house really doesn't need a boost of solar heat in September, October, November, March, April, or May, since during these transitional months, the solar home probably needs no purchased energy at all, or very little purchased energy. And, as indicated above, in summer months the sunspace may be more likely to be a cooling burden than a heating benefit. A sunspace's performance can be improved if a Solar Slab is used for its base and thermal mass. A small duct fan actuated by a thermostat at 50 degrees will in most cases transfer enough heat back into the sunspace to prevent it from freezing, provided that the sunspace and the Solar Slab are properly sized and constructed.

Special Difficulties in Sunspace Construction

Whenever glass is placed at an angle, the thermal stresses and temperature variations are substantially increased, and the force of gravity is effectively pulling the glazing panes or panels sideways to the direction they were designed to accomodate, making it difficult to keep seals from leaking. Only quality rooftop windows and rooftop fixed glass made for tilted use should be used. Because of the expense of commercial glazing units and ancillary products, many attempts to reduce costs have been made by do-it-yourself builders who re-use glass panels out of patio doors and set them in wooden frames to reduce costs.

Most warranties from window manufacturers are voided when glass that has been designed and manufactured to be placed vertically is placed at an angle. Glass expands at approximately the same rate as aluminum. Attempts to set tilted glass in wooden frames with wooden mull caps most likely will fail, because the glass and wood have incompatible coefficients of expansion. The glass will expand more rapidly than a wooden mull cap; the sealant used between the glass and the mull cap will crack, which will result in a water leak. In addition, in tilted glass the manufacturer's seal between the two panes of glass is also subjected to extraordinary thermal and gravitational stresses, and is likewise prone to leak. Have you ever driven by a homemade sunspace and noticed that the glass is fogged up? That is due to the failure of the factory seal between the dual panes. Commercially manufactured roof-top units are specifically designed and tested for tilted use, are warrantied against water leakage and seal failure, and are made out of tempered safety glass. Glass placed at an angle should always be tempered safety glass to prevent possible injury.

It's Not All Bad News—Sunspaces are Fun

Does this mean that homeowners should never add a sunspace or greenhouse? No, not at all. Sunspaces are fun to have; they provide a place to grow flowers year-round and to start spring seedlings. They provide a place to simply luxuriate in 90-degree heat when the outside temperature is in the teens on sunny winter afternoons. They provide an uplift to the spirit, when plants are bathed in sunlight and

Sunspace interior.

blooming in the dead of winter. And sunspaces present no special heating or cooling challenges in most regions in the relatively mild months of spring and autumn.

If you understand the possible benefits, and are willing to address the challenges, a sunspace may be "just what the doctor ordered." But if you believe that adding a sunspace is going to pay for itself by heating your house, you may want to reconsider.

Finally, another popular use for sunspaces is as retrofits on older homes. After hearing me out all through an explanation of the costs and difficulties like the explanation above, a prospective sunspace buyer responded, "I understand completely what you have said, but my husband and I own an ancient 'Four-square' home that is hopelessly inefficient. We have no hope of ever being able to afford a new home, and all I want is to have at least one place in my home that's warm when the sun is out." Pretty hard to say no to that.

IDEAL VERSUS
ACTUAL CIRCUMSTANCES

So far we have presumed the existence of ideal conditions under which to build a solar home. We have described a naturally heated and cooled home that takes full advantage of what is available to us, from the vantage point of both macro- and micro-environments.

Approach your home building project in this manner. Try to utilize all of the elements that are there to work with, in the best possible ways, and build the most environmentally sensitive home possible for a given location and set of circumstances. Try to think positively about each aspect of your site, your design, and your energy options. Remember that the sun is everywhere, and with careful planning you can build a home that harmonizes with solar energy.

But let's go over a few examples that demonstrate less than ideal situations. Suppose the garage or other structure has to be placed in such a way that it will obscure all the east-facing glass. The practical remedy is to rotate the home counter-clockwise so that the south-facing glass is about 15 to 20 degrees off of true south, with the south elevation now facing south-southeast. This will allow your south-facing glass to begin to collect energy earlier in the day. Conversely, if your west-facing glass for some reason will be obstructed, you can rotate the home 15 to 20 degrees clockwise to allow the south-facing glass to collect compensatory heat from the afternoon's westerly sun.

If you live in a region where it frequently may be necessary to use air conditioning for summer cooling, you can reduce morning and afternoon solar gain by shading the east- and west-facing glass with plantings of deciduous trees, and use of thermo-Shutters or other window insulation. You can also consider reducing the amount of east- and west-facing glass. The calculations in chapter 5 will permit you to evaluate during your design process the benefits of adding or removing these windows.

Orientation—the Key to Solar Design

Probably the biggest "no-no" is to buy north-facing land or sites located in deep, sunless valleys or canyons. Homesites with primarily northern exposures just don't get "bathed" by the sun. One of my former clients bought a lot in Maine, with a view of the ocean, and it wasn't until the builder visited the site with a compass that the man discovered that what he had imagined was a south view of the ocean was a north view. By this time the man was too far committed not to build his retirement home on that site. Given this challenge, we selected a saltbox design, and placed an array of roof windows in the long slope of the side that is normally the unglazed north roof, which in this situation was faced south. The high side of the saltbox that normally faces south was actually facing north, giving the residents full benefit of the ocean view. The amount of glass on what was now the north elevation was drastically reduced from the design specifications, and fitted with thermo-shutters. The home performed reasonably well, though the situation was far from ideal. Our solution was the best that could be managed with existing circumstances, and truth be told, these homeowners would not have ended up better off with a conventional instead of a solar home in that same situation.

The real moral of this story is to always take a compass with you when you are looking at house sites. There really is no substitute for a site with a good southern exposure.

OTHER WAYS TO USE ENERGY WISELY

Up to now we have mainly talked about storing the sun's free heat in the Solar Slab. Certain kinds of commercial or manufacturing processes generate excess "purchased" energy during the day, which if not vented outside will overheat the building. Why not store this excess purchased energy for nighttime use after the workday is over? For instance, consider the examples of an office building filled with heat-producing electronic equipment such as computers, or a dormitory building that is required by code to produce surplus hot water, or a library that has lighting requirements that result in excess lamp-generated heat. Why not circulate such waste or byproduct heat to other parts of the building, and/or store excess heat? A Solar Slab allows the storage of so-called waste heat for later use. The challenge of solar design is to consider every aspect of the planned building's energy situation over the lifetime of the structure.

Sometimes energy goals requirements appear to conflict. The library, for example, needs to provide a high degree of quality lighting to meet standards; but these lights give off excess heat. By circulating the air that has been warmed with already purchased electric-light energy through the Solar Slab, heat can be stored for later use rather than vented to the outside.

Solar Principle # 9

9

Use the materials you would use for a conventional home, but in ways that maximize energy efficiency and solar gain.

With exactly the same construction materials, it is possible to build an energy-efficient, sunny, and easy-to-maintain solar home or a energy-gluttonous, dark, and costly-to-maintain house. When designing a solar home, rearrange and reallocate materials to serve dual functions - adding solar benefits as well as addressing architectural or aesthetic goals. Placing a majority of the home's windows on the south side is an example. The carefully designed and constructed solar home need not cost any more to build than a comparably sized non-solar conventional home.

Wind power is another form of solar energy. Here is an old-time wind-powered water pump. New technologies allow people to use these age-old sources of energy. As with contemporary photovoltaics, which convert sunlight into storable and useable electricity, today's micro-sized wind turbines are very practical and affordable for home-scale use.

Another example: The college dormitory has a high hot water requirement for showering. In order to meet the demand, a large amount of hot water capacity is needed; however, showering usually takes place for a short period of time in the morning or evening, while the rest of the time hot water is stored in water heater tanks and kept up to temperature with periodic applications of electric or fossil-fuel energy. A solution to this problem is to use water-to-air heat exchangers for space heating, utilizing the domestic hot water for more than one "end-use," thereby eliminating the need for a separate furnace. It is also entirely practical, and very cost-effective, to use solar thermal techniques for heating or at least preheating water with sunshine, which in some regions can reduce conventional water heating expenses dramatically.

Examine all available heat sources, and maximize your provisions for benefiting from the specific conditions of your site. Rearrange the materials already committed to the building project in order to efficiently collect and store heat. Whether building a solar home or an office capable of storing excess purchased energy, we should use every technique available to reduce our use of finite and expensive fuels.

Solar Electricity

In most parts of the U.S., the present cost of having a power company provide electricity to a remote homesite is in excess of $24,000 per mile of added powerline. A viable alternative is to live "off-the-grid," producing your own electricity with solar photovoltaic modules. Early solar electric systems used 12-volt technology developed for recreational vehicles and boats. This required major lifestyle adjustments, as all the electrical equipment in the home had to be specially designed to run on 12-volt power.

Recent advances in storage battery technology, high-tech control equipment, and highly reliable DC/AC inverters have now made the off-the-grid home a very attractive option. With the use of a properly sized inverter, direct current generated by sun-tracking solar electric modules is converted to ordinary 115-volt alternating current, allowing the use of ordinary electrical appliances.

It is now entirely practical to live comfortably off-the-grid by producing solar electricity for storage in batteries, and utilizing solar space heating, a domestic solar hot water system, propane gas for refrigeration and cooking, and backing up the whole arrangement with a propane- or gasoline-powered generator. And with the right wind conditions and access to a year-round stream, an ideal site would even permit residents to harvest wind energy and hydroelectricity with the new micro-turbines, which are perfectly sized for household needs.

While we have concentrated in this book on the challenges and opportunities of solar home heating and cooling, hopefully the examples given here will help readers view the prospect of building energy-efficient and environmentally sensitive buildings with a greater sense of possibility and determination.

10

INTERIOR DESIGN FOR
YEAR-ROUND COMFORT

By Cornelia C. Kachadorian

There are a number of special factors to consider when thinking about interior design for a solar home, yet many of these considerations could really apply to all types of homes.

The primary challenge with a solar home is the deliberate access given to sun, with the greater exposure of interiors to sunlight, with all of its component radiation. Ultraviolet rays are principally responsible for fading fabrics and other materials, and infrared rays heat up surfaces they strike, while the visible spectrum of light ranges between the ultraviolet and infrared. One can find UV-reflecting glass on the market today, which helps reduce damage, but this glass does not block all the effects of ultraviolet. Infrared rays heat whatever they touch, making exposed portions of furniture hotter than their shaded areas.

On the other hand, natural light in the visible spectrum presents a lighting medium of great potential.

USE SUNLIGHT
AS A DECORATIVE ELEMENT

As emphasized throughout this book, solar homes' windows are oriented toward the east, south, and west, with a minimum of windows on the northern exposure. The characteristics of sunshine change throughout the day and the year, varying in intensity, color, and angle. Window light combined with well-chosen and well-placed supplemental lighting can provide exquisite results with minimal costs.

Because of its more horizontal angle, winter sunlight penetrates significantly deeper into the home but for a shorter duration than summer light. Winter light is whiter than summer light due to atmospheric quality, clarity, the absence of foliage colors, and reflection off snow. Winter shadows are blue.

By contrast, high-angled summer sun reaches minimally beyond the windowsills, resulting in dark summer interiors. For this reason, "summer houses" are traditionally decorated in light colors, luring the light inward. Light-colored surfaces in rooms on the sunny side of the house will bounce sunlight into the back of rooms. Dark furnishings will stop this flow of light, absorbing it and effectively punching a hole in the sunlight. In addition, the colors in summer foliage plus the increased moisture in the air bring more various tonal complexities to summertime sunlight.

Spring and fall have their own particular kind of radiance, with intermediate solar intensity and penetration into the rooms. These two seasons particularly lend their color to interior brilliance.

DESIGNING WITH THE SUN: WHERE TO BEGIN

Maximize your decorating dollars by choosing sun-resistant, light-neutral colors for expensive features. For example, make sure that expensive rugs, upholstery, and wall coverings are warrantied to resist fading. Certain fabrics and rugs are actually designed to mellow handsomely with time and exposure. Less expensive items, such as pillows, throw rugs, curtains, vases, and plants, can be changed with the season.

When looking for large-ticket decorating elements, get written details from the manufacturer on fabric and material stability. Olefin rug and upholstery fabrics, for instance, are stain-resistant and hold dyes well; however, they lose structural integrity with ultraviolet exposure. An olefin rug may continue to look the same color from a distance yet have lost its pile into the air after only a year's exposure. Certain traditional natural fibers, including wool and cotton, have been shown to withstand solar exposure very well. However, it is important to check with each manufacturer on dye processes. Silk often disintegrates with exposure. Cotton and linen may yellow unless treated.

Many furnishings, particularly dark-toned fabrics, are subject to uneven heating as the sun hits one side while the remainder is in shadow. Differential heating expands the fibers on the warm side, while the cool side remains normal. Glues and finishes are subjected to greater stresses, and wood dries out, shrinking as its moisture departs. Maintain wood pieces with a quality furniture oil. Check the joints and re-glue them when they become loose, as this will prevent breakage.

The character of reflected light is dependent upon surface texture. Shiny, highly polished surfaces such as glass, high-gloss paint, and bright urethanes reflect a high percentage of incident light (the angle of reflection of course equals the angle of incidence). These are hard-light reflections, carrying a lot of zap, and can be used for special effects.

Consider your choice of exterior surroundings such as decks, lawn furniture, flora, and ponds as part of the color scheme of the adjacent interiors. Light reflected off exterior colors and surfaces tints the space inside the home.

WINDOW DECOR

In a solar home, windows are calculated to function as more than merely panes of glass. Windows are utilized as solar collectors, collecting light and heat to minimize the home's reliance upon conventional sources of backup fuel.

Windows of traditional homes are mainly decorative, and are often partially covered with curtains, draperies, or blinds. Functional solar home windows require different treatment. Because these windows' surface area has been calculated into the total home energy dynamic, they must be

viewed as heating and lighting "generators," which carry energy both inward and outward.

Thermo-shutters (see chapter 4) are insulated, inward-folding shutters designed to block heat loss at night, or excessive daytime heat gain. These can be used as attractive decorative surfaces, adding angular interest to the window-area design. Whether formal or casual, thermo-shutter treatment will set the stage for further room decor. They can be curtained, mirrored, muraled, bulletin-boarded, wallpapered, painted, stained, or mounted with rugs for studio sound-proofing.

Mounting draperies on the thermo-shutters will dampen interior-based sound, as would drapes placed across a window. The thermo-shutters' wooden construction makes the need for heavy linings unnecessary, saving drapery construction costs.

At times of intense sun, thermo-shutters can be partially closed to screen the sunlight, effectively bouncing heat and light outside while allowing cool breezes to enter. To compensate for this additional shading, lightweight, semi-transparent curtains mounted on the thermo-shutters will capture the light, diffusing it throughout the room. Hard-edged window openings cast stronger shadows and crisper light. Translucent, fluffy curtains mounted on the thermo-shutters will diffuse harsh light, softening the glare. Remember that all home interiors appear darker in the summer than in the winter due to the high angle of summer sun.

Adjustable "Venetian" blinds present interesting possibilities. Blinds cut down on the percentage of solar heating provided, but can be very pleasant modulators when the sun is too harsh. They come in traditional horizontal slats, in very narrow vertical slats that reach from floor to ceiling, and in all sorts of other varieties. New tiny-slatted vertical blinds add a formal architectural dimension to light management. Blinds are available in many materials, with numerous colors and textures to choose from. Blinds are built to alter the reflective angle, to bounce light away from areas where it is unwelcome, toward the outside or toward a part of the room where accents of light can be useful. Their slats are easily adjustable, and the flexibility they provide can be quite attractive for someone who enjoys stage managing and fine-tuning the ambient light.

SUPPLEMENTAL LIGHTING

Fewer sources of purchased lighting are needed in a home that utilizes sunlight effectively. The daytime use of living spaces will have been planned to be in phase with solar incidence. Nighttime lighting will be relatively economical if the effects of light in various contexts has been considered, for instance, if a majority of light colors have been used as backgrounds.

Think of light as an architectural and a sculptural medium. Judicious lighting creates a stage set that will highlight special areas of activity. Work centers will appear as focal points, bright and inviting when juxtaposed with a more subdued hallway. Light expresses and concentrates function: with the right lighting, a reading niche, a work of art, the center of the dining room table will function better, and also be more comfortable. Space will appear to ebb and flow through the "movement" of light. In fact, the relationships of the home's various spaces can be persuasively determined by patterns of lighting. Pools of light serve as paths to guide the eye and the feet.

Project areas need a wash of bright, non-glaring light. Surrounding walls painted light matte colors will reflect a generalized, soft brightness rather than the more acute brilliance of high-gloss paint. This softer brightness will help to prevent distracting shadows.

In some situations, the comfortable "warm" glow of incandescent lighting is hard to beat. On the other hand, in an energy-conscious household you may choose fluorescent lamps for their vastly superior energy efficiency and longevity. Fluorescent light was originally designed for indirect lighting of large spaces. Used directly, it can be hard on the eyes. Contemporary fluorescents are now available in full-spectrum band waves as well as several other "colors" that are less objectionable than the lurid or chilly originals. Be aware that fluorescent light can fade fabrics over time if it shines directly on them.

Recessed lights have both artistic and practical potential. The recesses are not difficult to incorporate if this is done while framing the house. It is worthwhile to spend time during the planning stage of your home design to consider all of the locations where you might want the option of recessed lighting. It is better to build in too many than too few.

Track lighting, originally designed for theaters, uses moveable and removeable fixtures that are available in a wide variety of commercial designs. These can be swiveled, switched around, and reoriented for different effects. The mounting strips into which the fixtures plug are installed on ceilings or walls, and because they are so versatile, they can bring light to the most challenging of locations. The track-to-fixture connection is often proprietary to individual manufacturers, so when selecting track lighting, be sure to pick a manufacturer that seems likely to be around for a while. There's a better chance that they will also be around later if you choose to add more fixtures or replace one that is broken.

Lighting placed above beams or shelves and directed toward the ceiling can dramatically enhance a room. Incandescent light reflected off the golden tones of wooden beams gives an atmosphere quite different from that of fluorescent light bounced off a white ceiling. Remember that light aimed upward toward a light-colored surface makes a room appear larger. A white ceiling seems to float at a distance, while a darker one appears lower.

Long, dark, northern winters can be made more pleasant with full-spectrum electric lighting, which unlike conventional lamps puts out a more complete range of bands in light, simulating the richness of daylight. As psychologists have published their research on light-deficit disorders, the market has begun to respond, and several choices of full-spectrum lamp are now available ("Ott lights" were the originals). Full-spectrum lighting might well be worth the investment for both home and workplace. The psychological lift these lights provide could result in increased productivity, health, and happiness. Full-spectrum lights have also been shown to help beat "cabin fever," a problem newly dignified by the term "seasonal affective disorder," or SAD.

Linear accent lighting is available in the form of tiny strands of "mini" lightbulbs encased in flexible clear tubing. These use very little

wattage, yet the filaments are so tiny that the incandescence is very white. Some people use tiny white Christmas lights all year as accents.

If you are not familiar with the full diversity of options now available in lighting (and there are an amazing number of products to choose from), you might decide to hire a lighting designer during the planning stages of your house design. An expert can help you sort through your ideas and preferences, and will make you aware of the new products that are constantly coming onto the market.

FABRICS, RUGS, AND WALLCOVERINGS

Fabrics, rugs, and wallcoverings that reflect ultraviolet light best are least likely to be harmed by it.

Ultraviolet rays and direct fluorescent lighting will fade many fabric dyes and paints while darkening varnish. Color-resistance to ultraviolet is dependent on the chemistry and technique of the dyeing process. One wallpaper manufacturer's representative expressed the color stability problem this way: "You're safer staying away from oranges, greens, and purples. And *anyone* knows enough to stay away from reds, yellows, and blues, of course." A number of fade-resistant dyes and dye/fabric combinations have been found to be remarkably stable. When examining written warranties, be sure to look specifically for guarantees of stability with exposure to sunlight.

Just as with paint, natural or earth-toned and light fabric and wallpaper tints have less pigment to fade, and thus show the fading process far less than do more color-saturated hues. Certain strong colors that usually fade quickly have proven more durable when used with special dyeing techniques in such tested materials as Dupont's Antron III. It is a good idea to look for warranties from the company that actually manufactures and dyes the fabrics or other materials, and not just to go by the type of material used. For instance, many companies use Dupont fabrics, but not all use the same dyeing and fabrication methods. Make sure the manufacturer stands behind its products with a warranty.

Floor Coverings

The Solar Slab described in this book may be covered with any type of floor covering. Technically, a slab that is painted black would absorb the most heat; but the negligible improvement in performance certainly does not justify living on a concrete surface painted black.

Most homes use a thick pad and carpet. Other homes have used wood parquet. Wide wooden boards may be used by gun-nailing two layers of 1 x 3-inch strapping onto the slab surface, and then attaching the boards by screwing into the strapping. The screws can then be hidden with ship's "bungs" or wood plugs. The result is a very attractive wide-board floor that has resiliency due to the spacing of the strapping.

A rug can set the theme and color scheme for a room, and should be chosen with care. Rugs constructed of top-quality wools, including fine orientals and fine American Indian rugs, constantly undergo a process of modification, softening, blending colors. It has been said that these rugs are artworks in process. Wools from mountain regions are known to be most durable, while those from the plains are softer and structurally weaker. Pile weight of wool rugs determines not only ruggedness but also the rug's insulating properties. Using good padding as underlayment, rotating of rugs to equalize exposure to light and traffic, and frequent vacuuming will increase longevity.

Commercially available carpeting for wall-to-wall applications makes a warm covering for the Solar Slab. Strong colors can be disappointing as they tend to fade. Light colors bring the incident light to all corners of the room, making spaces seem larger.

Brand names such as Zeflon 500, Solution Dyed Nylon, Zefran Acrylic Berber, Zeflon Subdued luster nylon, and Antron III, are recommended for areas of hard wear. There are more product names than products, so it is important to find the generic base. Again, be sure to check the warranties for ultraviolet resistance as well as fade resistance.

Fine quality wall-to-wall commercial wool carpeting is usually more expensive, but it is also more sumptuous and is more resistant to ultraviolet structural degradation. It is offered in piles, sculptured rugs, and Berbers. When made with natural wool colors it is highly resistant to fading. The tactile warmth and long life of wool, as well as its soundproofing capacity and wearability, are hard to surpass.

The following is a partial listing of particular rug types, with comments:

Tunisian Mergoumes: Thin, but very durable rugs, these are unobtrusive, thus they go with almost anything.

Moroccans: From the Atlas Mountains, Moroccans are made of very good wool, thick-tufted with a high pile. They are generally custom designed.

Kilims: Thin, but durable, Kilims are available in a wide variety of colors and patterns.

Solar Principle # 10

Remember that the principles of solar design are compatible with diverse styles of architecture and building techniques.

Solar homes need not look experimental or futuristic, nor do they require complicated, expensive, and hard-to-maintain gadgetry to function well and be comfortable year-round. In solar design, good planning and sensitivity to the surrounding environment are worth far more than special technologies or equipment.

Spanish: In colors that are rich without being harsh, often striated throughout pattern for pleasant toning with age, Spanish rugs tend to be made of good wool, and are available in a variety of sizes and patterns.

Orientals: In selecting a Persian rug for a sunny location, consider the softening of color values that will probably enhance the tonal quality with age. (Traditional orientals have been washed and dried in the strong near-eastern sun as part of their curing process.)

American Indian: Native Americans make woven, non-pile rugs in a wide range of density and patterns. Natural wool colors and natural dyes, though often preferred, are not always more stable than synthetic dyes. Be careful not to confuse these with Mexican or other imports, which are usually substantially inferior in quality.

Others: Thick cut Chinese, Indian, Pakistani, and Bulgarian rugs are usually acid-washed, and therefore weakened, but with careful selection, some can be quite good. Be sure to select thick, dark-colored pieces.

Fabrics

As mentioned earlier, when choosing fabrics for use in a solar home, remember that olefin fabrics have a tendency to degenerate over time, an effect familiar in yellow olefin water-ski ropes. By contrast, dacron was developed by Dupont to be resistant to sunlight, a quality that is coupled with dimensional stability, making dacron-based products worth investigating.

The marine line of Uniroyal's Naugahyde brand of fabrics was developed to stand up to intense solar exposure, and is mildew resistant as well. "Ranchero" is a breathable Naugahyde with the velvety look and feel of suede. Their "Bahamas" fabric has a rich leathery texture.

Genuine leather will need extra attention if it will be exposed to sunlight. Check with the manufacturer on its care.

Wall Coverings

Wall coverings add character and definition to interior spaces. The trick is to follow the basic color scheme of the room and to keep the wall treatment on the wall, visually. A glorious pattern in vibrant hues will probably jump out and hide artwork, making a room appear smaller as well. It is challenging to keep the whole room design in mind when picking a wall treatment, yet so much more can be added to a room's appeal by using appropriate paint and wallpapers. Angled wood on one wall, complimentary painted hues, book shelves backed with an accent color, and the lush monotonal textured papers that carry the softness of certain rugs higher into the living space . . . Enjoy yourself as you plan.

Wallpapers will be subject to fading in a solar home. Wallpapers made by Albert Van Luit & Co. have been tested for years in the intense sunlight of Southern California. Other manufacturers are following suit. Mylar-based papers have proven dimensionally stable, but be aware of the effects of metallic reflections, which can be very dark or very brilliant depending on light exposure.

Home interiors evolve as people live in them. Don't hurry to fill up the space. If furnishings are put somewhere "for the time being," they usually remain there for a long time. It is better to wait until the right solution presents itself.

A WORD ABOUT PLANTS

Due to the increased amount of sun in a solar home, the usual house plants may need to be placed in rooms with less exposure. Geraniums, plants that love heat and dryness, orange trees, hibiscus, herbs, catnip, and cacti will all thrive in the warm southern exposures, whereas Christmas cacti, oxalis, begonias, African violets, and gloxinias are not really contented unless removed from direct exposure. On the other hand, seedlings are delighted to germinate in a sunny spot, as long as their soil is kept moist.

Check with the nursery or florist if you have questions about which plants are best for your region.

The natural solar house is not hard to decorate, but it is important to know the variables that over time will affect your choice of materials and solutions. Whatever choices you make, your maintenance costs should be low and your level of satisfaction great. Pop an apple pie in the oven, turn on the music, and sit back and enjoy the total experience of your home.

Solar Design Worksheets

As discussed in the preface, those readers that are technically proficient may wish to utilize the information given in this book and proceed on to design a solar home. All the "tools" needed are in the appendices. Permission is granted by the author to photocopy the worksheets in Appendix #1 as you will need multiple copies to perform trial "runs" for any solar design attempted. The permission to copy is only extended to Appendix #1.

Worksheet 1

1. House Location: _____

2. Latitude: _____

3. Magnetic Deviation: _____

4. House Alignment: _____

5. Area (in square feet) of east-facing glass: _____

6. Area (in square feet) of west-facing glass: _____

7. Area (in square feet) of south-facing glass: _____

8. Area (in square feet) of north-facing glass: _____

9. Total area (in square feet) of glass: _____

10. Area (in square feet) of glass with nighttime insulation:_____

11. Manufacturer's U-value of window glass: _____   Patio glass: _____

12. Shade Coefficient of glass: _____

13. U-value of glass with nighttime insulation: _____

14. Area (in square feet) of exterior (heated) walls: _____

15. Net area (in square feet) of exterior (heated) walls: Subtract line 9 from line 14 = _____

16. Area (in square feet) of heated lower living-space concrete wall (in sidehill design): _____

17. Area (in square feet) of insulated flat ceiling (or angled ceiling if house has
    a cathedral ceiling): _____

18. Volume (in cubic feet) of the heated airspace of the house: _____

19. Outside Winter Design Temperature: _____

20. U-value of total framed wall area: _____

21. U-value of total roof/ceiling area: _____

22. U-value of total lower living-space concrete wall: _____

23. Total heat loss from home without nighttime insulation for glass (excluding lower concrete
    wall): _____

24. Total heat loss from home with nighttime insulation for glass (excluding lower concrete
    wall): _____

25. Clearness number: _____

26. Recommended size of furnace: _____

27. Total requirement (in kilowatt-hours) of electric backup heat: _____

28. Recommended size of woodstove: _____

29. Estimated annual fuel consumption: _____

30. Required thickness of poured concrete for Solar Slab: _____

Worksheet 2
R– and U–value Calculation

A. FRAMED WALL: R-VALUE

1. 15 MPH wind (outside)   0.17

2. Exterior siding: _____   _____

3. Rigid insulation: _____   _____

4. Exterior house wrap   _____

5. Exterior sheathing: _____   _____

6. Fiberglass insulation: _____   _____

7. Vapor barrier: _____   _____

8. Interior wall covering: _____l   _____

9. Still air (inside surface of wall)   0.68

        Total R-value: _____

U-value of wall =1/R =_____ Btus/hr • ft^2 • °F

(Increase U-value if framing or bridging loss is significant): _____

B. ROOF OR CEILING: R-VALUE

1. 15 MPH wind (outside)   0.17

2. Roofing material: _____   _____

3. Felt roofing paper: _____   _____

4. Roof sheathing: _____   _____

5. Fiberglass insulation: _____   _____

6. Vapor barrier : _____   _____

7. Inside roof or ceiling covering: _____   _____

8. Still air (inside suface of roof or ceiling)   0.68

                Total R-value: _____

U-value of roof or ceiling =1/R =_____ Btus/hr • ft^2 • °F

(Increase U-value if roof or ceiling framing or bridging loss is significant): _____

Worksheet 2
(continued)

C. GLASS WITH NIGHTTIME INSULATION

1. 15 MPH wind (outside)   0.17
2. Glass: _____   _____
3. Dead air space (between glass and insulating device)   _____
4. Insulating device: _____   _____
5. Still air (inside surface of insulating device)   0.68

Total R-value: _____

U-value of nighttime insulated glass (1 ÷ R): _____ Btus/hr • ft^2 • °F

D. LOWER LIVING-SPACE CONCRETE WALL: R-VALUE

1. Exterior rigid insulation: _____   _____
2. Concrete: _____ inches x 0.075   _____
3. Interior insulation: _____   _____
4. Vapor barrier: _____   _____
5. Interior wall covering: _____   _____
6. Still air (inside surface of wall)   _____

Total R-value: _____

U-value of Lower living-space concrete wall = 1/R = _____ Btus/hr • ft^2 • °F difference

Worksheet 3
House Heat Loss Calculation

1. EXTERIOR WALL HEAT LOSS

Area of exterior walls (from Worksheet 1, line 15) × framed wall U-value
(from Worksheet 2, section A)

_____ square feet × _____ Btus/hr • ft^2 • °F = _____ Btus/hr • °F

2. ROOF OR CEILING LOSS

Area of roof or ceiling (from Worksheet 1, line 17) × roof or ceiling U-value
(from Worksheet 2, section B)

_____ square feet × _____ Btus/hr • ft^2 • °F = _____ Btus/hr • °F

3. INFILTRATION LOSS USING VOLUME METHOD

Volume of heated space (from Worksheet 1, line 18) × specific heat of air × air changes per hour

_____ cubic feet × 0.018 Btus/ft^3 • °F × .67 air changes/hr = _____ Btus/hr • °F

4. HEAT LOSS THROUGH GLASS (WITHOUT NIGHT-TIME WINDOW INSULATION)

Area of window and patio door glass (from Worksheet 1, line 9) × U-value of glass
(from Worksheet 2, section C)

_____ square feet × _____ Btus/hr • ft^2 • °F = _____ Btus/hr • °F

5. TOTAL HEAT LOSS:

Walls _____ Btus/hr • °F
Roof or Ceiling _____ Btus/hr • °F
Infiltration _____ Btus/hr • °F
Glass _____ Btus/hr • °F
Wall framing or bridging loss (if significant) _____ Btus/hr • ft^2 • °F

Worksheet 3
(continued)

Roof and/or ceiling framing or bridging loss (if significant) _____ Btus/hr • °F

Solar Slab perimeter loss (if significant) _____ Btus/hr • °F

Combined total rate of heat loss= _____ Btus/hr • °F

For a total of the house's predicted Heat Loss Without Nighttime Glass Insulation, multiply the above combined total rate of heat loss by 24 hours per day:

_____ Btus/hr • °F × 24 hr/day = _____ Btus/°F • day

6. REDUCTION OF HEAT LOSS DUE TO NIGHTTIME GLASS INSULATION
(applicable only if nighttime insulation used)

The Heat Loss Credit for insulated glass can be calculated as follows:

Area of glass with nighttime insulation (from Worksheet 1, line 10) × [U-value of glass without nighttime insulation (from Worksheet 1, line 11) – U-value of glass with nighttime insulation (from Worksheet 2, section C)] × number of hours that nighttime insulation will be used

_____ square feet × (_____ Btus/hr • ft² • °F –_____ Btus/hr • ft² • °F) × _____ hours per day = _____ Btus/°F • day

Using the Heat Loss Credit just derived, the Total Heat Loss With Nighttime Insulation is calculated as follows:

Heat Loss Without Nighttime Glass Insulation (from section 5, above) – the Heat Loss Credit

_____ Btus/°F • day – _____ Btus/°F • day = _____ Btus/°F • day

7. ADDITIONAL HEAT LOSS IN SIDEHILL DESIGN

In a sidehill situation, the heat loss through the lower living-space concrete wall is a constant. For simplicity, let's call this the "Lower Concrete Wall Loss" or LCWL, which can be calculated as follows:

(continued on next page)

Worksheet 3
(continued)

Area of lower living-space concrete wall (from Worksheet 1, line 16) × U-value of lower living-space concrete wall (from Worksheet 1, line 22) × difference between inside and outside temperatures (or 65 degrees – 45 degrees)

_____square feet × _____ Btus/hr • ft^2 • °F x 20 degrees = _____ Btus/hour

8. DESIGN CHECK

Calculate the total area of the east-, west-, and south-facing glass as a percentage of the gross upper and lower heated wall area:

(_____) square feet of E, W, and S glass (from Worksheet 1, lines 5, 6, and 7) ÷

(_____) square feet of wall (from Worksheet 1, lines 14 and 16) × 100 = 291/

2280 × 100 =_____ percent

The resulting percentage should be between 10 and 20 percent. _____

Worksheet 4
Solar-Supplied Heat Gain

1. Using appendix 6, enter the percent sunshine for your home site:

Month	% Sunshine
September	_____
October	_____
November	_____
December	_____
January	_____
February	_____
March	_____
April	_____
May	_____

2. From appendix 2, enter the east, south, and west half-day totals of Solar Heat Gain Factors for your home site latitude. (Read the table from top to bottom for sunrise to noon and from bottom to top for noon to sunset.) Assuming that your home faces south, multiply the south half-day total SHGF by 2. Ignore the west SHGFs for the AM and likewise ignore the east SHGFs for the PM (therefore, the east SHGF will equal the west SHGF).

Month	East	South (x2)	West
September	_____	_____	_____
October	_____	_____	_____
November	_____	_____	_____
December	_____	_____	_____
January	_____	_____	_____
February	_____	_____	_____
March	_____	_____	_____
April	_____	_____	_____
May	_____	_____	_____

Multiply the SHGFs given above by the area (in square feet) of glass on each elevation, and obtain a total for each month (square feet × Btus per square foot × days per month) = Btus per month

(continued next page)

Worksheet 4
(continued)

Month	Days	Square feet of East Glass × East SHGF × Days per Month		Square feet of South Glass × South SHGF × Days per Month		Square feet of West Glass × West SHGF × Days per Month		Total (in millions of Btus)
Sep	30	_____	+	_____	+	_____	=	_____
Oct	31	_____	+	_____	+	_____	=	_____
Nov	30	_____	+	_____	+	_____	=	_____
Dec	31	_____	+	_____	+	_____	=	_____
Jan	31	_____	+	_____	+	_____	=	_____
Feb	28	_____	+	_____	+	_____	=	_____
Mar	31	_____	+	_____	+	_____	=	_____
Apr	30	_____	+	_____	+	_____	=	_____
May	31	_____	+	_____	+	_____	=	_____

Tabulate the Solar Heat Gain for each month. Multiply the percentage of sunshine × the monthly total Btus × the Shade Factor X the Clearness Number:

Month	% Sunshine (as decimal)		Total Btus/month (from above)		Shade Factor		Clearness Number		Total (millions of Btus)
Sept	_____	×	_____	×	_____	×	_____	=	_____
Oct	_____	×	_____	×	_____	×	_____	=	_____
Nov	_____	×	_____	×	_____	×	_____	=	_____
Dec	_____	×	_____	×	_____	×	_____	=	_____
Jan	_____	×	_____	×	_____	×	_____	=	_____
Feb	_____	×	_____	×	_____	×	_____	=	_____
Mar	_____	×	_____	×	_____	×	_____	=	_____
Apr	_____	×	_____	×	_____	×	_____	=	_____
May	_____	×	_____	×	_____	×	_____	=	_____

Worksheet 5
House Heat Load Calculation

Using appendix 5, enter the monthly degree days for your house location.

Monthly Heat Load (in Btus) = Total House Loss (in Btus/°F • day) × degree days + lower sidehill concrete wall loss or LCWL (from Worksheet 3, line 7) _____ ,Btus per hour × 24 hours × days per month

If this is a sidehill design, first calculate the monthly heat loss through the lower concrete wall (MCWL) as follows:

Month	LCWL (in Btus)		Hours per day		Days per month		MCWL (millions of Btus)
Sep	_____	×	24 hours	×	30 Days	=	_____
Oct	_____	×	24 hours	×	31 Days	=	_____
Nov	_____	×	24 hours	×	30 Days	=	_____
Dec	_____	×	24 hours	×	31 Days	=	_____
Jan	_____	×	24 hours	×	31 Days	=	_____
Feb	_____	×	24 hours	×	28 Days	=	_____
Mar	_____	×	24 hours	×	31 Days	=	_____
Apr	_____	×	24 hours	×	30 Days	=	_____
May	_____	×	24 hours	×	31 Days	=	_____

Month	Total House Heat Loss (in Btus)		Degree Days		MCWL		Monthly Heat Load (millions of Btus)
Sep	_____	×	_____	+	_____	=	_____
Oct	_____	×	_____	+	_____	=	_____
Nov	_____	×	_____	+	_____	=	_____
Dec	_____	×	_____	+	_____	=	_____
Jan	_____	×	_____	+	_____	=	_____
Feb	_____	×	_____	+	_____	=	_____
Mar	_____	×	_____	+	_____	=	_____
Apr	_____	×	_____	+	_____	=	_____
May	_____	×	_____	+	_____	=	_____
					Total	=	_____

Worksheet 6
House Solar Performance Summary

From Worksheets 4 and 5, enter the total monthly heat load and the figure for solar-supplied heat. Subtract the monthly solar-supplied figure from the total heat load. If the difference is less than "0," enter "0" in the last column.

Month	HEAT LOAD (millions Btus) FROM WORKSHEET 5	SOLAR SUPPLIED (millions Btus) FROM WORKSHEET 4	DIFFERENCE: NOT SOLAR SUPPLIED (millions Btus)
Sep	_____	_____	_____
Oct	_____	_____	_____
Nov	_____	_____	_____
Dec	_____	_____	_____
Jan	_____	_____	_____
Feb	_____	_____	_____
Mar	_____	_____	_____
Apr	_____	_____	_____
May	_____	_____	_____
	Total = _____	Total = _____	

Difference: Not Solar Supplied = Btus to be supplied by purchased fuel

Totals are:

A. Total Purchased Fuel (from column 3, above) _____ Btus

B. Total Heat Load (from column 1, above) _____ Btus

C. % Purchased Fuel (A ÷ B × 100) _____ ÷ _____ x 100 = _____%

D. % Solar (100 – C)   100 - _____ = _____%

Worksheet 7
Backup Heat and Annual Fuel Usage Calculation

1. NET AVAILABLE BTUS FOR VARIOUS FUELS

A. #2 fuel oil: (theoretical heat energy = 140,000 Btus per gallon). Assuming 70% combustion efficiency, the net heat will be 0.70 × 140,000= 98,000 Btus per gallon.

B. Propane gas: (theoretical heat energy = 91,500 Btus per gallon). Assuming 75% combustion efficiency, the net heat will be 0.75 × 91,500 = 68,625 Btus per gallon.

C. Electricity (theoretical heat energy = net heat in this case): 3,415 Btus per kilowatt-hour.

D. Split and dry hardwood: Average net heat energy is 17,000,000 Btus per cord (a cord is 128 cubic feet), or _____ Btus/cord for the specific firewood to be burned.

2. FOR COMBUSTION EFFICIENCY IN STEP 2, BELOW, USE THE FOLLOWING VALUES OR SUBSTITUTE MANUFACTURER'S SPECIFIED EFFICIENCY:

Oil furnace: .70
Propane gas furnace: .75
Electric resistance heaters or electric furnace: 1.00
Woodstove: .85

3. SIZING THE CONVENTIONAL BACKUP HEAT EQUIPMENT

The appropriate furnace size (in Btus per hour) can be calculated as follows:

Step 1.

Total Heat Loss (from Worksheet 3, line 5*) _____ Btus/°F • day ÷ 24 hr/day × (72 − _____ °F Outside Winter Design Temperature) + Sidehill Lower Concrete Wall Loss** _____ Btus per hour = _____ Btus per hour

*Use Total Heat Loss without taking nighttime insulation credit
**Area of lower concrete wall (Worksheet 1, line 16) _____ square feet X U-value of lower concrete wall _____ (Btus/hr • ft² • °F) × (72 − 45 Degrees) = _____ Btus per hour

Step 2.

The answer from Step _____ Btus per hour ÷ combustion efficiency (as a decimal, from section 2, above) = _____ Btus per hour ÷ _____ = _____ Btus per hour

Rounded for simplicity to the nearest thousand:

Furnace Size = _____ Btus per hour***

*** Btus per hour net at bonnet. Increase slightly for duct and other losses.

(continued next page)

4. SIZING A WOODSTOVE

The recommended woodstove size can be calculated as follows:

Step 1.

Take the average of Heat Loss (from Worksheet 3, lines 5 and 6) (11,126 + 10,019) ÷ 2 Btus per hour ÷ 24 hours per day × (72 - outside Design Temperature) _____ degrees + sidehill LCWL (from section 1, above) _____ Btus per hour = _____ Btus per hour

Step 2.

Answer from Step 1 _____ Btus per hour ÷ .85 (combustion efficiency from section 2, above) = _____ Btus per hour

Rounded for simplicity the nearest thousand:

Woodstove size = _____ Btus per hour

5. ANNUAL FUEL CONSUMPTION

Total Purchased Fuel (from Worksheet 6, line A) ÷ net available heat energy in Btus per gallon, kilowatt-hour, or cord (from section 1, above) = annual fuel consumption in Btus*

*Monthly totals can also be obtained using the same method working with Worksheet 6, column 1.

SUMMARY:

Annual Purchased Oil Consumption (if 100% source of backup heat):

_____ Btus ÷ 98,000 Btus per gallon = _____ gallons of oil

Annual Electricity Consumption (if 100% source of backup heat):

_____ Btus ÷ 3,415 Btus per kilowatt-hour = _____ kilowatt-hours

Annual Firewood Consumption (if 100% source of backup heat):

_____ Btus ÷ _____ Btus per cord + 0.5 cord (to be conservative) = _____ cords

To calculate the cost of these various sources of backup heat, simply multiply your totals for this section by the present rate in your area for 1 gallon, 1 kilowatt-hour, or 1 cord of split and dried hardwood firewood.

Worksheet 8
Sizing the Solar Slab

1. DETERMINING THE TOTAL INSOLATION FOR YOUR HOUSE ON A SUNNY DAY IN FEBRUARY

A. Insolation for a representative February day*:

East-facing glass _____ square feet × East SHGF ½-day total _____ Btus per square feet + South-facing glass _____ square feet × South SHGF ½-day total × 2 _____ Btus per square feet + West-facing glass _____ square feet × West SHGF ½-day total _____ Btus per square feet = _____ Btus

*Obtain your Solar Heat Gain Factors (SHGFs) for February from Worksheet 4, part 2.

B. Peak Insolation for February day:

Multiply result from A (from above) _____ Btus × Shade Factor (as a decimal) _____ × Clearness Number (as a decimal) _____ = _____ Btus

2. DETERMINING THE PREDICTED HEAT LOSS OF THE HOUSE (WHILE COLLECTING THE BTUS INDICATED IN SECTION 1, ABOVE)

A. Calculate the heat loss from 7:00 AM to 5:00 PM as follows:

_____ Btus/hr • °F (from Worksheet 3, lines 6 or 5, if no nighttime glass insulation is used) ÷ 24 hours per day _____ Btus/°F • day × (68 – average Outdoor Winter Design Temperature for house location (from appendix 5) _____ degrees) × 10 hours = _____ Btus

B. If using a sidehill design, add the Lower Concrete Wall Loss (from Worksheet 3, line 7) _____ Btus per hour × 10 hours = _____
10-hour heat loss in Btus

C. Then add A + B = _____ Btus

3. DETERMINING THE EXCESS AVAILABLE HEAT TO STORE IN THE SOLAR SLAB:

Total from section 1, above _____ Btus – Total from section 2, above _____ Btus = _____ Btus

(continued on next page)

4. DETERMINING THE VOLUME OF THE SOLAR SLAB

Total from section 3, above _____ Btus ÷ 30 Btus/ft^3 • °F* ÷ 8 degrees** = _____ cubic feet

*Specific Heat of Solar Slab (combination of 12-inch concrete blocks and poured concrete over blocks)
**Desired Maximum Temperature Difference

5. DETERMINING THE APPROPRIATE SLAB THICKNESS (MINIMUM 4 INCHES)

T = total thickness in feet
l = length in feet
w = width in feet
t = thickness of poured concrete over 12-inch blocks

A. T = Total Volume (from section 4, above) _____ cubic feet ÷ [0.85 × area of 1st-floor Solar Slab _____ square feet (using outside dimensions)] = _____ feet
Convert Total to inches: _____ feet x 12 inches/foot = _____ inches

B. t = T (from A, above) _____ inches – 6 inches* = _____ inches

*12-inch blocks are approximately ½-solid concrete

Solar Intensity and Solar Heat Gain Factors for 16 to 64 degrees North Latitude

Reprinted with permission of the American Society of Heating, Refrigeration and Air-Conditioning Engineers from the 1993 ASHRAE *Handbook of Fundamentals*, Tables 12–18.

Date	Solar Time	Direct Normal Btu/(h·ft²)	N	NNE	NE	ENE	E	ESE	SE	SSE	S	SSW	SW	WSW	W	WNW	NW	NNW	Hor.	Solar Time
Jan	0700	141	5	6	44	92	124	134	126	96	49	6	5	5	5	5	5	5	14	1700
	0800	262	14	15	55	147	210	240	233	189	114	25	14	14	14	14	14	14	79	1600
	0900	300	21	21	32	122	200	244	251	219	152	58	22	21	21	21	21	21	150	1500
	1000	317	26	26	27	66	150	209	233	223	178	102	31	26	26	26	26	26	203	1400
	1100	325	29	29	29	31	77	148	195	210	194	146	75	31	29	29	29	29	236	1300
	1200	327	30	30	30	30	32	72	139	184	199	184	138	72	32	30	30	30	248	1200
HALF DAY TOTALS			110	112	196	461	760	1000	1096	1020	781	426	211	127	111	110	110	110	805	
Feb	0700	182	8	17	84	138	169	172	150	103	36	8	8	8	8	8	8	8	25	1700
	0800	273	17	19	96	180	231	247	224	166	77	18	17	17	17	17	17	17	101	1600
	0900	305	23	24	64	153	214	242	233	188	110	30	23	23	23	23	23	23	174	1500
	1000	319	28	29	33	92	161	202	211	188	134	61	30	28	28	28	28	28	229	1400
	1100	326	32	32	32	37	83	136	167	172	149	102	49	33	32	32	32	32	263	1300
	1200	328	33	33	33	33	34	60	107	142	154	142	106	60	34	33	33	33	275	1200
HALF DAY TOTALS			124	137	321	609	865	1023	1034	885	582	287	174	132	124	124	124	124	930	
Mar	0700	201	11	53	124	172	192	183	145	82	15	10	10	10	10	10	10	10	40	1700
	0800	272	20	50	140	205	239	235	195	123	35	19	19	19	19	19	19	19	120	1600
	0900	299	26	35	109	179	218	225	197	138	57	27	26	26	26	26	26	26	192	1500
	1000	312	31	33	61	120	165	182	172	134	76	34	32	31	31	31	31	31	247	1400
	1100	318	34	35	36	53	87	114	125	116	89	55	36	35	34	34	34	34	280	1300
	1200	320	35	35	36	36	37	47	69	87	93	86	68	47	37	36	36	35	291	1200
HALF DAY TOTALS			141	226	494	755	928	975	879	643	319	187	153	142	139	139	139	139	1025	
Apr	0600	14	2	8	12	14	14	12	8	2	1	1	1	1	1	1	1	1	1	1800
	0700	197	24	94	153	187	191	167	117	45	14	13	13	13	13	13	13	13	53	1700
	0800	256	27	99	172	216	227	204	150	69	24	22	22	22	22	22	22	22	131	1600
	0900	280	31	79	149	193	208	193	147	77	31	29	29	29	29	29	29	29	197	1500
	1000	293	35	54	102	141	158	151	120	73	37	34	33	33	33	33	33	33	249	1400
	1100	299	38	40	54	72	86	88	78	60	43	38	38	36	36	36	36	37	279	1300
	1200	301	39	39	39	40	40	41	43	45	45	45	43	41	40	39	39	39	289	1200
HALF DAY TOTALS			179	403	674	859	922	851	653	352	174	159	157	156	155	155	155	156	1057	
May	0600	44	14	30	41	45	43	34	19	4	3	3	3	3	3	3	3	5	5	1800
	0700	193	50	120	168	191	185	150	92	24	16	16	16	16	16	16	16	17	62	1700
	0800	244	52	132	189	218	215	179	115	38	25	24	24	24	24	24	25	25	135	1600
	0900	268	49	116	171	198	197	167	109	45	32	30	30	30	30	30	30	32	197	1500
	1000	280	47	89	130	151	150	126	84	44	37	35	35	35	35	35	35	37	245	1400
	1100	286	47	63	79	87	83	70	52	41	40	39	38	38	38	39	39	41	273	1300
	1200	288	46	46	44	43	42	41	41	41	41	41	41	41	42	43	44	46	282	1200
HALF DAY TOTALS			283	575	804	916	897	748	493	217	172	167	167	167	167	168	169	176	1058	
Jun	0600	53	20	39	52	55	51	39	20	4	4	4	4	4	4	4	4	7	7	1800
	0700	188	62	128	172	190	179	141	80	20	16	16	16	16	16	16	16	18	64	1700
	0800	238	66	142	194	217	207	167	99	31	25	25	25	25	25	25	25	27	135	1600
	0900	261	63	130	178	198	190	154	93	37	31	31	31	31	31	31	31	33	194	1500
	1000	273	59	104	140	154	145	115	70	39	37	36	36	36	36	36	36	38	241	1400
	1100	279	57	76	90	92	82	63	46	41	40	39	39	39	39	40	41	43	268	1300
	1200	281	57	55	50	45	43	42	41	41	41	41	41	42	42	45	50	55	277	1200
HALF DAY TOTALS			356	648	850	929	876	700	430	194	174	171	171	171	172	173	176	190	1049	
Jul	0600	41	14	29	39	42	40	31	18	4	3	3	3	3	3	3	3	6	6	1800
	0700	184	51	118	164	185	179	145	88	23	16	16	16	16	16	16	16	17	62	1700
	0800	236	55	132	187	214	210	174	111	37	25	25	25	25	25	25	25	26	133	1600
	0900	259	52	117	170	196	193	163	106	44	32	31	31	31	31	31	31	33	194	1500
	1000	272	50	92	131	151	148	123	81	44	38	36	36	36	36	36	36	38	241	1400
	1100	278	49	66	81	88	83	69	52	42	41	40	39	39	39	40	40	42	269	1300
	1200	279	49	48	46	44	43	42	42	42	42	42	42	42	43	44	46	48	277	1200
HALF DAY TOTALS			296	580	799	903	878	729	478	215	176	172	171	171	171	172	173	182	1043	
Aug	0600	11	2	7	10	12	12	10	6	2	1	1	1	1	1	1	1	1	1	1800
	0700	180	26	92	145	176	180	156	109	42	15	14	14	14	14	14	14	14	53	1700
	0800	240	30	100	168	209	219	196	143	65	25	23	23	23	23	23	23	23	128	1600
	0900	266	33	82	148	190	203	187	142	74	33	30	30	30	30	30	30	30	193	1500
	1000	279	37	58	104	140	155	147	117	71	39	36	35	35	35	35	35	35	243	1400
	1100	285	40	43	57	75	86	87	76	59	44	40	39	38	38	38	38	39	273	1300
	1200	287	41	41	41	42	42	43	44	45	46	45	44	43	42	41	41	41	282	1200
HALF DAY TOTALS			191	410	666	837	891	817	624	339	180	167	165	164	163	163	163	164	1033	
Sep	0700	179	12	50	114	158	176	168	133	76	15	11	11	11	11	11	11	11	39	1700
	0800	253	21	49	134	196	227	224	186	119	36	20	20	20	20	20	20	20	116	1600
	0900	281	28	36	106	173	211	217	191	134	57	28	27	27	27	27	27	27	185	1500
	1000	295	32	34	61	118	161	178	168	132	76	35	33	32	32	32	32	32	238	1400
	1100	302	35	36	37	54	86	113	123	114	88	56	38	36	35	35	35	35	271	1300
	1200	304	36	36	37	38	39	49	69	86	93	86	69	48	39	38	37	36	282	1200
HALF DAY TOTALS			146	226	475	722	885	931	842	622	319	192	159	148	145	144	144	144	991	
Oct	0700	166	8	18	79	128	156	159	139	95	33	9	8	8	8	8	8	8	25	1700
	0800	259	17	20	95	174	223	237	215	159	74	19	17	17	17	17	17	17	99	1600
	0900	292	24	25	65	150	209	235	225	182	106	31	24	24	24	24	24	24	170	1500
	1000	307	29	30	34	92	158	197	205	183	130	60	31	29	29	29	29	29	224	1400
	1100	314	32	32	33	39	83	133	163	167	145	100	49	34	32	32	32	32	258	1300
	1200	316	33	33	33	34	35	60	105	139	150	138	104	60	35	34	33	33	270	1200
HALF DAY TOTALS			127	141	318	592	836	986	996	852	563	283	175	136	128	127	127	127	911	
Nov	0700	134	5	6	43	89	119	129	120	92	47	6	5	5	5	5	5	5	14	1700
	0800	255	15	15	55	145	206	235	228	185	111	25	15	15	15	15	15	15	78	1600
	0900	295	21	21	33	121	197	241	247	215	150	57	22	21	21	21	21	21	149	1500
	1000	312	26	26	28	67	147	206	230	220	176	100	31	26	26	26	26	26	201	1400
	1100	320	29	29	29	31	77	146	192	207	191	144	74	31	29	29	29	29	234	1300
	1200	322	30	30	30	30	32	72	137	181	196	181	137	72	32	30	30	30	246	1200
HALF DAY TOTALS			112	113	197	456	749	983	1077	1001	767	420	210	128	112	112	112	112	799	
Dec	0700	118	4	5	30	72	101	112	107	85	48	7	4	4	4	4	4	4	10	1700
	0800	255	13	14	41	132	198	233	231	193	124	33	13	13	13	13	13	13	69	1600
	0900	297	20	20	25	108	191	241	254	227	165	72	21	20	20	20	20	20	138	1500
	1000	315	25	25	26	56	144	208	239	233	192	117	35	25	25	25	25	25	191	1400
	1100	323	28	28	28	29	73	150	202	221	207	161	86	30	28	28	28	28	223	1300
	1200	325	29	29	29	29	30	77	149	197	212	196	149	76	30	29	29	29	234	1200
HALF DAY TOTALS			104	105	159	402	710	975	1099	1050	836	484	228	125	105	104	104	104	748	
			N	NNW	NW	WNW	W	WSW	SW	SSW	S	SSE	SE	ESE	E	ENE	NE	NNE	Hor.	PM

Notes: 1. Clearness number = 1.00; Ground reflectance = 0.20.   2. Figures shown are for 21st day of each month.

Table 13 Solar Intensity (E_{DN}) and Solar Heat Gain Factors (SHGF) for 24° North Latitude

Date	Solar Time	Direct Normal Btu/(h·ft²)	N	NNE	NE	ENE	E	ESE	SE	SSE	S	SSW	SW	WSW	W	WNW	NW	NNW	Hor.	Solar Time
Jan	0700	71	2	3	21	45	62	67	63	49	25	3	2	2	2	2	2	2	5	1700
	0800	239	12	12	41	128	190	221	218	181	114	28	12	12	12	12	12	12	55	1600
	0900	288	18	18	23	106	190	240	253	227	166	73	19	18	18	18	18	18	121	1500
	1000	308	23	23	24	53	144	211	245	241	200	125	38	24	23	23	23	23	172	1400
	1100	317	26	26	26	27	73	156	211	234	220	173	95	29	26	26	26	26	204	1300
	1200	320	27	27	27	27	29	82	160	210	227	210	160	81	29	27	27	27	214	1200
	HALF DAY TOTALS		95	96	148	372	671	942	1076	1039	840	505	241	120	96	95	95	95	664	
Feb	0700	153	6	12	67	114	141	145	128	90	33	6	6	6	6	6	6	6	17	1700
	0800	262	15	16	80	165	220	240	224	172	89	17	15	15	15	15	15	15	83	1600
	0900	297	21	22	46	138	208	244	243	205	133	42	22	21	21	21	21	21	153	1500
	1000	314	26	26	28	76	157	209	228	213	165	87	28	26	26	26	26	26	205	1400
	1100	321	29	29	29	31	80	148	191	203	185	137	68	31	29	29	29	29	238	1300
	1200	323	30	30	30	30	32	70	134	177	192	177	133	70	32	30	30	30	249	1200
	HALF DAY TOTALS		113	119	257	527	806	1011	1072	965	699	374	200	127	113	113	113	113	820	
Mar	0700	194	11	45	115	164	186	180	145	86	17	10	10	10	10	10	10	10	36	1700
	0800	267	18	35	124	195	234	237	204	138	48	19	18	18	18	18	18	18	112	1600
	0900	295	25	27	85	165	215	232	214	163	82	27	25	25	25	25	25	25	180	1500
	1000	309	30	31	41	103	162	194	195	168	112	47	31	30	30	30	30	30	232	1400
	1100	315	33	33	34	42	85	129	154	155	139	86	43	34	33	33	33	33	264	1300
	1200	317	34	34	34	34	35	56	96	126	137	126	95	56	35	34	34	34	275	1200
	HALF DAY TOTALS		133	189	422	693	906	1011	970	778	458	249	169	139	133	133	133	133	962	
Apr	0600	40	6	21	33	39	39	33	22	7	2	2	2	2	2	2	2	2	4	1800
	0700	203	20	88	151	189	197	176	127	55	15	14	14	14	14	14	14	14	58	1700
	0800	256	24	80	159	209	228	212	164	88	24	22	22	22	22	22	22	22	132	1600
	0900	280	30	54	126	181	208	203	169	105	39	29	28	28	28	28	28	28	195	1500
	1000	292	34	37	75	125	157	165	148	107	56	35	33	33	33	33	33	33	244	1400
	1100	298	36	37	40	59	85	103	106	94	70	45	38	37	36	36	36	36	274	1300
	1200	299	37	37	38	38	39	46	59	70	75	70	58	45	39	38	38	37	283	1200
	HALF DAY TOTALS		168	339	607	826	940	924	773	494	244	180	163	157	155	155	154	154	1048	
May	0600	86	25	57	79	87	84	66	38	8	6	6	6	6	6	6	6	6	13	1800
	0700	203	43	117	171	199	196	163	105	32	17	17	17	17	17	17	17	18	73	1700
	0800	248	38	114	178	214	218	190	132	54	26	25	25	25	25	25	25	26	142	1600
	0900	269	35	88	150	188	198	179	132	66	33	31	31	31	31	31	31	31	201	1500
	1000	280	38	59	103	137	150	141	111	67	39	36	35	35	35	35	35	36	247	1400
	1100	286	40	43	55	72	83	84	75	58	44	40	39	38	38	38	38	39	274	1300
	1200	288	41	41	41	41	42	43	44	46	46	46	44	43	42	41	41	41	282	1200
	HALF DAY TOTALS		238	492	749	909	943	840	614	308	187	176	174	173	172	172	172	175	1089	
Jun	0600	97	36	70	93	101	94	73	39	8	7	7	7	7	7	7	7	8	17	1800
	0700	201	55	127	177	199	192	155	94	26	18	18	18	18	18	18	18	20	77	1700
	0800	242	50	126	184	214	212	179	117	43	27	26	26	26	26	26	26	27	145	1600
	0900	263	43	102	158	189	192	168	116	53	34	32	32	32	32	32	32	33	201	1500
	1000	274	41	72	113	140	146	131	96	55	39	36	36	36	36	36	36	38	245	1400
	1100	279	42	50	65	77	82	77	64	49	42	41	40	39	39	39	40	41	271	1300
	1200	281	43	43	43	43	43	43	43	43	43	43	43	43	43	43	43	43	279	1200
	HALF DAY TOTALS		284	562	802	933	932	797	544	255	187	181	180	179	179	179	180	187	1096	
Jul	0600	81	26	56	76	84	80	63	36	8	6	6	6	6	6	6	6	7	13	1800
	0700	195	45	116	168	194	190	158	101	31	18	18	18	18	18	18	18	19	73	1700
	0800	239	41	115	176	210	213	185	128	52	27	26	26	26	26	26	26	26	141	1600
	0900	261	37	90	150	186	195	175	129	64	34	32	32	32	32	32	32	32	198	1500
	1000	272	39	62	104	137	149	139	108	65	39	37	36	36	36	36	36	37	243	1400
	1100	278	41	44	58	73	83	83	73	57	44	41	40	39	39	39	39	40	270	1300
	1200	280	42	42	42	43	43	44	45	46	46	46	45	43	43	42	42	42	278	1200
	HALF DAY TOTALS		247	498	746	897	925	820	595	300	191	181	178	177	177	177	177	181	1076	
Aug	0600	35	6	20	30	35	35	30	19	6	2	2	2	2	2	2	2	2	4	1800
	0700	186	22	87	144	179	186	165	119	51	16	15	15	15	15	15	15	15	58	1700
	0800	241	26	82	156	203	220	204	157	84	26	24	24	24	24	24	24	24	130	1600
	0900	265	32	57	126	178	202	197	162	101	39	31	30	30	30	30	30	30	191	1500
	1000	278	36	40	78	125	155	161	143	103	55	37	35	35	35	35	35	35	239	1400
	1100	284	38	39	42	61	85	101	104	91	68	46	40	38	37	37	37	37	268	1300
	1200	286	38	39	40	40	41	47	58	69	72	68	58	47	41	40	40	39	277	1200
	HALF DAY TOTALS		179	347	601	806	910	889	740	473	243	186	171	165	164	163	163	162	1028	
Sep	0800	248	19	36	119	185	222	225	194	132	48	20	19	19	19	19	19	19	108	1600
	0900	278	26	28	84	160	207	223	206	158	81	28	26	26	26	26	26	26	174	1500
	1000	292	31	32	42	101	158	188	190	163	110	48	32	31	31	31	31	31	224	1400
	1100	299	34	34	35	43	84	127	151	151	128	86	44	35	34	34	34	34	256	1300
	1200	301	35	35	35	36	37	57	95	124	134	124	94	57	37	36	35	35	266	1200
	HALF DAY TOTALS		139	190	406	661	863	964	927	749	451	251	174	145	139	138	138	138	930	
Oct	0700	138	6	12	62	104	129	133	117	82	31	7	6	6	6	6	6	6	17	1700
	0800	247	16	17	79	159	211	230	214	164	85	17	16	16	16	16	16	16	82	1600
	0900	284	22	23	47	135	202	237	235	198	128	41	23	22	22	22	22	22	150	1500
	1000	301	27	27	29	77	154	204	222	207	160	85	29	27	27	27	27	27	201	1400
	1100	309	30	30	30	33	80	145	186	198	180	133	67	32	30	30	30	30	233	1300
	1200	311	31	31	31	31	33	70	131	173	187	172	130	69	33	31	31	31	244	1200
	HALF DAY TOTALS		116	123	255	512	778	974	1032	929	675	367	200	131	117	116	116	116	804	
Nov	0700	67	2	3	20	43	59	64	60	46	24	3	2	2	2	2	2	2	5	1700
	0800	232	12	13	42	126	186	216	213	177	111	28	12	12	12	12	12	12	55	1600
	0900	282	19	19	23	106	187	236	249	223	163	71	20	19	19	19	19	19	120	1500
	1000	303	23	23	24	53	143	209	241	237	197	123	37	24	23	23	23	23	171	1400
	1100	312	26	26	26	28	73	154	209	230	217	171	93	29	26	26	26	26	202	1300
	1200	315	27	27	27	27	29	81	158	207	224	207	158	80	29	27	27	27	213	1200
	HALF DAY TOTALS		97	97	149	368	661	926	1056	1020	825	497	239	121	98	97	97	97	659	
Dec	0700	30	1	1	7	18	25	28	27	21	12	2	1	1	1	1	1	1	2	1700
	0800	225	10	10	29	112	174	208	209	178	118	35	11	10	10	10	10	10	44	1600
	0900	281	17	17	19	93	180	234	252	231	174	84	18	17	17	17	17	17	107	1500
	1000	304	22	22	22	44	137	209	247	247	209	137	44	22	22	22	22	22	157	1400
	1100	314	25	25	25	26	69	156	216	241	230	183	104	29	25	25	25	25	188	1300
	1200	317	26	26	26	26	27	85	167	219	237	219	167	84	27	26	26	26	199	1200
	HALF DAY TOTALS		88	88	118	313	611	899	1054	1042	868	550	257	117	89	88	88	88	598	
			N	NNW	NW	WNW	W	WSW	SW	SSW	S	SSE	SE	ESE	E	ENE	NE	NNE	Hor.	PM

Notes: 1. Clearness number = 1.00; Ground reflectance = 0.20. 2. Figures shown are for 21st day of each month.

Table 14   Solar Intensity (E_{DN}) and Solar Heat Gain Factors (SHGF) for 32° North Latitude

Date	Solar Time	Direct Normal Btu/(h·ft²)	N	NNE	NE	ENE	E	ESE	SE	SSE	S	SSW	SW	WSW	W	WNW	NW	NNW	Hor.	Solar Time
Jan	0700	1	0	0	0	1	1	1	1	1	0	0	0	0	0	0	0	0	0	1700
	0800	203	9	9	29	105	160	189	189	159	103	28	9	9	9	9	9	9	32	1600
	0900	269	15	15	17	91	175	229	246	225	169	82	17	15	15	15	15	15	88	1500
	1000	295	20	20	20	41	135	209	249	250	212	141	46	20	20	20	20	20	136	1400
	1100	306	23	23	23	24	68	159	221	238	238	191	110	29	23	23	23	23	166	1300
	1200	310	24	24	24	24	25	88	174	228	246	228	174	88	25	24	24	24	176	1200
	HALF DAY TOTALS		79	79	107	284	570	856	1015	1014	853	553	264	112	80	79	79	79	512	
Feb	0700	112	4	7	47	82	102	106	95	67	26	4	4	4	4	4	4	4	9	1700
	0800	245	13	14	65	149	205	228	216	170	95	17	13	13	13	13	13	13	64	1600
	0900	287	19	19	32	122	199	242	248	216	149	55	20	19	19	19	19	19	127	1500
	1000	305	24	24	25	62	151	213	241	232	189	112	31	24	24	24	24	24	176	1400
	1100	314	26	26	26	28	76	156	208	227	212	165	87	28	26	26	26	26	207	1300
	1200	316	27	27	27	27	29	79	155	204	221	204	155	79	29	27	27	27	217	1200
	HALF DAY TOTALS		100	103	201	445	735	978	1080	1010	780	452	228	122	100	100	100	100	691	
Mar	0700	185	10	37	105	153	176	173	142	88	20	9	9	9	9	9	9	9	32	1700
	0800	260	17	25	107	183	227	237	209	150	62	18	17	17	17	17	17	17	100	1600
	0900	290	23	25	64	151	210	237	227	183	107	30	23	23	23	23	23	23	164	1500
	1000	304	28	28	30	87	158	202	215	195	144	70	29	28	28	28	28	28	211	1400
	1100	311	31	31	31	34	82	142	179	188	168	120	59	32	31	31	31	31	242	1300
	1200	313	32	32	32	32	33	66	122	162	176	162	122	66	33	32	32	32	252	1200
	HALF DAY TOTALS		124	162	359	629	875	1033	1041	888	589	326	193	136	125	124	124	124	874	
Apr	0600	66	9	35	54	65	66	56	38	12	4	3	3	3	3	3	3	3	7	1800
	0700	206	17	80	146	188	200	182	136	65	16	14	14	14	14	14	14	14	61	1700
	0800	255	23	61	144	200	227	219	177	107	30	22	22	22	22	22	22	22	129	1600
	0900	278	28	36	103	168	206	212	187	133	58	29	28	28	28	28	28	28	188	1500
	1000	290	32	34	52	108	155	177	172	141	87	39	33	32	32	32	32	32	233	1400
	1100	295	35	35	36	47	83	118	135	132	108	70	40	36	35	35	35	35	262	1300
	1200	297	36	36	36	37	38	53	82	106	115	106	82	53	38	37	36	36	271	1200
	HALF DAY TOTALS		161	296	550	792	952	992	889	645	360	228	177	157	153	152	152	152	1015	
May	0600	119	33	77	108	121	116	94	56	13	8	8	8	8	8	8	8	9	21	1800
	0700	211	36	111	170	202	204	174	118	42	19	18	18	18	18	18	18	19	81	1700
	0800	250	29	94	165	208	220	199	149	73	27	25	25	25	25	25	25	25	146	1600
	0900	269	33	61	128	177	198	190	155	93	37	32	31	31	31	31	31	31	201	1500
	1000	280	36	40	76	121	150	156	138	99	54	37	35	35	35	35	35	35	243	1400
	1100	285	38	39	42	59	83	99	102	90	68	47	40	39	37	37	37	37	269	1300
	1200	286	38	39	40	40	41	47	59	70	74	70	59	47	41	40	40	39	277	1200
	HALF DAY TOTALS		222	438	702	900	985	933	747	447	250	199	183	177	175	174	174	175	1098	
Jun	0600	131	44	92	123	135	127	99	55	12	10	10	10	10	10	10	10	11	28	1800
	0700	210	47	122	176	204	201	168	108	35	20	20	20	20	20	20	20	21	88	1700
	0800	245	36	106	171	208	214	189	135	60	28	27	27	27	27	27	27	27	151	1600
	0900	264	35	74	137	178	193	180	139	77	35	32	32	32	32	32	32	32	204	1500
	1000	274	38	47	86	125	146	145	123	83	45	38	36	36	36	36	36	36	244	1400
	1100	279	40	41	47	64	82	91	89	75	56	43	41	40	39	39	39	39	269	1300
	1200	280	41	41	41	42	42	46	52	58	60	58	52	46	42	42	41	41	276	1200
	HALF DAY TOTALS		261	504	762	935	985	897	678	372	225	197	189	185	184	184	183	186	1122	
Jul	0600	113	34	76	105	117	113	90	53	12	9	9	9	9	9	9	9	9	22	1800
	0700	203	38	111	167	198	198	169	114	41	20	19	19	19	19	19	19	19	81	1700
	0800	241	31	95	163	204	215	194	145	70	28	26	26	26	26	26	26	26	145	1600
	0900	261	34	64	129	175	195	186	150	90	37	32	32	32	32	32	32	32	198	1500
	1000	271	37	42	78	121	148	153	134	96	53	38	36	36	36	36	36	36	240	1400
	1100	277	39	40	43	60	83	98	99	88	66	47	41	40	38	38	38	38	265	1300
	1200	279	40	40	41	41	42	48	58	68	72	68	58	48	42	41	41	40	273	1200
	HALF DAY TOTALS		231	444	701	890	967	912	726	433	248	202	187	182	180	179	179	180	1088	
Aug	0600	59	10	33	50	60	60	51	34	11	4	4	4	4	4	4	4	4	8	1800
	0700	190	19	79	141	179	190	172	128	61	17	15	15	15	15	15	15	15	61	1700
	0800	240	25	63	141	195	219	210	170	102	31	23	23	23	23	23	23	23	128	1600
	0900	263	30	39	104	166	200	206	181	127	57	31	29	29	29	29	29	29	185	1500
	1000	276	34	36	55	109	153	173	167	136	84	40	35	34	34	34	34	34	229	1400
	1100	282	36	37	39	50	84	116	131	127	104	69	41	38	36	36	36	36	256	1300
	1200	284	37	37	37	39	40	54	81	103	111	103	81	54	40	39	37	37	265	1200
	HALF DAY TOTALS		171	303	546	774	922	955	854	618	352	231	184	166	162	161	160	160	999	
Sep	0700	163	10	35	96	139	159	156	128	80	20	10	10	10	10	10	10	10	31	1700
	0800	240	18	26	103	173	215	224	198	143	60	19	18	18	18	18	18	18	96	1600
	0900	272	24	26	64	146	202	227	218	177	105	31	24	24	24	24	24	24	158	1500
	1000	287	29	29	32	86	154	196	208	189	141	70	31	29	29	29	29	29	204	1400
	1100	294	32	32	32	36	81	139	174	182	163	118	59	34	32	32	32	32	234	1300
	1200	296	33	33	33	33	35	66	120	158	171	158	120	66	35	33	33	33	244	1200
	HALF DAY TOTALS		130	164	345	598	831	982	993	852	574	325	197	142	130	129	129	129	845	
Oct	0700	99	4	7	43	74	92	96	85	60	24	5	4	4	4	4	4	4	10	1700
	0800	229	13	15	63	143	195	217	206	162	90	17	13	13	13	13	13	13	63	1600
	0900	273	20	20	33	120	193	234	239	208	144	54	21	20	20	20	20	20	125	1500
	1000	293	24	24	26	62	147	207	234	225	183	109	32	24	24	24	24	24	173	1400
	1100	302	27	27	27	29	76	152	203	221	207	160	85	29	27	27	27	27	203	1300
	1200	304	28	28	28	28	30	78	151	199	215	199	151	78	30	28	28	28	213	1200
	HALF DAY TOTALS		103	106	200	433	708	941	1038	972	753	441	226	125	104	103	103	103	679	
Nov	0700	2	0	0	0	1	1	1	1	1	1	0	0	0	0	0	0	0	0	1700
	0800	196	9	9	29	103	156	184	184	155	100	27	9	9	9	9	9	9	32	1600
	0900	263	16	16	17	90	173	225	241	221	166	80	17	16	16	16	16	16	88	1500
	1000	289	20	20	21	41	134	206	245	246	209	138	45	21	20	20	20	20	136	1400
	1100	301	23	23	23	24	67	157	218	234	234	188	109	29	23	23	23	23	165	1300
	1200	304	24	24	24	24	25	87	171	224	243	224	171	87	25	24	24	24	175	1200
	HALF DAY TOTALS		80	81	108	282	561	841	996	996	838	544	261	113	81	80	80	80	509	
Dec	0800	176	7	7	19	84	135	163	166	143	97	31	7	7	7	7	7	7	22	1600
	0900	257	14	14	15	77	162	218	238	222	171	89	15	14	14	14	14	14	72	1500
	1000	288	18	18	18	34	127	204	246	251	216	148	52	19	18	18	18	18	119	1400
	1100	301	21	21	21	22	63	157	222	252	243	197	116	29	21	21	21	21	148	1300
	1200	304	22	22	22	22	23	89	177	232	252	232	177	89	23	22	22	22	158	1200
	HALF DAY TOTALS		71	71	84	227	500	792	965	986	852	578	275	107	71	71	71	71	440	
			N	NNW	NW	WNW	W	WSW	SW	SSW	S	SSE	SE	ESE	E	ENE	NE	NNE	Hor.	PM

Notes: 1. Clearness number = 1.00; Ground reflectance = 0.20.   2. Figures shown are for 21st day of each month.

Table 15 Solar Intensity (E_{DN}) and Solar Heat Gain Factors (SHGF) for 40° North Latitude

Date	Solar Time	Direct Normal Btu/(h·ft²)	N	NNE	NE	ENE	E	ESE	SE	SSE	S	SSW	SW	WSW	W	WNW	NW	NNW	Hor.	Solar Time
Jan	0800	142	5	5	17	71	111	132	133	114	75	22	6	5	5	5	5	5	14	1600
	0900	239	12	12	13	74	154	205	224	209	160	82	13	12	12	12	12	12	55	1500
	1000	274	16	16	16	31	124	199	241	246	213	146	51	17	16	16	16	16	96	1400
	1100	289	19	19	19	20	61	156	222	252	244	198	118	28	19	19	19	19	124	1300
	1200	294	20	20	20	20	21	90	179	234	254	234	179	90	21	20	20	20	133	1200
	HALF DAY TOTALS		61	61	73	199	452	734	904	932	813	561	273	101	62	61	61	61	354	
Feb	0700	55	2	3	23	40	51	53	47	34	14	2	2	2	2	2	2	2	4	1700
	0800	219	10	11	50	129	183	206	199	160	94	18	10	10	10	10	10	10	43	1600
	0900	271	16	16	22	107	186	234	245	218	157	66	17	16	16	16	16	16	98	1500
	1000	294	21	21	21	49	143	211	246	243	203	129	38	21	21	21	21	21	143	1400
	1100	304	23	23	23	24	71	160	219	244	231	184	103	27	23	23	23	23	171	1300
	1200	307	24	24	24	24	25	86	170	222	241	222	170	86	25	24	24	24	180	1200
	HALF DAY TOTALS		84	86	152	361	648	916	1049	1015	821	508	250	114	85	84	84	84	548	
Mar	0700	171	9	29	93	140	163	161	135	86	22	8	8	8	8	8	8	8	26	1700
	0800	250	16	18	91	169	218	232	211	157	74	17	16	16	16	16	16	16	85	1600
	0900	282	21	22	47	136	203	238	236	198	128	40	22	21	21	21	21	21	143	1500
	1000	297	25	25	27	72	153	207	229	216	171	95	29	25	25	25	25	25	186	1400
	1100	305	28	28	28	30	78	151	198	213	197	150	77	30	28	28	28	28	213	1300
	1200	307	29	29	29	29	31	75	145	191	206	191	145	75	31	29	29	29	223	1200
	HALF DAY TOTALS		114	139	302	563	832	1035	1087	968	694	403	220	132	114	113	113	113	764	
Apr	0600	89	11	46	72	87	88	76	52	18	5	5	5	5	5	5	5	5	11	1800
	0700	206	16	71	140	185	201	186	143	75	16	14	14	14	14	14	14	14	61	1700
	0800	252	22	44	128	190	224	223	188	124	41	22	21	21	21	21	21	21	123	1600
	0900	274	27	29	80	155	202	219	203	156	83	29	27	27	27	27	27	27	177	1500
	1000	286	31	31	37	92	152	187	193	170	121	56	32	31	31	31	31	41	217	1400
	1100	292	33	33	34	39	81	130	160	166	146	102	52	35	33	33	33	33	243	1300
	1200	293	34	34	34	34	36	62	108	142	154	142	108	62	36	34	34	34	252	1200
	HALF DAY TOTALS		154	265	501	758	957	1051	994	782	488	296	199	157	148	147	147	147	957	
May	0500	1	0	1	1	1	1	1	0	0	0	0	0	0	0	0	0	0	0	1900
	0600	144	36	90	128	145	141	115	71	18	10	10	10	10	10	10	10	11	31	1800
	0700	216	28	102	165	202	209	184	131	54	20	19	19	19	19	19	19	19	87	1700
	0800	250	27	73	149	199	220	208	164	93	29	25	25	25	25	25	25	25	146	1600
	0900	267	31	42	105	164	197	200	175	121	53	32	30	30	30	30	30	30	195	1500
	1000	277	34	36	54	105	148	168	163	133	83	40	35	34	34	34	34	34	234	1400
	1100	283	36	36	38	48	81	113	130	127	105	70	42	38	36	36	36	36	257	1300
	1200	284	37	37	37	38	40	54	82	104	113	104	82	54	40	38	37	37	265	1200
	HALF DAY TOTALS		215	404	666	893	1024	1025	881	601	358	247	200	180	176	175	174	175	1083	
Jun	0500	22	10	17	21	22	20	14	6	2	1	1	1	1	1	1	1	2	3	1900
	0600	155	48	104	143	159	151	121	70	17	13	13	13	13	13	13	13	14	40	1800
	0700	216	37	113	172	205	207	178	122	46	22	21	21	21	21	21	21	21	97	1700
	0800	246	30	85	156	201	216	199	152	80	29	27	27	27	27	27	27	27	153	1600
	0900	263	33	51	114	166	192	190	161	105	45	33	32	32	32	32	32	32	201	1500
	1000	272	35	38	63	109	145	158	148	116	69	39	36	35	35	35	35	35	238	1400
	1100	277	38	39	40	52	81	105	116	110	88	60	41	39	38	38	38	38	260	1300
	1200	279	38	38	38	40	41	52	72	89	95	89	72	52	41	40	38	38	267	1200
	HALF DAY TOTALS		253	470	734	941	1038	999	818	523	315	236	204	191	188	187	186	188	1126	
Jul	0500	2	1	2	2	2	2	1	1	0	0	0	0	0	0	0	0	0	0	1900
	0600	138	37	89	125	142	137	112	68	18	11	11	11	11	11	11	11	12	32	1800
	0700	208	30	102	163	198	204	179	127	53	21	20	20	20	20	20	20	20	88	1700
	0800	241	28	75	148	196	216	203	160	90	30	26	26	26	26	26	26	26	145	1600
	0900	259	32	44	106	163	193	196	170	118	52	33	31	31	31	31	31	31	194	1500
	1000	269	35	37	56	106	146	165	159	129	81	41	36	35	35	35	35	35	231	1400
	1100	275	37	38	40	50	81	111	127	123	102	69	43	39	37	37	37	37	254	1300
	1200	276	38	38	38	40	41	55	80	101	109	101	80	55	41	40	38	38	262	1200
	HALF DAY TOTALS		223	411	666	885	1008	1003	858	584	352	248	204	186	181	180	180	181	1076	
Aug	0600	81	12	44	68	81	82	71	48	17	6	5	5	5	5	5	5	5	12	1800
	0700	191	17	71	135	177	191	177	135	70	17	16	16	16	16	16	16	16	62	1700
	0800	237	24	47	126	185	216	214	180	118	41	23	23	23	23	23	23	23	122	1600
	0900	260	28	31	82	153	197	212	196	151	80	31	28	28	28	28	28	28	174	1500
	1000	272	32	33	40	93	150	182	187	165	116	56	34	32	32	32	32	32	214	1400
	1100	278	35	35	36	41	81	128	156	160	141	99	52	37	35	35	35	35	239	1300
	1200	280	35	35	35	36	38	63	106	138	149	138	106	63	38	36	35	35	247	1200
	HALF DAY TOTALS		164	273	498	741	928	1013	956	751	474	296	205	166	157	156	156	156	946	
Sep	0700	149	9	27	84	125	146	144	121	77	21	9	9	9	9	9	9	9	25	1700
	0800	230	17	19	87	160	205	218	199	148	71	18	17	17	17	17	17	17	82	1600
	0900	263	22	23	47	131	194	227	226	190	124	41	23	22	22	22	22	22	138	1500
	1000	280	27	27	28	71	148	200	221	209	165	93	30	27	27	27	27	27	180	1400
	1100	287	29	29	29	31	78	147	192	207	191	146	77	31	29	29	29	29	206	1300
	1200	290	30	30	30	30	32	75	142	185	200	185	142	75	32	30	30	30	215	1200
	HALF DAY TOTALS		119	142	291	534	787	980	1033	925	672	396	222	137	119	118	118	118	738	
Oct	0700	48	2	3	20	36	45	47	42	30	12	2	2	2	2	2	2	2	4	1700
	0800	204	11	12	49	123	173	195	188	151	89	18	11	11	11	11	11	11	43	1600
	0900	257	17	17	23	104	180	225	235	209	151	64	18	17	17	17	17	17	97	1500
	1000	280	21	21	22	50	139	205	238	235	196	125	38	22	21	21	21	21	140	1400
	1100	291	24	24	24	25	71	156	212	236	224	178	101	28	24	24	24	24	168	1300
	1200	294	25	25	25	25	27	85	165	216	234	216	165	85	27	25	25	25	177	1200
	HALF DAY TOTALS		88	89	152	351	623	878	1006	974	791	493	247	117	89	88	88	88	540	
Nov	0800	136	5	5	18	69	108	128	129	110	72	21	6	5	5	5	5	5	14	1600
	0900	232	12	12	13	73	151	201	219	204	156	80	13	12	12	12	12	12	55	1500
	1000	268	16	16	16	31	122	196	237	242	209	143	50	17	16	16	16	16	96	1400
	1100	283	19	19	19	20	61	154	218	248	240	194	116	28	19	19	19	19	123	1300
	1200	288	20	20	20	20	21	89	176	231	250	231	176	89	21	20	20	20	132	1200
	HALF DAY TOTALS		63	63	75	198	445	721	887	914	798	551	269	101	63	63	63	63	354	
Dec	0800	89	3	3	8	41	67	82	84	73	50	17	3	3	3	3	3	3	6	1600
	0900	217	10	10	11	60	135	185	205	194	151	83	13	10	10	10	10	10	39	1500
	1000	261	14	14	14	25	113	188	232	239	210	146	55	15	14	14	14	14	77	1400
	1100	280	17	17	17	17	56	151	217	249	242	198	120	28	17	17	17	17	104	1300
	1200	285	18	18	18	18	19	89	178	233	253	233	178	89	19	18	18	18	113	1200
	HALF DAY TOTALS		52	52	56	146	374	649	822	867	775	557	276	94	53	52	52	52	282	
			N	NNW	NW	WNW	W	WSW	SW	SSW	S	SSE	SE	ESE	E	ENE	NE	NNE	Hor.	PM

Notes: 1. Clearness number = 1.00; Ground reflectance = 0.20.　　　　2. Figures shown are for 21st day of each month.

Table 16 Solar Intensity (E_{DN}) and Solar Heat Gain Factors (SHGF) for 48° North Latitude

Date	Solar Time	Direct Normal Btu/(h·ft²)	N	NNE	NE	ENE	E	ESE	SE	SSE	S	SSW	SW	WSW	W	WNW	NW	NNW	Hor.	Solar Time
Jan	0800	37	1	1	4	18	29	34	35	30	20	6	1	1	1	1	1	1	2	1600
	0900	185	8	8	8	53	118	160	176	166	129	69	10	8	8	8	8	8	25	1500
	1000	239	12	12	12	22	106	175	216	223	195	136	50	12	12	12	12	12	55	1400
	1100	261	14	14	14	15	53	144	208	239	233	190	116	26	14	14	14	14	77	1300
	1200	267	15	15	15	15	16	86	171	226	245	226	171	86	16	15	15	15	85	1200
	HALF DAY TOTALS		43	43	46	117	316	567	729	776	701	512	259	85	43	43	43	43	203	
Feb	0700	4	0	0	1	3	3	3	3	2	1	0	0	0	0	0	0	0	0	1700
	0800	180	8	8	36	103	149	170	166	136	82	17	8	8	8	8	8	8	25	1600
	0900	247	13	13	16	90	168	216	230	209	155	71	14	13	13	13	13	13	66	1500
	1000	275	17	17	17	38	131	203	242	244	207	138	44	18	17	17	17	17	105	1400
	1100	288	19	19	19	20	65	158	221	249	239	192	113	27	19	19	19	19	130	1300
	1200	292	20	20	20	20	22	89	176	231	250	231	176	89	22	20	20	20	138	1200
	HALF DAY TOTALS		68	68	107	274	541	816	968	967	813	531	261	104	68	68	68	68	395	
Mar	0700	153	7	22	80	123	145	145	123	80	23	7	7	7	7	7	7	7	20	1700
	0800	236	14	15	76	154	204	222	206	158	82	15	14	14	14	14	14	14	68	1600
	0900	270	19	19	3	121	193	234	239	207	142	52	20	19	19	19	19	19	118	1500
	1000	287	23	23	24	58	146	208	237	231	189	115	33	23	23	23	23	23	156	1400
	1100	295	25	25	25	26	74	156	210	232	218	172	94	28	25	25	25	25	180	1300
	1200	298	26	26	26	26	27	83	161	211	228	211	161	83	27	26	26	26	188	1200
	HALF DAY TOTALS		100	118	250	494	775	1012	1100	1014	767	465	244	126	101	100	100	100	636	
Apr	0600	108	12	53	86	105	107	93	64	23	6	6	6	6	6	6	6	6	15	1800
	0700	205	15	61	132	180	199	189	148	84	18	14	14	14	14	14	14	14	60	1700
	0800	247	20	32	111	179	219	225	196	138	55	21	20	20	20	20	20	20	114	1600
	0900	268	25	26	60	141	197	223	215	176	106	33	25	25	25	25	25	25	161	1500
	1000	280	28	28	31	77	148	193	209	194	150	80	31	28	28	28	28	28	196	1400
	1100	286	31	31	31	33	78	140	181	193	177	133	69	33	31	31	31	31	218	1300
	1200	288	31	31	31	31	34	71	131	172	186	172	131	71	34	31	31	31	226	1200
	HALF DAY TOTALS		147	242	461	724	957	1098	1081	895	605	370	226	156	141	140	140	140	875	
May	0500	41	17	31	40	42	39	29	14	3	3	3	3	3	3	3	3	3	5	1900
	0600	162	35	97	141	162	160	133	85	24	12	12	12	12	12	12	12	13	40	1800
	0700	219	23	90	158	200	212	191	142	68	21	19	19	19	19	19	19	19	91	1700
	0800	248	26	54	132	190	218	214	178	113	38	25	25	25	25	25	25	25	142	1600
	0900	264	29	32	82	151	194	208	192	147	77	32	29	29	29	29	29	29	185	1500
	1000	274	33	34	39	90	145	178	184	163	116	57	35	33	33	33	33	33	219	1400
	1100	279	35	35	36	40	79	126	155	160	142	101	54	37	35	35	35	35	240	1300
	1200	280	35	35	35	36	38	63	107	139	150	139	107	63	38	36	35	35	247	1200
	HALF DAY TOTALS		215	388	645	893	1065	1114	1007	749	483	316	225	184	174	173	173	174	1045	
Jun	0500	77	35	61	76	80	72	53	24	6	5	5	5	5	5	5	5	8	12	1900
	0600	172	46	110	155	175	169	138	84	22	14	14	14	14	14	14	14	16	51	1800
	0700	220	29	101	165	204	211	187	135	60	23	21	21	21	21	21	21	21	103	1700
	0800	246	29	64	139	191	215	206	168	101	34	27	27	27	27	27	27	27	152	1600
	0900	261	31	36	91	153	190	199	180	133	66	33	31	31	31	31	31	31	193	1500
	1000	269	34	36	45	94	143	169	171	148	101	50	36	34	34	34	34	34	225	1400
	1100	274	36	36	38	44	79	118	142	145	126	88	49	38	36	36	36	36	246	1300
	1200	275	37	37	37	38	40	60	96	124	134	124	96	60	40	38	37	37	252	1200
	HALF DAY TOTALS		257	459	722	955	1095	1102	955	678	436	299	228	197	189	188	188	191	1108	
Jul	0500	43	18	33	42	45	41	30	15	3	3	3	3	3	3	3	3	4	6	1900
	0600	156	37	96	138	159	156	129	82	24	13	13	13	13	13	13	13	14	41	1800
	0700	211	25	90	156	196	207	186	138	66	22	20	20	20	20	20	20	20	92	1700
	0800	240	27	56	132	187	214	209	174	110	38	26	26	26	26	26	26	26	142	1600
	0900	256	30	34	83	149	191	204	187	143	75	33	30	30	30	30	30	30	184	1500
	1000	266	34	35	41	90	143	174	180	158	113	56	36	34	34	34	34	34	217	1400
	1100	271	36	36	37	42	79	124	151	156	138	99	54	38	36	36	36	36	237	1300
	1200	272	36	36	36	37	39	63	104	136	146	136	104	63	39	37	36	36	244	1200
	HALF DAY TOTALS		223	395	646	886	1050	1092	983	730	474	315	229	190	181	179	179	180	1042	
Aug	0600	99	13	51	81	98	100	87	60	22	7	7	7	7	7	7	7	7	16	1800
	0700	190	17	61	128	172	190	179	141	79	19	15	15	15	15	15	15	15	61	1700
	0800	232	22	34	110	174	211	216	188	132	53	23	22	22	22	22	22	22	114	1600
	0900	154	27	28	63	139	192	216	108	169	102	34	27	27	27	27	27	27	159	1500
	1000	266	30	30	33	78	145	188	203	188	144	78	33	30	30	30	30	30	193	1400
	1100	272	32	32	32	36	78	137	175	187	171	129	68	35	32	32	32	32	215	1300
	1200	274	33	33	33	33	36	71	128	167	189	167	128	71	36	33	33	33	223	1200
	HALF DAY TOTALS		157	251	459	709	929	1060	1040	862	587	366	231	165	151	149	149	149	869	
Sep	0700	131	8	21	71	108	128	128	108	71	21	8	7	7	7	7	7	7	20	1700
	0800	215	15	16	72	144	191	207	193	148	77	16	15	15	15	15	15	15	65	1600
	0900	251	20	20	34	116	184	223	227	197	136	52	21	20	20	20	20	20	114	1500
	1000	269	24	24	25	58	141	200	228	221	182	112	34	24	24	24	24	24	151	1400
	1100	278	26	26	26	28	73	151	203	223	210	166	92	29	26	26	26	26	174	1300
	1200	280	27	27	27	27	29	82	156	204	220	204	156	82	29	27	27	27	182	1200
	HALF DAY TOTALS		105	121	240	465	729	953	1040	963	737	453	243	131	106	105	105	105	614	
Oct	0700	4	0	0	2	3	4	4	3	2	1	0	0	0	0	0	0	0	0	1700
	0800	165	8	9	35	96	139	159	155	126	77	16	8	8	8	8	8	8	25	1600
	0900	233	14	14	16	88	161	207	220	199	148	68	15	14	14	14	14	14	66	1500
	1000	262	18	18	18	39	128	196	233	234	199	133	43	18	18	18	18	18	104	1400
	1100	274	20	20	20	21	64	153	213	241	231	186	109	27	20	20	20	20	128	1300
	1200	278	21	21	21	21	23	87	171	223	242	223	171	87	23	21	21	21	136	1200
	HALF DAY TOTALS		71	71	108	266	519	780	925	925	779	513	256	106	72	71	71	71	391	
Nov	0800	36	1	1	4	18	29	34	35	30	20	6	1	1	1	1	1	1	2	1600
	0900	179	8	8	9	52	115	156	171	161	125	67	10	8	8	8	8	8	26	1500
	1000	233	12	12	12	22	104	172	212	218	191	133	49	13	12	12	12	12	55	1400
	1100	255	15	15	15	15	52	142	204	234	228	186	114	26	15	15	15	15	77	1300
	1200	261	15	15	15	15	17	85	168	222	240	222	168	85	17	15	15	15	85	1200
	HALF DAY TOTALS		44	44	47	117	310	555	713	760	686	502	255	85	44	44	44	44	204	
Dec	0900	140	5	5	6	36	86	120	133	127	100	56	8	5	5	5	5	5	13	1500
	1000	214	10	10	10	16	91	156	194	201	179	126	49	10	10	10	10	10	38	1400
	1100	242	12	12	12	13	46	134	195	225	220	180	111	25	12	12	12	12	57	1300
	1200	250	13	13	13	13	14	81	163	215	233	215	168	81	14	13	13	13	65	1200
	HALF DAY TOTALS		33	33	34	73	233	458	610	665	616	468	247	76	34	33	33	33	141	
			N	NNW	NW	WNW	W	WSW	SW	SSW	S	SSE	SE	ESE	E	ENE	NE	NNE	Hor.	PM

Notes: 1. Clearness number = 1.00; Ground reflectance = 0.20.

2. Figures shown are for 21st day of each month.

Table 17 Solar Intensity (E_{DN}) and Solar Heat Gain Factors (SHGF) for 56° North Latitude

Date	Solar Time	Direct Normal Btu/(h·ft²)	N	NNE	NE	ENE	E	ESE	SE	SSE	S	SSW	SW	WSW	W	WNW	NW	NNW	Hor.	Solar Time
Jan	0900	78	3	3	3	21	49	67	74	70	55	30	4	3	3	3	3	3	5	1500
	1000	170	7	7	7	13	74	126	156	162	143	100	38	7	7	7	7	7	21	1400
	1100	207	9	9	9	10	40	116	169	194	190	156	96	21	9	9	9	9	34	1300
	1200	217	10	10	10	10	11	71	144	190	205	190	144	71	11	10	10	10	40	1200
	HALF DAY TOTALS		23	23	24	46	163	343	468	517	487	378	206	61	24	23	23	23	80	
Feb	0800	115	4	4	21	64	95	109	107	88	55	12	4	4	4	4	4	4	10	1600
	0900	203	10	10	11	71	139	183	197	182	136	66	10	10	10	10	10	10	36	1500
	1000	246	13	13	13	28	115	184	223	227	196	133	45	14	13	13	13	13	65	1400
	1100	262	15	15	15	16	57	148	210	239	232	188	112	25	15	15	15	15	84	1300
	1200	267	16	16	16	16	17	86	171	225	244	225	171	86	17	16	16	16	91	1200
	HALF DAY TOTALS		49	50	66	182	409	666	821	846	737	509	253	89	50	49	49	49	241	
Mar	0700	128	6	16	65	101	121	122	105	70	21	6	6	6	6	6	6	6	14	1700
	0800	215	12	13	61	136	185	205	194	152	84	15	12	12	12	12	12	12	49	1600
	0900	253	16	16	23	105	179	224	233	207	148	61	17	16	16	16	16	16	89	1500
	1000	272	19	19	20	46	136	203	238	236	198	128	39	20	19	19	19	19	122	1400
	1100	282	21	21	21	22	68	156	215	241	230	184	106	27	21	21	21	21	142	1300
	1200	284	22	22	22	22	24	86	170	222	241	222	170	86	24	22	22	22	149	1200
	HALF DAY TOTALS		85	97	200	419	699	956	1071	1016	800	502	258	118	86	85	85	85	491	
Apr	0600	122	13	58	95	118	121	107	75	29	7	7	7	7	7	7	7	7	18	1800
	0700	201	15	51	123	173	195	188	152	91	21	14	14	14	14	14	14	14	56	1700
	0800	239	19	23	95	167	211	223	201	148	68	20	19	19	19	19	19	19	101	1600
	0900	260	23	24	44	126	190	223	223	189	126	44	24	23	23	23	23	23	140	1500
	1000	272	26	26	27	63	142	196	220	212	171	102	33	26	26	26	26	26	170	1400
	1100	278	28	28	28	30	74	147	195	213	200	156	86	31	28	28	28	28	189	1300
	1200	280	28	28	28	28	31	79	149	194	210	194	149	79	31	28	28	28	195	1200
	HALF DAY TOTALS		139	226	430	694	951	1132	1147	982	699	437	252	154	132	131	131	131	772	
May	0500	93	36	68	89	95	88	66	33	7	6	6	6	6	6	6	6	7	14	1900
	0600	175	33	99	148	174	173	147	97	31	14	14	14	14	14	14	14	14	48	1800
	0700	219	21	77	149	195	212	197	152	81	22	19	19	19	19	19	19	19	92	1700
	0800	244	25	38	115	179	215	218	189	131	52	25	24	24	24	24	24	24	135	1600
	0900	259	28	30	62	136	189	213	206	168	102	36	28	28	28	28	28	28	171	1500
	1000	268	31	31	33	75	141	185	200	187	145	80	33	31	31	31	31	31	199	1400
	1100	273	32	32	32	35	76	135	174	187	172	131	71	35	32	32	32	32	216	1300
	1200	275	33	33	33	33	36	71	129	168	181	168	129	71	36	33	33	33	222	1200
	HALF DAY TOTALS		222	391	644	906	1112	1202	1120	878	604	392	256	187	172	170	170	173	986	
Jun	0400	21	13	19	22	21	18	11	3	1	1	1	1	1	1	1	2	5	3	2000
	0500	122	53	94	119	126	115	85	40	10	9	9	9	9	9	9	9	12	25	1900
	0600	185	42	111	160	185	182	152	97	30	16	16	16	16	16	16	16	17	62	1800
	0700	222	25	86	156	199	213	195	147	74	24	22	22	22	22	22	22	22	105	1700
	0800	243	27	46	122	181	213	213	181	122	46	27	26	26	26	26	26	26	146	1600
	0900	257	30	32	69	139	187	206	196	156	91	34	30	30	30	30	30	30	181	1500
	1000	265	33	33	36	79	139	178	190	174	132	71	35	33	33	33	33	33	208	1400
	1100	269	34	34	35	38	76	129	164	174	159	119	65	37	34	34	34	34	225	1300
	1200	271	35	35	35	35	38	68	119	155	168	155	119	68	38	35	35	35	231	1200
	HALF DAY TOTALS		275	473	738	989	1162	1207	1082	822	562	376	260	203	190	189	189	196	1070	
Jul	0500	91	37	69	89	95	88	66	33	8	7	7	7	7	7	7	7	8	16	1900
	0600	169	34	98	145	170	170	143	95	31	15	14	14	14	14	14	14	15	50	1800
	0700	212	23	77	147	192	208	193	148	79	23	20	20	20	20	20	20	20	93	1700
	0800	237	26	40	115	177	211	214	185	128	51	26	25	25	25	25	25	25	135	1600
	0900	252	29	31	63	135	186	209	201	164	99	36	29	29	29	29	29	29	171	1500
	1000	261	32	32	34	76	139	181	196	182	142	78	35	32	32	32	32	32	198	1400
	1100	265	33	33	33	37	76	133	171	183	168	128	70	36	33	33	33	33	215	1300
	1200	267	34	34	34	34	37	71	126	164	177	164	126	71	37	34	34	34	221	1200
	HALF DAY TOTALS		231	398	646	901	1097	1180	1096	859	593	390	259	193	179	177	177	180	987	
Aug	0500	1	0	1	1	1	1	1	0	0	0	0	0	0	0	0	0	0	0	1900
	0600	112	14	56	91	111	114	101	71	28	8	8	8	8	8	8	8	8	20	1800
	0700	187	16	51	119	165	186	179	144	86	22	15	15	15	15	15	15	15	58	1700
	0800	225	20	25	94	162	203	214	192	142	66	22	20	20	20	20	20	20	101	1600
	0900	246	25	26	46	124	184	216	215	182	121	44	26	25	25	25	25	25	140	1500
	1000	258	28	28	30	65	139	191	213	204	165	99	34	28	28	28	28	28	169	1400
	1100	264	30	30	30	32	74	143	189	206	193	152	84	33	30	30	30	30	187	1300
	1200	266	30	30	30	30	30	78	155	188	203	188	145	78	33	30	30	30	198	1200
	HALF DAY TOTALS		149	235	429	680	923	1092	1104	946	678	431	256	163	142	140	140	141	771	
Sep	0700	107	6	15	56	87	104	105	90	60	19	6	6	6	6	6	6	6	14	1700
	0800	194	12	14	58	126	171	189	179	140	78	16	12	12	12	12	12	12	48	1600
	0900	233	17	17	24	100	170	211	220	195	140	59	18	17	17	17	17	17	86	1500
	1000	253	20	20	21	46	131	194	227	225	189	123	39	21	20	20	20	20	118	1400
	1100	263	22	22	22	24	67	150	206	230	220	176	103	28	22	22	22	22	137	1300
	1200	266	23	23	23	23	25	85	163	213	231	213	163	85	25	23	23	23	144	1200
	HALF DAY TOTALS		89	99	191	391	652	893	1004	958	761	484	255	121	90	89	89	89	474	
Oct	0800	104	4	5	20	59	87	100	98	81	50	11	4	4	4	4	4	4	10	1600
	0900	193	10	10	11	68	132	173	186	171	129	63	11	10	10	10	10	10	37	1500
	1000	231	14	14	14	28	111	176	213	216	186	127	44	14	14	14	14	14	64	1400
	1100	248	16	16	16	17	56	142	202	229	222	180	108	25	16	16	16	16	84	1300
	1200	253	16	16	16	16	18	83	164	216	234	216	164	83	18	16	16	16	91	1200
	HALF DAY TOTALS		52	52	68	177	390	633	779	804	702	487	246	90	53	52	52	52	240	
Nov	0900	76	3	3	3	21	48	66	72	69	54	29	4	3	3	3	3	3	6	1500
	1000	165	7	7	7	13	72	122	152	157	139	98	37	7	7	7	7	7	21	1400
	1100	201	9	9	9	10	39	113	165	190	186	152	94	21	9	9	9	9	35	1300
	1200	211	10	10	10	10	11	70	140	186	200	186	140	70	11	10	10	10	40	1200
	HALF DAY TOTALS		24	24	24	47	161	336	457	505	475	369	202	61	24	24	24	24	81	
Dec	0900	5	0	0	0	1	3	4	5	5	4	2	0	0	0	0	0	0	0	1500
	1000	113	4	4	4	7	47	82	103	107	96	68	27	4	4	4	4	4	9	1400
	1100	166	6	6	6	7	30	92	135	156	154	127	78	17	6	6	6	6	19	1300
	1200	180	7	7	7	7	8	59	120	159	171	159	120	59	8	7	7	7	23	1200
	HALF DAY TOTALS		14	14	14	20	88	217	311	354	343	277	163	47	15	14	14	14	40	
			N	NNW	NW	WNW	W	WSW	SW	SSW	S	SSE	SE	ESE	E	ENE	NE	NNE	Hor.	PM

Notes: 1. Clearness number = 1.00; Ground reflectance = 0.20. 2. Figures shown are for 21st day of each month.

Table 18 Solar Intensity (E_{DN}) and Solar Heat Gain Factors (SHGF) for 64° North Latitude

Date	Solar Time	Direct Normal Btu/(h·ft²)	N	NNE	NE	ENE	E	ESE	SE	SSE	S	SSW	SW	WSW	W	WNW	NW	NNW	Hor.	Solar Time
Jan	1000	22	1	1	1	1	9	16	20	21	19	13	5	1	1	1	1	1	1	1400
	1100	81	3	3	3	3	15	45	67	77	75	62	38	8	3	3	3	3	6	1300
	1200	100	3	3	3	3	4	33	67	89	96	89	67	33	4	3	3	3	8	1200
	HALF DAY TOTALS		5	5	5	6	25	79	121	142	141	119	75	23	5	5	5	5	11	
Feb	0800	18	1	1	3	10	15	17	17	14	9	2	1	1	1	1	1	1	1	1600
	0900	134	5	5	6	43	89	118	128	119	90	45	6	5	5	5	5	5	13	1500
	1000	190	8	8	8	18	87	144	176	180	157	108	38	9	8	8	8	8	28	1400
	1100	215	10	10	10	11	44	122	177	202	197	160	97	20	10	10	10	10	41	1300
	1200	222	11	11	11	11	12	73	147	194	210	194	147	73	12	11	11	11	45	1200
	HALF DAY TOTALS		29	30	33	89	244	446	578	617	560	411	212	66	30	29	29	29	106	
Mar	0700	95	4	11	47	74	90	91	79	53	17	4	4	4	4	4	4	4	9	1700
	0800	185	9	10	46	113	158	177	170	135	78	14	9	9	9	9	9	9	32	1600
	0900	227	13	13	16	88	159	203	215	194	143	64	14	13	13	13	13	13	59	1500
	1000	249	16	16	16	35	122	190	226	228	194	130	42	16	16	16	16	16	84	1400
	1100	260	17	17	17	18	60	148	209	236	228	184	109	25	17	17	17	17	99	1300
	1200	263	18	18	18	18	19	85	168	221	239	221	168	85	19	18	18	18	105	1200
	HALF DAY TOTALS		68	74	150	334	596	854	984	958	779	504	257	104	68	68	68	68	335	
Apr	0500	27	8	18	24	27	26	20	12	2	1	1	1	1	1	1	1	1	2	1900
	0600	133	12	59	102	127	132	118	84	35	8	8	8	8	8	8	8	8	21	1800
	0700	194	14	41	113	163	189	185	153	96	25	13	13	13	13	13	13	13	51	1700
	0800	228	17	19	79	153	201	217	201	153	79	19	17	17	17	17	17	17	85	1600
	0900	248	21	21	32	111	180	219	225	197	138	55	22	21	21	21	21	21	116	1500
	1000	260	23	23	24	51	134	194	225	221	185	118	38	24	23	23	23	23	140	1400
	1100	266	24	24	24	26	68	148	202	225	214	171	99	29	24	24	24	24	155	1300
	1200	268	25	25	25	25	27	83	159	208	224	208	159	83	27	25	25	25	160	1200
	HALF DAY TOTALS		131	218	410	671	943	1150	1186	1036	763	487	273	149	121	120	120	120	651	
May	0400	51	30	44	51	51	43	28	8	3	3	3	3	3	3	3	10	6	2000
	0500	132	48	95	125	135	125	96	50	11	9	9	9	9	9	9	9	11	26	1900
	0600	185	28	97	150	181	183	158	109	40	15	15	15	15	15	15	15	15	55	1800
	0700	218	21	63	138	189	211	201	161	94	24	19	19	19	19	19	19	19	90	1700
	0800	239	23	28	97	167	209	220	198	146	68	25	23	23	23	23	23	23	124	1600
	0900	252	26	27	45	122	183	215	215	184	123	46	27	26	26	26	26	26	152	1500
	1000	261	28	28	30	61	135	188	212	205	167	102	36	28	28	28	28	28	174	1400
	1100	265	30	30	30	32	72	141	188	207	195	154	87	33	30	30	30	30	188	1300
	1200	267	30	30	30	30	33	78	146	189	204	189	146	78	33	30	30	30	192	1200
	HALF DAY TOTALS		247	425	680	950	1177	1291	1218	985	708	465	288	191	169	168	168	176	911	
Jun	0300	21	17	21	22	20	14	6	2	1	1	1	1	1	1	1	2	10	3	2100
	0400	93	53	83	96	94	78	50	14	7	7	7	7	7	7	7	7	21	16	2000
	0500	154	62	114	148	158	145	110	55	14	12	12	12	12	12	12	12	14	39	1900
	0600	194	36	107	162	191	192	163	110	39	18	17	17	17	17	17	17	18	71	1800
	0700	221	24	71	145	193	213	200	158	89	25	22	22	22	22	22	22	22	105	1700
	0800	239	25	33	104	170	208	216	192	139	62	27	25	25	25	25	25	25	137	1600
	0900	251	28	29	51	124	181	210	208	175	115	43	29	28	28	28	28	28	165	1500
	1000	258	30	30	32	65	134	183	204	195	157	94	36	30	30	30	30	30	186	1400
	1100	262	32	32	32	34	72	137	180	196	184	144	82	35	32	32	32	32	199	1300
	1200	263	32	32	32	32	35	76	138	179	193	179	138	76	35	32	32	32	203	1200
	HALF DAY TOTALS		326	538	806	1066	1256	1318	1195	947	679	455	297	212	192	191	192	216	1021	
Jul	0400	53	32	47	55	54	46	29	9	4	4	4	4	4	4	4	11	8	2000
	0500	128	49	94	123	133	124	95	50	11	10	10	10	10	10	10	10	11	28	1900
	0600	179	30	96	148	177	180	155	106	39	16	15	15	15	15	15	15	15	57	1800
	0700	211	22	64	137	186	207	197	157	92	25	20	20	20	20	20	20	20	92	1700
	0800	231	24	30	97	165	205	215	193	142	67	26	24	24	24	24	24	24	124	1600
	0900	245	27	28	47	121	180	211	211	179	120	46	28	27	27	27	27	27	152	1500
	1000	253	29	29	31	62	134	185	208	200	164	100	37	29	29	29	29	29	174	1400
	1100	257	31	31	31	33	72	139	185	202	191	151	86	34	31	31	31	31	187	1300
	1200	259	31	31	31	31	34	78	143	185	200	185	143	78	34	31	31	31	192	1200
	HALF DAY TOTALS		258	434	684	946	1163	1269	1193	965	697	462	292	198	177	175	175	185	918	
Aug	0500	29	9	20	27	30	28	22	13	2	2	2	2	2	2	2	2	2	3	1900
	0600	123	13	58	97	121	125	111	80	34	9	9	9	9	9	9	9	9	23	1800
	0700	181	15	42	109	157	180	176	145	92	26	14	14	14	14	14	14	14	53	1700
	0800	214	19	21	78	148	193	208	192	147	76	21	19	19	19	19	19	19	87	1600
	0900	234	22	22	34	109	174	211	217	189	133	55	22	22	22	22	22	22	117	1500
	1000	246	25	25	26	52	131	188	217	214	178	114	39	25	25	25	25	25	140	1400
	1100	252	26	26	26	28	69	144	196	217	207	166	97	31	26	26	26	26	154	1300
	1200	254	27	27	27	27	29	82	155	201	217	201	155	82	29	27	27	27	159	1200
	HALF DAY TOTALS		142	226	410	657	914	1109	1141	997	740	478	275	158	131	130	130	130	656	
Sep	0700	77	4	10	39	62	74	75	65	44	15	4	4	4	4	4	4	4	8	1700
	0800	163	10	10	43	103	143	160	154	123	71	14	10	10	10	10	10	10	31	1600
	0900	206	14	14	17	83	148	189	200	181	133	61	15	14	14	14	14	14	57	1500
	1000	229	16	16	17	35	116	179	213	214	183	123	41	17	16	16	16	16	81	1400
	1100	240	18	18	18	19	59	141	198	224	216	174	104	26	18	18	18	18	96	1300
	1200	244	19	19	19	19	21	82	160	209	227	209	160	82	21	19	19	19	101	1200
	HALF DAY TOTALS		71	77	142	307	547	787	910	891	731	480	249	106	72	71	71	71	324	
Oct	0800	17	1	1	3	10	14	16	16	13	8	2	1	1	1	1	1	1	1	1600
	0900	122	5	5	6	40	82	109	118	110	83	42	6	5	5	5	5	5	13	1500
	1000	176	9	9	9	18	83	135	165	169	147	102	36	9	9	9	9	9	29	1400
	1100	201	11	11	11	11	43	116	167	191	186	152	92	20	11	11	11	11	41	1300
	1200	208	11	11	11	11	13	70	140	184	199	184	140	70	13	11	11	11	46	1200
	HALF DAY TOTALS		31	31	34	86	231	420	542	580	527	388	202	66	32	31	31	31	108	
Nov	1000	23	1	1	1	1	10	17	21	22	20	14	5	1	1	1	1	1	1	1400
	1100	79	3	3	3	3	15	44	65	75	74	61	37	8	3	3	3	3	6	1300
	1200	97	4	4	4	4	4	32	66	87	93	87	66	32	4	4	4	4	8	1200
	HALF DAY TOTALS		5	5	5	6	26	79	120	141	140	117	74	23	6	5	5	5	11	
Dec	1100	4	0	0	0	0	1	2	3	4	4	3	2	0	0	0	0	0	0	1300
	1200	16	0	0	0	0	1	5	14	15	14	11	5	1	0	0	0	0	1	1200
	HALF DAY TOTALS		0	0	0	0	1	5	9	11	11	10	7	3	0	0	0	0	1	
			N	NNW	NW	WNW	W	WSW	SW	SSW	S	SSE	SE	ESE	E	ENE	NE	NNE	Hor.	PM

Notes: 1. Clearness number = 1.00; Ground reflectance = 0.20.

2. Figures shown are for 21st day of each month.

Thermal Properties of Typical Building and Insulating Materials (Design Values)

Selected from American Society of Heating, Refrigerating and Air-Conditioning Engineers (ASHRAE), 1993 *Handbook of Fundamentals,* Table 4.

BUILDING BOARD

Description	Density LBS/FT³	Conductivity (k) $\frac{\text{BTUS} \times \text{INCH}}{\text{HR} \times \text{FT}^2 \times °\text{F}}$	Conductance (C) $\frac{\text{BTUS}}{\text{HR} \times \text{FT}^2 \times °\text{F}}$	Resistance (R) per inch thickness $\frac{°\text{F} \times \text{FT}^2 \times \text{HR}}{\text{BTUS} \times \text{INCH}}$	Resistance (R) for thickness listed $\frac{°\text{F} \times \text{FT}^2 \times \text{HR}}{\text{BTUS}}$	Specific Heat $\frac{\text{BTUS}}{\text{LBS} \times °\text{F}}$
Gypsum or Plaster board						
0.375 in.	50	—	3.10	—	0.32	0.26
0.5 in.	50	—	2.22	—	0.45	—
0.625 in.	50	—	1.78	—	0.56	—
Plywood (Douglas Fir)	34	0.80	—	1.25	—	0.29
Plywood (Douglas Fir)						
0.25 in.	34	—	3.20	—	0.31	—
0.375 in.	34	—	2.13	—	0.47	—
0.5 in.	34	—	1.60	—	0.62	—
0.625 in.	34	—	1.29	—	0.77	—
Plywood or wood panels						
0.75 in.	34	—	1.07	—	0.93	0.29
Particleboard						
(medium density)	50	0.94	—	1.06	—	0.31

BUILDING MEMBRANE

Description	Density LBS/FT³	Conductivity (k)	Conductance (C)	Resistance (R) per inch thickness	Resistance (R) for thickness listed	Specific Heat
Vapor-seal, plastic film	—	—	—	—	negligible	—

INSULATING MATERIALS

Blanket and Batt

Description	Density LBS/FT³	Conductivity (k)	Conductance (C)	Resistance (R) per inch thickness	Resistance (R) for thickness listed	Specific Heat
Mineral fiber, fibrous form processed from rock, slag, or glass						
approx. 3–4 in.	0.4–2.0	—	0.091	—	11.00	—
approx. 3.5 in.	0.4–2.0	—	0.077	—	13.00	—
approx. 3.5 in.	1.2–1.6	—	0.067	—	15.00	—
approx. 5.5–6.5 in.	0.4–2.0	—	0.053	—	19.00	—
approx. 5.5 in.	0.6–1.0	—	0.048	—	21.00	—
approx. 6–7.5 in.	0.4–2.0	—	0.045	—	22.00	—
approx. 8.25–10 in.	0.4–2.0	—	0.033	—	30.00	—
approx. 10–13 in.	0.4–2.0	—	0.026	—	38.00	—

Board

Description	Density LBS/FT³	Conductivity (k)	Conductance (C)	Resistance (R) per inch thickness	Resistance (R) for thickness listed	Specific Heat
Expanded polystyrene, extruded (smooth skin surface)	1.8–3.5	0.20	—	5.00	—	0.29
Expanded polystyrene, molded beads	1.25	0.25	—	4.00	—	—

DESCRIPTION	DENSITY LBS/FT³	CONDUCTIVITY (κ) BTUS × INCH HR × FT² × °F	CONDUCTANCE (C) BTUS HR × FT² × °F	RESISTANCE (R) PER INCH THICKNESS °F × FT² × HR BTUS × INCH	RESISTANCE (R) FOR THICKNESS LISTED °F × FT² × HR BTUS	SPECIFIC HEAT BTUS LBS × °F
ROOFING						
Asphalt roll roofing	70	—	6.50	—	0.15	0.36
Asphalt shingles	70	—	2.27	—	0.44	0.30
Wood shingles, plain and plastic film faced	—	—	1.06	—	0.94	0.31
MASONRY MATERIALS						
Concrete Blocks						
Normal weight aggregate (sand & gravel)						
8 in., 33-36 lb,						
2 or 3 cores	126-136	—	0.90–1.03	—	1.11–0.97	0.22
12 in., 50 lb, 2 cores	125	—	0.81	—	1.23	0.22
Concrete						
Sand and gravel or stone aggregate concretes						
(Concretes with more than 50% quartz or quartzite sand have conductivities in the higher end of the range.)						
	150	10.0–20.0	—	0.10–0.05	—	—
	140	9.0–18.0	—	0.11–0.06	—	0.19–0.24
	130	7.0–13.0	—	0.14–0.08	—	—

	DENSITY	CONDUCTIVITY	CONDUCTANCE	RESISTANCE PER INCH	RESISTANCE FOR THICKNESS	SPECIFIC HEAT
WOODS						
Hardwoods						
Oak	41.2–46.8	1.12–1.25	—	0.89–0.80	—	0.39
Birch	42.6–45.4	1.16–1.22	—	0.87–0.82	—	
Maple	39.8–44.0	1.09–1.19	—	0.92–0.84	—	
Ash	38.4–41.9	1.06–1.14	—	0.94–0.88	—	
Softwoods						
Southern Pine	35.6–41.2	1.00–1.12	—	1.00–0.89	—	0.39
Douglas Fir-Larch	33.5–36.3	0.95–1.01	—	1.06–0.99	—	
Southern Cypress	31.4–32.1	0.90–0.92	—	1.11–1.09	—	
Hem-Fir, Spruce-Pine-Fir	24.5–31.4	0.74–0.90	—	1.35–1.11	—	
West Coast Woods, Cedars	21.7–31.4	0.68–0.90	—	1.48–1.11	—	
California Redwood	24.5–28.0	0.74–0.82	—	1.35–1.22	—	

North Latitude, Elevation, and Outside Winter Design Temperature for Selected Cities in the U.S. and Canada

Adapted and reprinted from the *Cooling and Heating Manual*, U. S. Department of Housing and Urban Development Office of Policy Development and Research.

State and City	Latitude °	Latitude ′	Elevation (feet)	Outside Winter Design Temperature (°F)	State and City	Latitude °	Latitude ′	Elevation (feet)	Outside Winter Design Temperature (°F)
ALABAMA					**DELAWARE**				
Anniston	33	4	599	5	Wilmington	39	4	78	0
Birmingham	33	3	610	10	**DISTRICT OF COLUMBIA**				
Mobile	30	4	211	15	Washington	38	5	14	0
Montgomery	32	2	195	10	**FLORIDA**				
ARIZONA					Jacksonville	30	3	24	25
Flagstaff	35	1	6,973	-10	Key West	24	3	6	45
Phoenix	33	3	1,117	25	Miami	25	5	7	35
Tucson	33	1	2,584	25	Pensacola	30	3	13	20
Winslow	35	0	4,880	-10	Tallahassee	30	2	58	25
Yuma	32	4	199	30	Tampa	28	0	19	30
ARKANSAS					**GEORGIA**				
Fort Smith	35	2	449	10	Atlanta	33	4	1,005	10
Little Rock	34	4	257	5	Augusta	33	2	143	10
CALIFORNIA					Macon	32	4	356	15
Bakersfield	35	2	495	25	Savannah	32	1	52	20
Eureka	41	0	217	30	**IDAHO**				
Fresno	36	5	326	25	Boise	43	3	2,842	-10
Los Angeles	34	0	99	35	Lewiston	46	2	1,413	5
Oakland	37	4	3	30	Pocatello	43	0	4,444	-5
Sacramento	38	3	17	30	Twin Falls	42	3	4,148	-10
San Diego	32	4	19	35	**ILLINOIS**				
San Francisco	37	4	8	35	Chicago	41	5	594	-10
San Jose	37	2	70	25	Danville	40	1	558	-5
COLORADO					Moline	41	3	582	-10
Denver	39	5	5,283	-10	Peoria	40	4	652	-10
Fort Collins	40	4	5,001	-30	Springfield	39	5	587	-10
Grand Junction	39	1	4,849	-15	**INDIANA**				
Pueblo	38	2	4,639	-20	Evansville	38	0	381	0
CONNECTICUT					Fort Wayne	41	0	791	-10
Bridgeport	41	1	7	0	Indianapolis	39	4	793	-10
Hartford	41	5	15	0	South Bend	41	4	773	-5
New Haven	41	2	6	0					
Waterbury	41	3	605	-15					

State and City	Latitude °	Latitude '	Elevation (feet)	Outside Winter Design Temperature (°F)	State and City	Latitude °	Latitude '	Elevation (feet)	Outside Winter Design Temperature (°F)
IOWA					Springfield	42	1	247	-10
Cedar Rapids	41	5	863	-5	Worcester	42	2	986	0
Des Moines	41	3	948	-15					
Dubuque	42	2	1,065	-20	**MICHIGAN**				
Fort Dodge	42	3	1,111	-20	Alpena	45	0	689	-10
Keokuk	40	2	526	-10	Detroit	42	2	633	-10
Sioux City	42	2	1,095	-20	Escanaba	45	4	594	-15
Waterloo	42	3	868	-15	Flint	43	0	766	-10
					Grand Rapids	42	5	681	-10
KANSAS					Kalamazoo	42	1	930	-5
Dodge City	37	5	2,594	-10	Lansing	42	5	852	-10
Salina	38	5	1,271	-15	Marquette	46	3	677	-10
Topeka	39	0	877	-10	Sault Ste. Marie	46	3	721	-20
Wichita	37	4	1,321	-10					
					MINNESOTA				
KENTUCKY					Alexandria	45	5	1,421	-25
Lexington	38	0	979	0	Duluth	46	5	1,426	-25
Louisville	38	1	474	0	Minneapolis	44	5	822	-20
					St. Cloud	45	4	1,034	-25
LOUISIANA					St. Paul	44	5	822	-20
Alexandria	31	2	92	20					
New Orleans	30	0	3	20	**MISSISSIPPI**				
Shreveport	32	3	252	20	Jackson	32	2	330	15
					Meridian	32	2	294	10
MAINE					Vicksburg	32	2	234	10
Millinocket	45	4	405	-20					
Portland	43	4	61	-5	**MISSOURI**				
Waterville	44	3	89	-15	Columbia	39	0	778	-10
					Kansas City	39	1	742	-10
MARYLAND					St. Joseph	39	5	809	-10
Baltimore	39	1	146	0	St. Louis	38	5	535	0
Frederick	39	2	294	-5	Springfield	37	1	1,265	-10
Salisbury	38	2	52	10					
					MONTANA				
MASSACHUSETTS					Billings	45	5	3,567	-25
Boston	42	2	15	0	Butte	46	0	5,526	-20
Fall River	41	4	190	-10	Great Falls	47	3	3,664	-20
Lowell	42	3	90	-15	Havre	48	3	2,488	-30
New Bedford	41	4	70	0					

State and City	Latitude °	Latitude '	Elevation (feet)	Outside Winter Design Temperature (°F)	State and City	Latitude °	Latitude '	Elevation (feet)	Outside Winter Design Temperature (°F)
Helena	46	4	3,893	-20	Jamestown	42	1	1,390	-10
Kalispell	48	2	2,965	-20	New York City	40	5	132	0
Miles City	46	3	2,629	-35	Oneonta	42	3	1,150	-15
Missoula	46	5	3,200	-20	Oswego	43	3	300	-10
					Rochester	43	1	543	-5
NEBRASKA					Syracuse	43	1	424	-10
Grand Island	41	0	1,841	-20	Watertown	44	0	497	-15
Lincoln	40	5	1,150	-10					
Norfolk	42	0	1,532	-15	**NORTH CAROLINA**				
North Platte	41	1	2,779	-20	Asheville	35	3	2,170	0
Omaha	41	2	978	-10	Charlotte	35	1	735	10
					Greensboro	36	1	897	10
NEVADA					Raleigh	35	5	433	10
Las Vegas	36	1	2,162	20	Wilmington	34	2	30	15
Reno	39	3	4,404	-5					
Tonopah	38	0	5,426	5	**NORTH DAKOTA**				
Winnemucca	40	5	4,299	-15	Bismark	46	5	1,647	-30
					Devils Lake	48	1	1,471	-30
NEW HAMPSHIRE					Fargo	46	5	900	-25
Berlin	44	3	1,110	-25	Grand Forks	48	0	832	-25
Concord	43	1	339	-15	Williston	48	1	1,877	-35
Keene	43	0	490	-20					
					OHIO				
NEW JERSEY					Akron	41	0	1,210	-5
Atlantic City	39	3	11	5	Cincinnati	39	1	761	0
Newark	40	4	11	0	Cleveland	41	2	777	0
Trenton	40	1	144	0	Columbus	40	0	812	-10
					Dayton	39	5	997	0
NEW MEXICO					Lima	40	4	860	-5
Albuquerque	35	0	5,310	0	Sandusky	41	3	606	0
Roswell	33	2	3,643	-10					
Santa Fe	35	4	7,045	0	**OKLAHOMA**				
					Ardmore	34	2	880	10
NEW YORK					Bartlesville	36	5	715	-10
Albany	42	5	277	-10	Oklahoma City	35	2	1,280	0
Binghamton	42	1	858	-10	Tulsa	36	1	650	0
Buffalo	43	0	705	-5					
Cortland	42	4	1,129	-10	**OREGON**				
Glens Falls	43	2	321	-15	Baker	44	5	3,368	-5
Ithaca	42	3	950	-15					

State and City	Latitude °	Latitude '	Elevation (feet)	Outside Winter Design Temperature (°F)	State and City	Latitude °	Latitude '	Elevation (feet)	Outside Winter Design Temperature (°F)
Eugene	44	1	364	-15	Brownsville	25	5	16	30
Pendleton	45	4	1,492	-15	Corpus Christi	27	5	43	20
Portland	45	4	21	10	Dallas	32	5	481	0
					Del Rio	29	2	1,072	15
PENNSYLVANIA					El Paso	31	5	3,918	10
Altoona	40	2	1,468	-5	Fort Worth	32	5	544	10
Erie	42	1	732	-5	Galveston	29	2	5	20
Harrisburg	40	1	335	0	Houston	29	4	50	20
New Castle	41	0	825	0	Palestine	31	5	580	15
Philadelphia	39	5	7	0	Port Arthur	30	0	16	20
Pittsburgh	40	3	1,137	0	San Antonio	29	3	792	20
Reading	40	2	226	0					
Scranton	41	2	940	-5	**UTAH**				
Warren	41	5	1,280	-15	Logan	41	4	4,775	-15
Williamsport	41	1	527	-5	Ogden	41	1	4,400	-10
					Salt Lake City	40	5	4,220	-10
RHODE ISLAND									
Providence	41	4	55	0	**VERMONT**				
					Burlington	44	3	331	-10
SOUTH CAROLINA					Rutland	43	3	620	-20
Charleston	32	5	41	15					
Columbia	34	0	217	10	**VIRGINIA**				
Greenville	34	5	957	10	Lynchburg	37	2	947	5
					Norfolk	36	5	26	15
SOUTH DAKOTA					Richmond	37	3	162	15
Huron	44	3	1,282	-20	Roanoke	37	2	1,174	0
Rapid City	44	0	3,165	-20					
Sioux Falls	43	4	1,420	-20	**WASHINGTON**				
					Seattle	47	3	386	15
TENNESSEE					Spokane	47	4	2,357	-15
Chattanooga	35	0	670	10	Tacoma	47	1	350	15
Knoxville	35	5	980	0	Walla Walla	46	1	1,185	-10
Memphis	35	0	263	0	Yakima	46	3	1,061	5
Nashville	36	1	577	0					
					WEST VIRGINIA				
TEXAS					Charleston	38	2	939	0
Abilene	32	3	1,759	15	Elkins	38	5	1,970	-10
Amarillo	35	1	3,607	-10	Huntington	38	2	565	-5
Austin	30	2	597	20	Martinsburg	39	2	537	-5

State/Province and City	Latitude °	Latitude '	Elevation (feet)	Outside Winter Design Temperatures (°F)	State/Province and City	Latitude °	Latitude '	Elevation (feet)	Outside Winter Design Temperatures (°F)
Parkersburg	39	2	615	-10	Vancouver	49	11	0	11
Wheeling	40	1	659	-5					
					MANITOBA				
WISCONSIN					Winnipeg	49	54	814	-29
Ashland	46	3	650	-20					
Eau Claire	44	5	888	-20	**NEW FOUNDLAND**				
Green Bay	44	3	683	-20	Gander	48	57	482	-3
La Crosse	43	5	652	-25					
Madison	43	1	858	-15	**NOVA SCOTIA**				
Milwaukee	43	0	672	-15	Halifax	44	39	98	4
WYOMING					**ONTARIO**				
Casper	42	5	5,319	-20	Kapuskasing	49	25	95	-30
Cheyenne	41	1	6,126	-15	Toronto	43	41	577	0
Lander	42	5	5,563	-18					
Sheridan	44	5	3,942	-30	**QUEBEC**				
					Montreal	45	28	98	-9
ALBERTA									
Edmonton	53	34	2,218	-33	**SASKATCHEWAN**				
					Regina	50	26	1,893	-34
BRITISH COLUMBIA									
Prince George	53	53	2,218	-32					

Average Monthly and Yearly Degree Days for Cities in the U.S. and Canada

Reprinted with permission of the American Society of Heating, Refrigerating and Air-Conditioning Engineers from the 1981 ASHRAE *Handbook of Fundamentals.*

State	Station	Avg. Winter Temp[d]	July	Aug.	Sept.	Oct.	Nov.	Dec.	Jan.	Feb.	Mar.	Apr.	May	June	Yearly Total
Ala.	Birmingham .... A	54.2	0	0	6	93	363	555	592	462	363	108	9	0	2551
	Huntsville .... A	51.3	0	0	12	127	426	663	694	557	434	138	19	0	3070
	Mobile.............................. A	59.9	0	0	0	22	213	357	415	300	211	42	0	0	1560
	Montgomery....................... A	55.4	0	0	0	68	330	527	543	417	316	90	0	0	2291
Alaska	Anchorage .... A	23.0	245	291	516	930	1284	1572	1631	1316	1293	879	592	315	10864
	Fairbanks.......................... A	6.7	171	332	642	1203	1833	2254	2359	1901	1739	1068	555	222	14279
	Juneau.............................. A	32.1	301	338	483	725	921	1135	1237	1070	1073	810	601	381	9075
	Nome................................ A	13.1	481	496	693	1094	1455	1820	1879	1666	1770	1314	930	573	14171
Ariz.	Flagstaff .... A	35.6	46	68	201	558	867	1073	1169	991	911	651	437	180	7152
	Phoenix............................. A	58.5	0	0	0	22	234	415	474	328	217	75	0	0	1765
	Tucson .... A	58.1	0	0	0	25	231	406	471	344	242	75	6	0	1800
	Winslow .... A	43.0	0	0	6	245	711	1008	1054	770	601	291	96	0	4782
	Yuma .... A	64.2	0	0	0	0	108	264	307	190	90	15	0	0	974
Ark.	Fort Smith .... A	50.3	0	0	12	127	450	704	781	596	456	144	22	0	3292
	Little Rock......................... A	50.5	0	0	9	127	465	716	756	577	434	126	9	0	3219
	Texarkana.......................... A	54.2	0	0	0	78	345	561	626	468	350	105	0	0	2533
Calif.	Bakersfield .... A	55.4	0	0	0	37	282	502	546	364	267	105	19	0	2122
	Bishop.............................. A	46.0	0	0	48	260	576	797	874	680	555	306	143	36	4275
	Blue Canyon....................... A	42.2	28	37	108	347	594	781	896	795	806	597	412	195	5596
	Burbank............................ A	58.6	0	0	6	43	177	301	366	277	239	138	81	18	1646
	Eureka C	49.9	270	257	258	329	414	499	546	470	505	438	372	285	4643
	Fresno.............................. A	53.3	0	0	0	84	354	577	605	426	335	162	62	6	2611
	Long Beach .... A	57.8	0	0	9	47	171	316	397	311	264	171	93	24	1803
	Los Angeles .... A	57.4	28	28	42	78	180	291	372	302	288	219	158	81	2061
	Los Angeles C	60.3	0	0	6	31	132	229	310	230	202	123	68	18	1349
	Mt. Shasta C	41.2	25	34	123	406	696	902	983	784	738	525	347	159	5722
	Oakland .... A	53.5	53	50	45	127	309	481	527	400	353	255	180	90	2870
	Red Bluff .... A	53.8	0	0	0	53	318	555	605	428	341	168	47	0	2515
	Sacramento........................ A	53.9	0	0	0	56	321	546	583	414	332	178	72	0	2502
	Sacramento........................ C	54.4	0	0	0	62	312	533	561	392	310	173	76	0	2419
	Sandberg........................... C	46.8	0	0	30	202	480	691	778	661	620	426	264	57	4209
	San Diego.......................... A	59.5	9	0	21	43	135	236	298	235	214	135	90	42	1458
	San Francisco .... A	53.4	81	78	60	143	306	462	508	395	363	279	214	126	3015
	San Francisco C	55.1	192	174	102	118	231	388	443	336	319	279	239	180	3001
	Santa Maria .... A	54.3	99	93	96	146	270	391	459	370	363	282	233	165	2967
Colo.	Alamosa .... A	29.7	65	99	279	639	1065	1420	1476	1162	1020	696	440	168	8529
	Colorado Springs .... A	37.3	9	25	132	456	825	1032	1128	938	893	582	319	84	6423
	Denver .... A	37.6	6	9	117	428	819	1035	1132	938	887	558	288	66	6283
	Denver C	40.8	0	0	90	366	714	905	1004	851	800	492	254	48	5524
	Grand Junction .... A	39.3	0	0	30	313	786	1113	1209	907	729	387	146	21	5641
	Pueblo.............................. A	40.4	0	0	54	326	750	986	1085	871	772	429	174	15	5462
Conn.	Bridgeport .... A	39.9	0	0	66	307	615	986	1079	966	853	510	208	27	5617
	Hartford .... A	37.3	0	12	117	394	714	1101	1190	1042	908	519	205	33	6235
	New Haven .... A	39.0	0	12	87	347	648	1011	1097	991	871	543	245	45	5897
Del.	Wilmington........................ A	42.5	0	0	51	270	588	927	980	874	735	387	112	6	4930
D.C.	Washington .... A	45.7	0	0	33	217	519	834	871	762	626	288	74	0	4224
Fla.	Apalachicola....................... C	61.2	0	0	0	16	153	319	347	260	180	33	0	0	1308
	Daytona Beach.................... A	64.5	0	0	0	0	75	211	248	190	140	15	0	0	879
	Fort Myers .... A	68.6	0	0	0	0	24	109	146	101	62	0	0	0	442
	Jacksonville .... A	61.9	0	0	0	12	144	310	332	246	174	21	0	0	1239
	Key West .... A	73.1	0	0	0	0	0	28	40	31	9	0	0	0	108
	Lakeland........................... C	66.7	0	0	0	0	57	164	195	146	99	0	0	0	661
	Miami............................... A	71.1	0	0	0	0	0	65	74	56	19	0	0	0	214

[a] Data for United States cities from a publication of the United States Weather Bureau, *Monthly Normals of Temperature, Precipitation and Heating Degree Days*, 1962, are for the period 1931 to 1960 inclusive. These data also include information from the 1963 revisions to this publication, where available.

[b] Data for airport stations, A, and city stations, C, are both given where available.

[c] Data for Canadian cities were computed by the Climatology Division, Department of Transport from normal monthly mean temperatures, and the monthly values of heating degree days data were obtained using the National Research Council computer and a method devised by H. C. S. Thom of the United States Weather Bureau. The heating degree days are based on the period from 1931 to 1960.

[d] For period October to April, inclusive.

State	Station	Avg. Winter Temp[d]	July	Aug.	Sept.	Oct.	Nov.	Dec.	Jan.	Feb.	Mar.	Apr.	May	June	Yearly Total
Fla. (Cont'd)	Miami Beach C	72.5	0	0	0	0	0	40	56	36	9	0	0	0	141
	Orlando .... A	65.7	0	0	0	0	72	198	220	165	105	6	0	0	766
	Pensacola .... A	60.4	0	0	0	19	195	353	400	277	183	36	0	0	1463
	Tallahassee .... A	60.1	0	0	0	28	198	360	375	286	202	36	0	0	1485
	Tampa......................... A	66.4	0	0	0	0	60	171	202	148	102	0	0	0	683
	West Palm Beach......... A	68.4	0	0	0	0	6	65	87	64	31	0	0	0	253
Ga.	Athens .... A	51.8	0	0	12	115	405	632	642	529	431	141	22	0	2929
	Atlanta .... A	51.7	0	0	18	124	417	648	636	518	428	147	25	0	2961
	Augusta .... A	54.5	0	0	0	78	333	552	549	445	350	90	0	0	2397
	Columbus .... A	54.8	0	0	0	87	333	543	552	434	338	96	0	0	2383
	Macon .... A	56.2	0	0	0	71	297	502	505	403	295	63	0	0	2136
	Rome .... A	49.9	0	0	24	161	474	701	710	577	468	177	34	0	3326
	Savannah .... A	57.8	0	0	0	47	246	437	437	353	254	45	0	0	1819
	Thomasville C	60.0	0	0	0	25	198	366	394	305	208	33	0	0	1529
Hawaii	Lihue......................... A	72.7	0	0	0	0	0	0	0	0	0	0	0	0	0
	Honolulu .... A	74.2	0	0	0	0	0	0	0	0	0	0	0	0	0
	Hilo .... A	71.9	0	0	0	0	0	0	0	0	0	0	0	0	0
Idaho	Boise .... A	39.7	0	0	132	415	792	1017	1113	854	722	438	245	81	5809
	Lewiston .... A	41.0	0	0	123	403	756	933	1063	815	694	426	239	90	5542
	Pocatello .... A	34.8	0	0	172	493	900	1166	1324	1058	905	555	319	141	7033
Ill.	Cairo......................... C	47.9	0	0	36	164	513	791	856	680	539	195	47	0	3821
	Chicago (O'Hare)......... A	35.8	0	12	117	381	807	1166	1265	1086	939	534	260	72	6639
	Chicago (Midway) .... A	37.5	0	0	81	326	753	1113	1209	1044	890	480	211	48	6155
	Chicago........................ C	38.9	0	0	66	279	705	1051	1150	1000	868	489	226	48	5882
	Moline .... A	36.4	0	9	99	335	774	1181	1314	1100	918	450	189	39	6408
	Peoria .... A	38.1	0	6	87	326	759	1113	1218	1025	849	426	183	33	6025
	Rockford..................... A	34.8	6	9	114	400	837	1221	1333	1137	961	516	236	60	6830
	Springfield................... A	40.6	0	0	72	291	696	1023	1135	935	769	354	136	18	5429
Ind.	Evansville .... A	45.0	0	0	66	220	606	896	955	767	620	237	68	0	4435
	Fort Wayne .... A	37.3	0	9	105	378	783	1135	1178	1028	890	471	189	39	6205
	Indianapolis .... A	39.6	0	0	90	316	723	1051	1113	949	809	432	177	39	5699
	South Bend .... A	36.6	0	6	111	372	777	1125	1221	1070	933	525	239	60	6439
Iowa	Burlington .... A	37.6	0	0	93	322	768	1135	1259	1042	859	426	177	33	6114
	Des Moines .... A	35.5	0	6	96	363	828	1225	1370	1137	915	438	180	30	6588
	Dubuque .... A	32.7	12	31	156	450	906	1287	1420	1204	1026	546	260	78	7376
	Sioux City................... A	34.0	0	9	108	369	867	1240	1435	1198	989	483	214	39	6951
	Waterloo .... A	32.6	12	19	138	428	909	1296	1460	1221	1023	531	229	54	7320
Kans.	Concordia..................... A	40.4	0	0	57	276	705	1023	1163	935	781	372	149	18	5479
	Dodge City .... A	42.5	0	0	33	251	666	939	1051	840	719	354	124	9	4986
	Goodland .... A	37.8	0	6	81	381	810	1073	1166	955	884	507	236	42	6141
	Topeka .... A	41.7	0	0	57	270	672	980	1122	893	722	330	124	12	5182
	Wichita....................... A	44.2	0	0	33	229	618	905	1023	804	645	270	87	6	4620
Ky.	Covington..................... A	41.4	0	0	75	291	669	983	1035	893	756	390	149	24	5265
	Lexington .... A	43.8	0	0	54	239	609	902	946	818	685	325	105	0	4683
	Louisville .... A	44.0	0	0	54	248	609	890	930	818	682	315	105	9	4660
La.	Alexandria .... A	57.5	0	0	0	56	273	431	471	361	260	69	0	0	1921
	Baton Rouge .... A	59.8	0	0	0	31	216	369	409	294	208	33	0	0	1560
	Lake Charles .... A	60.5	0	0	0	19	210	341	381	274	195	39	0	0	1459
	New Orleans................. A	61.0	0	0	0	19	192	322	363	258	192	39	0	0	1385
	New Orleans................. C	61.8	0	0	0	12	165	291	344	241	177	24	0	0	1254
	Shreveport .... A	56.2	0	0	0	47	297	477	552	426	304	81	0	0	2184
Me.	Caribou........................ A	24.4	78	115	336	682	1044	1535	1690	1470	1308	858	468	183	9767
	Portland .... A	33.0	12	53	195	508	807	1215	1339	1182	1042	675	372	111	7511
Md.	Baltimore .... A	43.7	0	0	48	264	585	905	936	820	679	327	90	0	4654
	Baltimore C	46.2	0	0	27	189	486	806	859	762	629	288	65	0	4111
	Frederich .... A	42.0	0	0	66	307	624	955	995	876	741	384	127	12	5087
Mass.	Boston........................ A	40.0	0	9	60	316	603	983	1088	972	846	513	208	36	5634
	Nantucket................... A	40.2	12	22	93	332	573	896	992	941	896	621	384	129	5891
	Pittsfield................... A	32.6	25	59	219	524	831	1231	1339	1196	1063	660	326	105	7578
	Worcester .... A	34.7	6	34	147	450	774	1172	1271	1123	998	612	304	78	6969

State	Station	Avg. Winter Temp[d]	July	Aug.	Sept.	Oct.	Nov.	Dec.	Jan.	Feb.	Mar.	Apr.	May	June	Yearly Total
Mich.	Alpena .... A	29.7	68	105	273	580	912	1268	1404	1299	1218	777	446	156	8506
	Detroit (City) .... A	37.2	0	0	87	360	738	1088	1181	1058	936	522	220	42	6232
	Detroit (Wayne)............... A	37.1	0	0	96	353	738	1088	1194	1061	933	534	239	57	6293
	Detroit (Willow Run) .... A	37.2	0	0	90	357	750	1104	1190	1053	921	519	229	45	6258
	Escanaba........................ C	29.6	59	87	243	539	924	1293	1445	1296	1203	777	456	159	8481
	Flint .... A	33.1	16	40	159	465	843	1212	1330	1198	1066	639	319	90	7377
	Grand Rapids.................. A	34.9	9	28	135	434	804	1147	1259	1134	1011	579	279	75	6894
	Lansing .... A	34.8	6	22	138	431	813	1163	1262	1142	1011	579	273	69	6909
	Marquette....................... C	30.2	59	81	240	527	936	1268	1411	1268	1187	771	468	177	8393
	Muskegon........................ A	36.0	12	28	120	400	762	1088	1209	1100	995	594	310	78	6696
	Sault Ste. Marie .... A	27.7	96	105	279	580	951	1367	1525	1380	1277	810	477	201	9048
Minn.	Duluth .... A	23.4	71	109	330	632	1131	1581	1745	1518	1355	840	490	198	10000
	Minneapolis .... A	28.3	22	31	189	505	1014	1454	1631	1380	1166	621	288	81	8382
	Rochester .... A	28.8	25	34	186	474	1005	1438	1593	1366	1150	630	301	93	8295
Miss.	Jackson .... A	55.7	0	0	0	65	315	502	546	414	310	87	0	0	2239
	Meridian .... A	55.4	0	0	0	81	339	518	543	417	310	81	0	0	2289
	Vicksburg C	56.9	0	0	0	53	279	462	512	384	282	69	0	0	2041
Mo.	Columbia .... A	42.3	0	0	54	251	651	967	1076	874	716	324	121	12	5046
	Kansas City .... A	43.9	0	0	39	220	612	905	1032	818	682	294	109	0	4711
	St. Joseph .... A	40.3	0	6	60	285	708	1039	1172	949	769	348	133	15	5484
	St. Louis .... A	43.1	0	0	60	251	627	936	1026	848	704	312	121	15	4900
	St. Louis C	44.8	0	0	36	202	576	884	977	801	651	270	87	0	4484
	Springfield...................... A	44.5	0	0	45	223	600	877	973	781	660	291	105	6	4900
Mont.	Billings .... A	34.5	6	15	186	487	897	1135	1296	1100	970	570	285	102	7049
	Glasgow .... A	26.4	31	47	270	608	1104	1466	1711	1439	1187	648	335	150	8996
	Great Falls .... A	32.8	28	53	258	543	921	1169	1349	1154	1063	642	384	186	7750
	Havre .... A	28.1	28	53	306	595	1065	1367	1584	1364	1181	657	338	162	8700
	Havre C	29.8	19	37	252	539	1014	1321	1528	1305	1116	612	304	135	8182
	Helena............................ A	31.1	31	59	294	601	1002	1265	1438	1170	1042	651	381	195	8129
	Kalispell .... A	31.4	50	99	321	654	1020	1240	1401	1134	1029	639	397	207	8191
	Miles City .... A	31.2	6	6	174	502	972	1296	1504	1252	1057	579	276	99	7723
	Missoula .... A	31.5	34	74	303	651	1035	1287	1420	1120	970	621	391	219	8125
Neb.	Grand Island .... A	36.0	0	6	108	381	834	1172	1314	1089	908	462	211	45	6530
	Lincoln C	38.8	0	6	75	301	726	1066	1237	1016	834	402	171	30	5864
	Norfolk .... A	34.0	9	0	111	397	873	1234	1414	1179	983	498	233	48	6979
	North Platte .... A	35.5	0	6	123	440	885	1166	1271	1039	930	519	248	57	6684
	Omaha .... A	35.6	0	12	105	357	828	1175	1355	1126	939	465	208	42	6612
	Scottsbluff...................... A	35.9	0	0	138	459	876	1128	1231	1008	921	552	285	75	6673
	Valentine........................ A	32.6	9	12	165	493	942	1237	1395	1176	1045	579	288	84	7425
Nev.	Elko .... A	34.0	9	34	225	561	924	1197	1314	1036	911	621	409	192	7433
	Ely .... A	33.1	28	43	234	592	939	1184	1308	1075	977	672	456	225	7733
	Las Vegas .... A	53.5	0	0	0	78	387	617	688	487	335	111	6	0	2709
	Reno .... A	39.3	43	87	204	490	801	1026	1073	823	729	510	357	189	6332
	Winnemucca..................... A	36.7	0	34	210	536	876	1091	1172	916	837	573	363	153	6761
N.H.	Concord .... A	33.0	6	50	177	505	822	1240	1358	1184	1032	636	298	75	7383
	Mt. Washington Obsv.............	15.2	493	536	720	1057	1341	1742	1820	1663	1652	1260	930	603	13817
N.J.	Atlantic City .... A	43.2	0	0	39	251	549	880	936	848	741	420	133	15	4812
	Newark........................... A	42.8	0	0	30	248	573	921	983	876	729	381	118	0	4589
	Trenton........................... C	42.4	0	0	57	264	576	924	989	885	753	399	121	12	4980
N. M.	Albuquerque .... A	45.0	0	0	12	229	642	868	930	703	595	288	81	0	4348
	Clayton .... A	42.0	0	6	66	310	699	899	986	812	747	429	183	21	5158
	Raton .... A	38.1	9	28	126	431	825	1048	1116	904	834	543	301	63	6228
	Roswell .... A	47.5	0	0	18	202	573	806	840	641	481	201	31	0	3793
	Silver City .... A	48.0	0	0	6	183	525	729	791	605	518	261	87	0	3705
N.Y.	Albany .... A	34.6	0	19	138	440	777	1194	1311	1156	992	564	239	45	6875
	Albany C	37.2	0	9	102	375	699	1104	1218	1072	908	498	186	30	6201
	Binghamton .... A	33.9	22	65	201	471	810	1184	1277	1154	1045	645	313	99	7286
	Binghamton C	36.6	0	28	141	406	732	1107	1190	1081	949	543	229	45	6451
	Buffalo .... A	34.5	19	37	141	440	777	1156	1256	1145	1039	645	329	78	7062
	New York (Cent. Park)....... C	42.8	0	0	30	233	540	902	986	885	760	408	118	9	4871
	New York (La Guardia) ...... A	43.1	0	0	27	223	528	887	973	879	750	414	124	6	4811

State	Station	Avg. Winter Temp[d]	July	Aug.	Sept.	Oct.	Nov.	Dec.	Jan.	Feb.	Mar.	Apr.	May	June	Yearly Total
	New York (Kennedy) .... A	41.4	0	0	36	248	564	933	1029	935	815	480	167	12	5219
	Rochester .... A	35.4	9	31	126	415	747	1125	1234	1123	1014	597	279	48	6748
	Schenectady C	35.4	0	22	123	422	756	1159	1283	1131	970	543	211	30	6650
	Syracuse .... A	35.2	6	28	132	415	744	1153	1271	1140	1004	570	248	45	6756
N. C.	Asheville C	46.7	0	0	48	245	555	775	784	683	592	273	87	0	4042
	Cape Hatteras	53.3	0	0	0	78	273	521	580	518	440	177	25	0	2612
	Charlotte .... A	50.4	0	0	6	124	438	691	691	582	481	156	22	0	3191
	Greensboro .... A	47.5	0	0	33	192	513	778	784	672	552	234	47	0	3805
	Raleigh .... A	49.4	0	0	21	164	450	716	725	616	487	180	34	0	3393
	Wilmington .... A	54.6	0	0	0	74	291	521	546	462	357	96	0	0	2347
	Winston-Salem .... A	48.4	0	0	21	171	483	747	753	652	524	207	37	0	3595
N. D.	Bismarck .... A	26.6	34	28	222	577	1083	1463	1708	1442	1203	645	329	117	8851
	Devils Lake C	22.4	40	53	273	642	1191	1634	1872	1579	1345	753	381	138	9901
	Fargo .... A	24.8	28	37	219	574	1107	1569	1789	1520	1262	690	332	99	9226
	Williston .... A	25.2	31	43	261	601	1122	1513	1758	1473	1262	681	357	141	9243
Ohio	Akron-Canton .... A	38.1	0	9	96	381	726	1070	1138	1016	871	489	202	39	6037
	Cincinnati C	45.1	0	0	39	208	558	862	915	790	642	294	96	6	4410
	Cleveland .... A	37.2	9	25	105	384	738	1088	1159	1047	918	552	260	66	6351
	Columbus .... A	39.7	0	6	84	347	714	1039	1088	949	809	426	171	27	5660
	Columbus C	41.5	0	0	57	285	651	977	1032	902	760	396	136	15	5211
	Dayton .... A	39.8	0	6	78	310	696	1045	1097	955	809	429	167	30	5622
	Mansfield .... A	36.9	9	22	114	397	768	1110	1169	1042	924	543	245	60	6403
	Sandusky C	39.1	0	6	66	313	684	1032	1107	991	868	495	198	36	5796
	Toledo .... A	36.4	0	16	117	406	792	1138	1200	1056	924	543	242	60	6494
	Youngstown .... A	36.8	6	19	120	412	771	1104	1169	1047	921	540	248	60	6417
Okla.	Oklahoma City .... A	48.3	0	0	15	164	498	766	868	664	527	189	34	0	3725
	Tulsa .... A	47.7	0	0	18	158	522	787	893	683	539	213	47	0	3860
Ore.	Astoria .... A	45.6	146	130	210	375	561	679	753	622	636	480	363	231	5186
	Burns C	35.9	12	37	210	515	867	1113	1246	988	856	570	366	177	6957
	Eugene .... A	45.6	34	34	129	366	585	719	803	627	589	426	279	135	4726
	Meacham .... A	34.2	84	124	288	580	918	1091	1209	1005	983	726	527	339	7874
	Medford .... A	43.2	0	0	78	372	678	871	918	697	642	432	242	78	5008
	Pendleton .... A	42.6	0	0	111	350	711	884	1017	773	617	396	205	63	5127
	Portland .... A	45.6	25	28	114	335	597	735	825	644	586	396	245	105	4635
	Portland C	47.4	12	16	75	267	534	679	769	594	536	351	198	78	4109
	Roseburg .... A	46.3	22	16	105	329	567	713	766	608	570	405	267	123	4491
	Salem .... A	45.4	37	31	111	338	594	729	822	647	611	417	273	144	4754
Pa.	Allentown .... A	38.9	0	0	90	353	693	1045	1116	1002	849	471	167	24	5810
	Erie .... A	36.8	0	25	102	391	714	1063	1169	1081	973	585	288	60	6451
	Harrisburg .... A	41.2	0	0	63	298	648	992	1045	907	766	396	124	12	5251
	Philadelphia .... A	41.8	0	0	60	297	620	965	1016	889	747	392	118	40	5144
	Philadelphia C	44.5	0	0	30	205	513	856	924	823	691	351	93	0	4486
	Pittsburgh .... A	38.4	0	9	105	375	726	1063	1119	1002	874	480	195	39	5987
	Pittsburgh C	42.2	0	0	60	291	615	930	983	885	763	390	124	12	5053
	Reading C	42.4	0	0	54	257	597	939	1001	885	735	372	105	0	4945
	Scranton .... A	37.2	0	19	132	434	762	1104	1156	1028	893	498	195	33	6254
	Williamsport .... A	38.5	0	9	111	375	717	1073	1122	1002	856	468	177	24	5934
R. I.	Block Island .... A	40.1	0	16	78	307	594	902	1020	955	877	612	344	99	5804
	Providence .... A	38.8	0	16	96	372	660	1023	1110	988	868	534	236	51	5954
S. C.	Charleston .... A	56.4	0	0	0	59	282	471	487	389	291	54	0	0	2033
	Charleston C	57.9	0	0	0	34	210	425	443	367	273	42	0	0	1794
	Columbia .... A	54.0	0	0	0	84	345	577	570	470	357	81	0	0	2484
	Florence .... A	54.5	0	0	0	78	315	552	552	459	347	84	0	0	2387
	Greenville-Spartanburg .... A	51.6	0	0	6	121	399	651	660	546	446	132	19	0	2980
S. D.	Huron .... A	28.8	9	12	165	508	1014	1432	1628	1355	1125	600	288	87	8223
	Rapid City .... A	33.4	22	12	165	481	897	1172	1333	1145	1051	615	326	126	7345
	Sioux Falls .... A	30.6	19	25	168	462	972	1361	1544	1285	1082	573	270	78	7839
Tenn.	Bristol .... A	46.2	0	0	51	236	573	828	828	700	598	261	68	0	4143
	Chattanooga .... A	50.3	0	0	18	143	468	698	722	577	453	150	25	0	3254
	Knoxville .... A	49.2	0	0	30	171	489	725	732	613	493	198	43	0	3494
	Memphis .... A	50.5	0	0	18	130	447	698	729	585	456	147	22	0	3232

State or Prov.	Station	Avg. Winter Temp[d]	July	Aug.	Sept.	Oct.	Nov.	Dec.	Jan.	Feb.	Mar.	Apr.	May	June	Yearly Total
	Memphis C	51.6	0	0	12	102	396	648	710	568	434	129	16	0	3015
	Nashville .... A	48.9	0	0	30	158	495	732	778	644	512	189	40	0	3578
	Oak Ridge C	47.7	0	0	39	192	531	772	778	669	552	228	56	0	3817
Tex.	Abilene .... A	53.9	0	0	0	99	366	586	642	470	347	114	0	0	2624
	Amarillo .... A	47.0	0	0	18	205	570	797	877	664	546	252	56	0	3985
	Austin .... A	59.1	0	0	0	31	225	388	468	325	223	51	0	0	1711
	Brownsville .... A	67.7	0	0	0	0	66	149	205	106	74	0	0	0	600
	Corpus Christi .... A	64.6	0	0	0	0	120	220	291	174	109	0	0	0	914
	Dallas .... A	55.3	0	0	0	62	321	524	601	440	319	90	6	0	2363
	El Paso .... A	52.9	0	0	0	84	414	648	685	445	319	105	0	0	2700
	Fort Worth .... A	55.1	0	0	0	65	324	536	614	448	319	99	0	0	2405
	Galveston .... A	62.2	0	0	0	6	147	276	360	263	189	33	0	0	1274
	Galveston C	62.0	0	0	0	0	138	270	350	258	189	30	0	0	1235
	Houston .... A	61.0	0	0	0	6	183	307	384	288	192	36	0	0	1396
	Houston C	62.0	0	0	0	0	165	288	363	258	174	30	0	0	1278
	Laredo .... A	66.0	0	0	0	0	105	217	267	134	74	0	0	0	797
	Lubbock .... A	48.8	0	0	18	174	513	744	800	613	484	201	31	0	3578
	Midland .... A	53.8	0	0	0	87	381	592	651	468	322	90	0	0	2591
	Port Arthur .... A	60.5	0	0	0	22	207	329	384	274	192	39	0	0	1447
	San Angelo .... A	56.0	0	0	0	68	318	536	567	412	288	66	0	0	2255
	San Antonio .... A	60.1	0	0	0	31	204	363	428	286	195	39	0	0	1546
	Victoria .... A	62.7	0	0	0	6	150	270	344	230	152	21	0	0	1173
	Waco .... A	57.2	0	0	0	43	270	456	536	389	270	66	0	0	2030
	Wichita Falls .... A	53.0	0	0	0	99	381	632	698	518	378	120	6	0	2832
Utah	Milford .... A	36.5	0	0	99	443	867	1141	1252	988	822	519	279	87	6497
	Salt Lake City .... A	38.4	0	0	81	419	849	1082	1172	910	763	459	233	84	6052
	Wendover .... A	39.1	0	0	48	372	822	1091	1178	902	729	408	177	51	5778
Vt.	Burlington .... A	29.4	28	65	207	539	891	1349	1513	1333	1187	714	353	90	8269
Va.	Cape Henry C	50.0	0	0	0	112	360	645	694	633	536	246	53	0	3279
	Lynchburg .... A	46.0	0	0	51	223	540	822	849	731	605	267	78	0	4166
	Norfolk .... A	49.2	0	0	0	136	408	698	738	655	533	216	37	0	3421
	Richmond .... A	47.3	0	0	36	214	495	784	815	703	546	219	53	0	3865
	Roanoke .... A	46.1	0	0	51	229	549	825	834	722	614	261	65	0	4150
Wash.	Olympia .... A	44.2	68	71	198	422	636	753	834	675	645	450	307	177	5236
	Seattle-Tacoma .... A	44.2	56	62	162	391	633	750	828	678	657	474	295	159	5145
	Seattle C	46.9	50	47	129	329	543	657	738	599	577	396	242	117	4424
	Spokane .... A	36.5	9	25	168	493	879	1082	1231	980	834	531	288	135	6655
	Walla Walla C	43.8	0	0	87	310	681	843	986	745	589	342	177	45	4805
	Yakima .... A	39.1	0	12	144	450	828	1039	1163	868	713	435	220	69	5941
W. Va.	Charleston .... A	44.8	0	0	63	254	591	865	880	770	648	300	96	9	4476
	Elkins .... A	40.1	9	25	135	400	729	992	1008	896	791	444	198	48	5675
	Huntington .... A	45.0	0	0	63	257	585	856	880	764	636	294	99	12	4446
	Parkersburg C	43.5	0	0	60	264	606	905	942	826	691	339	115	6	4754
Wisc.	Green Bay .... A	30.3	28	50	174	484	924	1333	1494	1313	1141	654	335	99	8029
	La Crosse .... A	31.5	12	19	153	437	924	1339	1504	1277	1070	540	245	69	7589
	Madison .... A	30.9	25	40	174	474	930	1330	1473	1274	1113	618	310	102	7863
	Milwaukee .... A	32.6	43	47	174	471	876	1252	1376	1193	1054	642	372	135	7635
Wyo.	Casper .... A	33.4	6	16	192	524	942	1169	1290	1084	1020	657	381	129	7410
	Cheyenne .... A	34.2	28	37	219	543	909	1085	1212	1042	1026	702	428	150	7381
	Lander .... A	31.4	6	19	204	555	1020	1299	1417	1145	1017	654	381	153	7870
	Sheridan .... A	32.5	25	31	219	539	948	1200	1355	1154	1051	642	366	150	7680
Alta.	Banff C	—	220	295	498	797	1185	1485	1624	1364	1237	855	589	402	10551
	Calgary .... A	—	109	186	402	719	1110	1389	1575	1379	1268	798	477	291	9703
	Edmonton .... A	—	74	180	411	738	1215	1603	1810	1520	1330	765	400	222	10268
	Lethbridge .... A	—	56	112	318	611	1011	1277	1497	1291	1159	696	403	213	8644
B. C.	Kamloops .... A	—	22	40	189	546	894	1138	1314	1057	818	462	217	102	6799
	Prince George* .... A	—	236	251	444	747	1110	1420	1612	1319	1122	747	468	279	9755
	Prince Rupert C	—	273	248	339	539	708	868	936	808	812	648	493	357	7029
	Vancouver* .... A	—	81	87	219	456	657	787	862	723	676	501	310	156	5515
	Victoria* .... A	—	136	140	225	462	663	775	840	718	691	504	341	204	5699
	Victoria C	—	172	184	243	426	607	723	805	668	660	487	354	250	5579

Average Monthly and Yearly Degree Days for Cities in the U.S. and Canada /

State or Prov.	Station	Avg. Winter Temp[d]	July	Aug.	Sept.	Oct.	Nov.	Dec.	Jan.	Feb.	Mar.	Apr.	May	June	Yearly Total
Man.	Brandon* .... A	—	47	90	357	747	1290	1792	2034	1737	1476	837	431	198	11036
	Churchill........................... A	—	360	375	681	1082	1620	2248	2558	2277	2130	1569	1153	675	16728
	The Pas............................. C	—	59	127	429	831	1440	1981	2232	1853	1624	969	508	228	12281
	Winnipeg .... A	—	38	71	322	683	1251	1757	2008	1719	1465	813	405	147	10679
N. B.	Fredericton* .... A	—	78	68	234	592	915	1392	1541	1379	1172	753	406	141	8671
	Moncton C	—	62	105	276	611	891	1342	1482	1336	1194	789	468	171	8727
	St. John C	—	109	102	246	527	807	1194	1370	1229	1097	756	490	249	8219
Nfld.	Argentia .... A	—	260	167	294	564	750	1001	1159	1085	1091	879	707	483	8440
	Corner Brook C	—	102	133	324	642	873	1194	1358	1283	1212	885	639	333	8978
	Gander .... A	—	121	152	330	670	909	1231	1370	1266	1243	939	657	366	9254
	Goose* .... A	—	130	205	444	843	1227	1745	1947	1689	1494	1074	741	348	11887
	St. John's* .... A	—	186	180	342	651	831	1113	1262	1170	1187	927	710	432	8991
N. W. T.	Aklavik C	—	273	459	807	1414	2064	2530	2632	2336	2282	1674	1063	483	18017
	Fort Norman C	—	164	341	666	1234	1959	2474	2592	2209	2058	1386	732	294	16109
	Resolution Island................ C	—	843	831	900	1113	1311	1724	2021	1850	1817	1488	1181	942	16021
N. S.	Halifax C	—	58	51	180	457	710	1074	1213	1122	1030	742	487	237	7361
	Sydney .... A	—	62	71	219	518	765	1113	1262	1206	1150	840	567	276	8049
	Yarmouth............................ A	—	102	115	225	471	696	1029	1156	1065	1004	726	493	258	7340
Ont.	Cochrane C	—	96	180	405	760	1233	1776	1978	1701	1528	963	570	222	11412
	Fort William .... A	—	90	133	366	694	1140	1597	1792	1557	1380	876	543	237	10405
	Kapuskasing C	—	74	171	405	756	1245	1807	2037	1735	1562	978	580	222	11572
	Kitchener C	—	16	59	177	505	855	1234	1342	1226	1101	663	322	66	7566
	London .... A	—	12	43	159	477	837	1206	1305	1198	1066	648	332	66	7349
	North Bay C	—	37	90	267	608	990	1507	1680	1463	1277	780	400	120	9219
	Ottawa C	—	25	81	222	567	936	1469	1624	1441	1231	708	341	90	8735
	Toronto C	—	7	18	151	439	760	1111	1233	1119	1013	616	298	62	6827
P.E.I.	Charlottetown...................... C	—	40	53	198	518	804	1215	1380	1274	1169	813	496	204	8164
	Summerside C	—	47	84	216	546	840	1246	1438	1291	1206	841	518	216	8488
Que.	Arvida............................... C	—	102	136	327	682	1074	1659	1879	1619	1407	891	521	231	10528
	Montreal* .... A	—	9	43	165	521	882	1392	1566	1381	1175	684	316	69	8203
	Montreal............................ C	—	16	28	165	496	864	1355	1510	1328	1138	657	288	54	7899
	Quebec* .... A	—	56	84	273	636	996	1516	1665	1477	1296	819	428	126	9372
	Quebec C	—	40	68	243	592	972	1473	1612	1418	1228	780	400	111	8937
Sasks	Prince Albert .... A	—	81	136	414	797	1368	1872	2108	1763	1559	867	446	219	11630
	Regina............................... A	—	78	93	360	741	1284	1711	1965	1687	1473	804	409	201	10806
	Saskatoon C	—	56	87	372	750	1302	1758	2006	1689	1463	798	403	186	10870
Y. T.	Dawson............................... C	—	164	326	645	1197	1875	2415	2561	2150	1838	1068	570	258	15067
	Mayo Landing C	—	208	366	648	1135	1794	2325	2427	1992	1665	1020	580	294	14454

*The data for these normals were from the full ten-year period 1951–1960, adjusted to the standard normal period 1931–1960.

Mean Percentage of Possible Sunshine for Selected Cities in the U.S. and Canada

Based on period of record through December 1959, except in a few instances. These charts and tabulation are derived from the "Normals, Means, and Extremes" table in U.S. Weather Bureau publication *Local Climatological Data*.

STATE/PROVINCE & CITY	JAN	FEB	MAR	APR	MAY	JUNE	JULY	AUG	SEPT	OCT	NOV	DEC
ALABAMA												
Birmingham	43	49	56	63	66	67	62	65	66	67	58	44
Montgomery	51	53	61	69	73	72	66	69	69	71	64	48
ALASKA												
Anchorage	39	46	56	58	50	51	45	39	35	32	33	29
Fairbanks	34	50	61	68	55	53	45	35	31	28	38	29
Juneau	30	32	39	37	34	35	28	30	25	18	21	18
Nome	44	46	48	53	51	48	32	26	34	35	36	30
ARIZONA												
Phoenix	76	79	83	88	93	94	84	84	89	88	84	77
Yuma	83	87	91	94	97	98	92	91	93	93	90	83
ARKANSAS												
Little Rock	44	53	57	62	67	72	71	73	71	74	58	47
CALIFORNIA												
Eureka	40	44	50	53	54	56	51	46	52	48	42	39
Fresno	46	63	72	83	89	94	97	97	93	87	73	47
Los Angeles	70	69	70	67	68	69	80	81	80	76	79	72
Red Bluff	50	60	65	75	79	86	95	94	89	77	64	50
Sacramento	44	57	67	76	82	90	96	95	92	82	65	44
San Diego	68	67	68	66	60	60	67	70	70	70	76	71
San Francisco	53	57	63	69	70	75	68	63	70	70	62	54
COLORADO												
Denver	67	67	65	63	61	69	68	68	71	71	67	65
Grand Junction	58	62	64	67	71	79	76	72	77	74	67	58
CONNECTICUT												
Hartford	46	55	56	54	57	60	62	60	57	55	46	46
DISTRICT OF COLUMBIA												
Washington	46	53	56	57	61	64	64	62	62	61	54	47
FLORIDA												
Apalachicola	59	62	62	71	77	70	64	63	62	74	66	53
Jacksonville	58	59	66	71	71	63	62	63	58	58	61	53
Key West	68	75	78	78	76	70	69	71	65	65	69	66
Miami Beach	66	72	73	73	68	62	65	67	62	62	65	65
Tampa	63	67	71	74	75	66	61	64	64	67	67	61
GEORGIA												
Atlanta	48	53	57	65	68	68	62	63	65	67	60	47
HAWAII												
Hilo	48	42	41	34	31	41	44	38	42	41	34	36
Honolulu	62	64	60	62	64	66	67	70	70	68	63	60
Lihue	48	48	48	46	51	60	58	59	67	58	51	49

STATE/PROVINCE & CITY	JAN	FEB	MAR	APR	MAY	JUNE	JULY	AUG	SEPT	OCT	NOV	DEC
IDAHO												
Boise	40	48	59	67	68	75	89	86	81	66	46	37
Pocatello	37	47	58	64	66	72	82	81	78	66	48	36
ILLINOIS												
Cairo	46	53	59	65	71	77	82	79	75	73	56	46
Chicago	44	49	53	56	63	69	73	70	65	61	47	41
Springfield	47	51	54	58	64	69	76	72	73	64	53	45
INDIANA												
Evansville	42	49	55	61	67	73	78	76	73	67	52	42
Fort Wayne	38	44	51	55	62	69	74	69	64	58	41	38
Indianapolis	41	47	49	55	62	68	74	70	68	64	48	39
IOWA												
Des Moines	56	56	56	59	62	66	75	70	64	64	53	48
Dubuque	48	52	52	58	60	63	73	67	61	55	44	40
Sioux City	55	58	58	59	63	67	75	72	67	65	53	50
KANSAS												
Concordia	60	60	62	63	65	73	79	76	72	70	64	58
Dodge City	67	66	68	68	68	74	78	78	76	75	70	67
Wichita	61	63	64	64	66	73	80	77	73	69	67	59
KENTUCKY												
Louisville	41	47	52	57	64	68	72	69	68	64	51	39
LOUISIANA												
New Orleans	49	50	57	63	66	64	58	60	64	70	60	46
Shreveport	48	54	58	60	69	78	79	80	79	77	65	60
MAINE												
Eastport	45	51	52	52	51	53	55	57	54	50	37	40
Portland	55	59	58	57	57	64	66	63	62	59	51	49
MASSACHUSETTS												
Boston	47	56	57	56	59	62	64	63	61	58	48	48
MICHIGAN												
Alpena	29	43	52	56	59	64	70	64	52	44	24	22
Detroit	34	42	48	52	58	65	69	66	61	54	35	29
Grand Rapids	26	37	48	54	60	66	72	67	58	50	31	22
Marquette	31	40	47	52	53	56	63	57	47	38	24	24
Sault Ste. Marie	28	44	50	54	54	59	63	58	45	36	21	22
MINNESOTA												
Duluth	47	55	60	58	58	60	68	63	53	47	36	40
Minneapolis	49	54	55	57	60	64	72	69	60	54	40	40
MISSISSIPPI												
Vicksburg	46	50	57	64	69	73	69	72	74	71	60	45

STATE/PROVINCE & CITY	JAN	FEB	MAR	APR	MAY	JUNE	JULY	AUG	SEPT	OCT	NOV	DEC
MISSOURI												
Kansas City	55	57	59	60	64	70	76	73	70	67	59	52
St. Louis	48	49	56	59	64	68	72	68	67	65	54	44
Springfield	48	54	57	60	63	69	77	72	71	65	58	48
MONTANA												
Havre	49	58	61	63	63	65	78	75	64	57	48	48
Helena	46	55	58	60	59	63	77	74	63	57	48	43
Kalispell	28	40	49	57	58	60	77	73	61	50	28	20
NEBRASKA												
Lincoln	57	59	60	60	63	69	76	71	67	66	59	55
North Platte	63	63	64	62	64	72	78	74	72	70	62	58
NEVADA												
Ely	61	64	68	65	67	79	79	81	81	73	67	62
Las Vegas	74	77	78	81	85	91	84	86	92	84	83	75
Reno	59	64	69	75	77	82	90	89	86	76	68	56
Winnemucca	52	60	64	70	76	83	90	90	86	75	62	53
NEW HAMPSHIRE												
Concord	48	53	55	53	51	56	57	58	55	50	43	43
NEW JERSEY												
Atlantic City	51	57	58	59	62	65	67	66	65	54	58	52
NEW MEXICO												
Albuquerque	70	72	72	76	79	84	76	75	81	85	79	70
Roswell	69	72	75	77	76	80	76	75	74	74	74	69
NEW YORK												
Albany	43	51	53	53	57	62	63	61	58	54	39	38
Binghamton	31	39	41	44	50	56	54	51	47	43	29	26
Buffalo	32	41	49	51	59	67	70	67	60	51	31	28
Canton	37	47	50	48	54	61	63	61	54	45	30	31
New York	49	56	57	59	62	65	66	64	64	61	53	50
Syracuse	31	38	45	50	58	64	67	63	58	47	29	26
NORTH CAROLINA												
Asheville	48	53	56	61	64	63	59	59	62	64	59	48
Raleigh	50	56	59	64	67	65	62	62	63	64	62	52
NORTH DAKOTA												
Bismark	52	58	56	57	58	61	73	69	62	59	49	48
Devils Lake	53	60	59	60	59	62	71	67	59	56	44	45
Fargo	47	55	56	58	62	63	73	69	60	57	39	46
Williston	51	59	60	63	66	66	78	75	65	60	48	48
OHIO												
Cincinnati	41	46	52	56	62	69	72	68	68	60	46	39

State/Province & City	Jan	Feb	Mar	Apr	May	June	July	Aug	Sept	Oct	Nov	Dec
Cleveland	29	36	45	52	61	67	71	68	62	54	32	25
Columbus	36	44	49	54	63	68	71	68	66	60	44	35
OKLAHOMA												
Oklahoma City	57	60	63	64	65	74	75	78	74	68	64	57
OREGON												
Baker	41	49	56	61	63	67	83	81	74	62	46	37
Portland	27	34	41	49	52	55	70	65	55	42	29	23
Roseburg	24	32	40	51	57	59	79	77	65	42	28	28
PENNSYLVANIA												
Harrisburg	43	52	55	57	61	63	68	63	62	58	47	43
Philadelphia	45	56	57	58	61	62	64	61	62	61	53	49
Pittsburgh	32	38	45	50	57	62	64	61	62	54	39	30
RHODE ISLAND												
Block Island	45	54	47	56	58	60	62	62	60	59	50	44
SOUTH CAROLINA												
Charleston	58	60	65	72	73	70	66	66	67	68	68	57
Columbia	53	57	62	68	69	68	63	65	64	68	64	51
SOUTH DAKOTA												
Huron	55	62	60	62	65	68	76	72	68	61	52	48
Rapid City	58	62	63	62	61	66	73	73	69	66	58	54
TENNESSEE												
Knoxville	42	49	53	59	64	66	64	59	64	64	53	41
Memphis	44	51	57	64	68	74	73	74	70	69	58	45
Nashville	42	47	54	60	65	69	69	68	69	65	55	42
TEXAS												
Abilene	64	68	73	66	73	86	83	85	73	71	72	66
Amarillo	71	71	75	75	75	82	81	81	79	76	76	70
Austin	46	50	57	60	62	72	76	79	70	70	57	49
Brownsville	44	49	51	57	65	73	78	78	67	70	54	44
Del Rio	53	55	61	63	60	66	75	80	69	66	58	52
El Paso	74	77	81	85	87	87	78	78	80	82	80	73
Fort Worth	56	57	65	66	67	75	78	78	74	70	63	58
Galveston	50	50	55	61	69	76	72	71	70	74	62	49
San Antonio	48	51	56	58	60	69	74	75	69	67	55	49
UTAH												
Salt Lake City	48	53	61	68	73	78	82	82	84	75	56	49
VERMONT												
Burlington	34	43	48	47	53	59	62	59	51	43	25	24
VIRGINIA												
Norfolk	50	57	60	63	67	66	66	66	63	64	60	51

State/Province & City	Jan	Feb	Mar	Apr	May	June	July	Aug	Sept	Oct	Nov	Dec
Richmond	49	55	59	63	67	66	65	62	63	64	58	50
WASHINGTON												
North Head	26	37	42	48	48	48	50	46	48	41	31	27
Seattle	27	34	42	48	53	48	62	56	53	36	28	24
Spokane	26	41	53	63	64	68	82	79	68	53	28	22
Tatoosh Island	26	36	39	45	47	46	48	44	47	38	26	23
Walla Walla	24	35	51	63	67	72	86	84	72	59	33	20
Yakima	34	49	62	70	72	74	86	86	74	61	38	29
WEST VIRGINIA												
Elkins	33	37	42	47	55	55	56	53	55	51	41	33
Parkersburg	30	36	42	49	56	60	63	60	60	53	37	29
WISCONSIN												
Green Bay	44	51	55	56	58	64	70	65	58	52	40	40
Madison	44	49	52	53	58	64	70	66	60	58	41	38
Milwaukee	44	48	53	56	60	65	73	67	62	56	44	39
WYOMING												
Cheyenne	65	66	64	61	59	68	70	68	69	69	65	63
Lander	66	70	71	66	65	74	76	75	72	67	61	62
Sheridan	56	61	62	61	61	67	76	74	67	60	53	52
Yellowstone Park	39	51	55	57	56	63	73	71	65	57	45	38
ALBERTA												
Edmonton	35	43	45	53	52	49	61	58	49	48	39	33
BRITISH COLUMBIA												
Prince George	22	31	36	44	50	47	52	53	43	31	22	18
Vancouver	16	26	30	41	47	43	56	56	46	32	19	13
MANITOBA												
Winnipeg	38	47	45	50	51	51	63	60	48	46	30	32
NEWFOUNDLAND												
Gander	26	29	29	28	32	33	41	40	38	33	23	23
NOVA SCOTIA												
Halifax	34	39	40	38	44	46	51	50	45	44	31	33
ONTARIO												
Kapuskasing	27	36	37	41	41	43	48	45	33	27	16	21
Toronto	27	35	38	42	48	56	61	60	53	45	29	27
QUEBEC												
Montreal	29	36	40	41	44	47	51	51	45	37	24	28
SASKATCHEWAN												
Regina	37	41	41	52	55	51	67	63	52	51	35	34

Isogonic Chart
(Magnetic Declination)

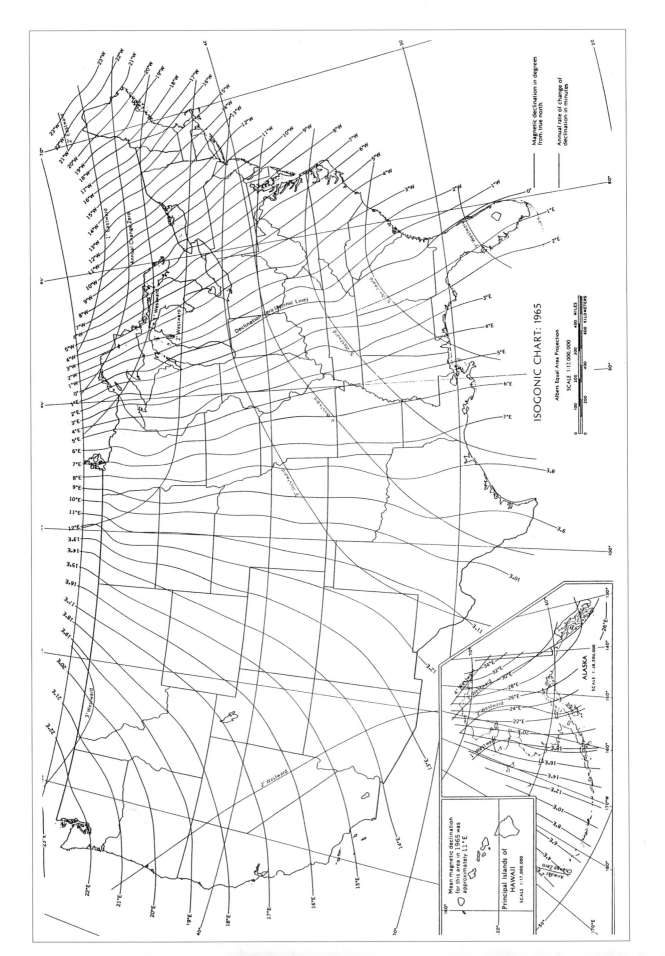

ISOGONIC CHART: 1965

Albers Equal Area Projection

SCALE 1:17,000,000

Magnetic declination in degrees
from true north

Annual rate of change of
declination in minutes

Principal Islands of
HAWAII
SCALE 1:17,000,000

Mean magnetic declination
for this area in 1965 was
approximately 11°E.

ALASKA
SCALE 1:8,500,000

Index